# Parallel Curriculum Units for

## Grades K–5

# Parallel Curriculum Units for

## Grades K–5

### Marcia B. Imbeau

CORWIN
A SAGE Company

FOR INFORMATION:

Corwin
A SAGE Company
2455 Teller Road
Thousand Oaks, California 91320
(800) 233-9936
Fax: (800) 417-2466
www.corwin.com

SAGE Ltd.
1 Oliver's Yard
55 City Road
London EC1Y 1SP
United Kingdom

SAGE India Pvt. Ltd.
B 1/I 1 Mohan Cooperative
Industrial Area
Mathura Road, New Delhi 110 044
India

SAGE Asia-Pacific Pte. Ltd.
33 Pekin Street #02-01
Far East Square
Singapore 048763

Acquisitions Editor:   Jessica Allan
Associate Editor:   Allison Scott
Editorial Assistant:   Lisa Whitney
Permissions Editor:   Karen Ehrmann
Production Editor:   Cassandra Margaret Seibel
Copy Editor:   Gretchen Treadwell
Typesetter:   C&M Digitals (P) Ltd.
Proofreader:   Jenifer Kooiman
Indexer:   Wendy Allex
Cover Designer:   Rose Storey

Library of Congress Cataloging-in-Publication Data

Imbeau, Marcia B.

Parallel curriculum units for grades K-5 / Marcia B. Imbeau.

p. cm.
Includes bibliographical references and index.

ISBN 978-1-4129-6383-1 (pbk.)

1. Curriculum planning—United States. 2. Education (Elementary)—United States. I. Title.

LB2806.15.I52 2011 372.19—dc22 2010040038

11 12 13 14 15 10 9 8 7 6 5 4 3 2 1

# Contents

About the Editor                                                                ix

About the Contributors                                                          xi

Introduction: A Brief History of the Parallel Curriculum Model (PCM)             1

1.  **Plants Alive**                                                            13
    *Christy D. McGee*
    Introduction to the Unit                                                    13
    Content Framework                                                           15
    Unit Assessments                                                            19
    Unit Sequence and Teacher Reflection                                        19
        Lesson 1.1: What Do We Know About Plants?                               19
        Lesson 1.2: Is It Alive?                                                20
        Lesson 1.3: What's In a Seed?                                           23
        Lesson 1.4: What Do Seeds Need to Grow?                                 25
        Lesson 1.5: Observing Germinating Plants                                27
        Lesson 1.6: Plant Parts!                                                29
        Lesson 1.7: The Needs of Every Living Thing                             31
        Lesson 1.8: The Adventures of a Seed                                    33
        Lesson 1.9: What's Inside Our Fruit?                                    35
        Lesson 1.10: What Do We Know About Plants? Revisited                    36
    Conclusion: Plant Fair                                                      37

2.  **Point of View Under Transition: Using the Work
    of Chris Van Allsburg**                                                     55
    *Laurie Boen*
    Introduction to the Unit                                                    55
    Content Framework                                                           56
    Unit Assessments                                                            59
    Unit Sequence and Teacher Reflection                                        59
        Lesson 2.1: What Is My Point of View? Parallel of Connections           59
        Lesson 2.2: What Is Point of View? Core Parallel                        62
        Lesson 2.3: Changing Point of View: Parallel of Practice                64
        Lesson 2.4: Look . . . I Am an Author! Parallel of Identity             66
        Lesson 2.5: Wrapping Up That Changing Point of View:
            Parallel of Practice                                                68

**3. Experience Poetry (Grades 2–5)**     **75**
*Leighann Pennington*
Introduction to the Unit     75
Content Framework     77
Unit Assessments     81
Unit Sequence and Teacher Reflection     82
    Lesson 3.1: Preassessment: "What I Know"
      Interest Inventory and "What I Love" and the Five Senses     82
    Lesson 3.2: Elements of Poetry     86
    Lesson 3.3: The Junk Festival and William Carlos
      Williams Poem Imitation     90
    Lesson 3.4: *Love That Dog* and Why Write Poetry?     93
    Lesson 3.5: Roller 'Roo Story and Poem Differentiation
      and Found Poems     95
    Lesson 3.6: Interactive Poetry Museum     97
References     100

**4. Getting to the Heart of Mathematical Numbers
and Operations (Grades 2–5)**     **115**
*Linda H. Eilers*
Introduction to the Unit     115
Content Framework     117
Unit Assessments     121
Unit Sequence and Teacher Reflection     121
    Prior to Lesson 4.1: Preassessment     121
    Lesson 4.1: Know When to Add, Subtract, Multiply, or Divide     122
    Lesson 4.2: Facilitating Easy Recall of Mathematical "Facts"     124
    Lesson 4.3: Building Conceptual Understanding of Algorithms     128
    Lesson 4.4: Relationships Between Operations     132
    Lesson 4.5: Connecting Problem Solving to the Real World     134
    Lesson 4.6: What Is a Mathematician?     135
    Lesson 4.7: The Tools of a Mathematician     137
    Lesson 4.8: The Ethics of the Use of the Tools of Mathematics     138
Reference     139

**5. Preserving Our Identity: Learning About the
History of Our State (Intermediate)**     **153**
*Jennifer Beasley*
Introduction to the Unit     153
Content Framework     158
Unit Assessments     160
Unit Sequence and Teacher Reflection     161
    Lesson 5.1: Introducing the Historical Method     161
    Lesson 5.2: Understanding the Tools of a Public
      Historian: Learning About Our Own Lives     163
    Lesson 5.3: Understanding the Tools of a Historian:
      Learning About Our State History     166

Lesson 5.4: Using Primary Sources                                    169
Lesson 5.5: If You're Not From . . . , You Don't Know . . .          174
Lesson 5.6: Making Our State Public: Culminating Project             176
References                                                            179

**6.   Conundrums in Criminalistics: Clues, Culprits,
and Conclusions (Grades 4–5)**                                       **195**
*Lisa DaVia Rubenstein*
Introduction to the Unit                                              195
Content Framework                                                     199
Unit Assessments                                                      200
Unit Sequence and Teacher Reflection                                 201
Lesson 6.1: The Universe of Knowledge                                201
Lesson 6.2: Thoughts and Tools of the Trade                          205
Lesson 6.3: Who's Who in Forensic Science?                           208
Lesson 6.4: Scene Analysis and Evidence Documentation                211
Lesson 6.5: Document Analysis                                         214
Lesson 6.6: DNA and Imprints                                         220
Lesson 6.7: Fingerprinting, Blood, Questions, and Evidence           225
Lesson 6.8: Meet a Forensic Scientist                                228
Lesson 6.9: Solve a Simulated Crime                                  230
References                                                            234

**Index**                                                            257

# About the Editor

**Marcia B. Imbeau** is an Associate Professor at the University of Arkansas, Fayetteville, where she teaches graduate courses in gifted education and elementary education. She is actively involved with university–public school partnerships and teaches in a local elementary school as a university liaison. Her professional experience includes serving as a field researcher for the National Research Center on the Gifted and Talented, elementary teaching in the regular classroom, teaching in programs for the gifted, and coordinating university-based and Saturday programs for advanced learners.

She has been a board member for the National Association for Gifted Children and has served as a governor at-large for the Council for Exceptional Children–The Association for the Gifted Division. She is a past president of Arkansans for Gifted and Talented Education, a state organization that supports appropriate instructional services for all students.

She is the author of *Designing a Professional Development Plan* (2006), and has coauthored various publications including *Leading and Managing a Differentiated Classroom* (2010), *The Parallel Curriculum Model (2nd ed.)* (2009), and *How to Use Differentiated Instruction With Students With Disabilities in the General Education Classroom* (2002) (a service publication for the Council for Exceptional Children). She is also a member of the ASCD's Differentiated Instruction Cadre, which provides support and training to schools interested in improving their efforts to meet the academically diverse learning needs of their students.

# About the Contributors

**Jennifer Beasley** is Assistant Professor in Curriculum and Instruction at the University of Arkansas. With more than seventeen years of experience in education as an elementary school teacher and a gifted facilitator, her work has given her many opportunities to develop challenging and engaging curriculum, and contributed directly to the unit she designed for this book. After receiving an MA in education administration and gifted education, she completed her doctoral work in educational psychology at the University of Virginia. Her professional contributions include serving as a regular columnist for the National Association for Gifted Children's publication *Teaching for High Potential* as well as facilitating workshops with schools and districts in the United States and internationally—specializing in gifted education, differentiation, and professional development. She was the recipient of the National Association for Gifted Children Curriculum Award in 2005.

**Laurie Boen** is Assistant Professor of preservice teachers at Southwest Baptist University, and works with students pursuing master's degrees in gifted education at Drury University. She is a second-generation educator, following in the footsteps of both her mother and her father. She earned a bachelor's degree at the University of Texas at the Permian Basin, Odessa; obtained a master's degree in gifted education from Drury University, Springfield, Missouri; and completed a doctorate in curriculum and instruction from the University of Arkansas, Fayetteville. She taught in public school for seventeen years; as a classroom teacher, she worked in heterogeneous classes at the elementary, junior high, and high school levels, and also in special classes for students identified as gifted learners. She also served as the coordinator for gifted programs in Grades K–12, and is an educational consultant for teachers on differentiated instruction and gifted education. Her work focuses on teachers and administrators who want to develop responsive classrooms and schools.

**Linda H. Eilers** is a Clinical Associate Professor at the University of Arkansas in Fayetteville, Arkansas, where she teaches courses in educational research and assessment. Prior to this position, she taught graduate and undergraduate mathematics methods courses at Mississippi College in Clinton and the University of Louisiana at Monroe, and was also a classroom teacher and curriculum coordinator for gifted education at a performing arts magnet school in Little Rock, Arkansas. In addition, she served as a consultant and member of the committee for program development for the Mathematics, Science and Computer Magnet School in Monroe, Louisiana. She received her BSE, MEd, and gifted certification from the University of Arkansas, Little Rock, and her PhD in curriculum and instruction from Louisiana State University in Baton Rouge. Her publications include journal articles on her research and work with teachers in classrooms and she has presented workshops on mathematics and children's literature at the National Council of Teachers of Mathematics annual conferences. She also participated in a multiyear National Science Foundation grant entitled Preparation of Elementary Mathematics Teachers (POEMT) at Florida International University, Miami, focusing on the National Council of Teachers of Mathematics' curriculum and evaluation standards. She currently serves as president of the Arkansas Reading Association, an affiliate of the International Reading Association.

**Christy D. McGee** is an Associate Professor at Bellarmine University in Louisville, Kentucky. She has taught in both elementary and high school settings. As an elementary teacher, her room housed many plants and animals. Children not only observed rats, rabbit, birds, cacti, ferns, and so forth; they were also responsible for their care. During her doctoral program, she was a research assistant on a National Science Foundation (NSF) grant that studied the effect of incorporating zoos into elementary and middle school biology curriculum. She currently teaches a science methodology course at the undergraduate level, and her undergraduate students spend several days and one night at the zoo during the semester. Alongside teaching, she is an active member of the National Association for Gifted Children (NAGC). She has served NAGC in several capacities, including chair of the Curriculum Studies Network, a member of the parents advisory and networks communication committees, and she currently serves as chair-elect of the Parent and Community Network.

**Leighann Pennington** teaches English to middle school students at Tarbut V' Torah Community Day School in Orange County, California. She studied creative writing at Miami University and earned an MEd in educational psychology, with an emphasis in gifted education, at the University of Virginia. For the past eight years, she has worked for the summer and online programs at Johns Hopkins University's Center for Talented Youth (JHU-CTY). In 2007, the Experience Poetry unit won the Curriculum Studies Award through the National Association for Gifted Children (NAGC). She has taught the Experience Poetry unit to students in Grades 2–6 at public and private schools and the Saturday enrichment programs in Virginia and California, as well as at the CTY summer programs. She has presented on the poetry unit and the Parallel Curriculum Model at the National Association for Gifted Children's Annual Conference and Best Practices Institute: Differentiating in Reading and Writing, and institutes on academic diversity at the University of Virginia. She has published articles about engaging students in reading and writing in *Parenting for High Potential, 2e: Twice Exceptional Newsletter, Virginia Association for the Gifted Newsletter, California Association of Independent Schools Faculty Newsletter, Dialogue,* and *SCOPE.*

**Lisa DaVia Rubenstein** is a Research Assistant for the National Research Center on the Gifted and Talented at the University of Connecticut, where she has developed curriculum and professional development resources for the What Works in Gifted Education research project. She teaches an online graduate course and also conducts workshops for teachers in the areas of differentiated instruction, program development, and Socratic seminars. She was previously a classroom teacher and a coordinator of a gifted education program in Pennsylvania, and is currently completing her doctorate in educational psychology from the University of Connecticut. Her research interests include motivation in gifted students and creativity.

# Introduction

## A Brief History of the Parallel Curriculum Model (PCM)

**W**hen *The Parallel Curriculum: A Design to Develop High Potential and Challenge High-Ability Learners* was published by Carol Ann Tomlinson in 2002, the six of us who coauthored the work knew we had found ideas in the model to be interesting, challenging, and worthy of a great deal more thought and articulation. Since the original book's publication over eight years ago, we have spent a great deal of time talking among ourselves and with other practitioners about the Parallel Curriculum Model (PCM). These colleagues were as passionate as we were about the nature of high-quality curriculum and the increasing need for such learning experiences for all students. Our colleagues offered us invaluable viewpoints, opinions, suggestions, and probing questions. We surely benefitted in countless ways from their expertise and insights.

Our conversations led to the publication of two new books about PCM in 2006. *Book I, The Parallel Curriculum in the Classroom: Essays for Application Across the Content Areas, K–12,* featured articles that we hope clarified and expanded upon selected aspects of the model. We continue to hope that it helps educators think more deeply about important facets of the model and some of its "nonnegotiable" components.

*Book II, The Parallel Curriculum in the Classroom: Units for Application Across the Content Areas, K–12,* invited readers to consider eight curriculum units that were designed using PCM. As we compiled the units, we sought to answer the question, "What is necessary in the design process of any parallel curriculum unit?"

We did not consider these units as off-the-shelf selections that a teacher might pick up and teach. Rather, we viewed the eight units as professional development tools helpful to any educator who wants to reflect on one way of creating thoughtful curriculum.

*Editor's Note:* A portion of the introduction was previously published in *Teaching for High Potential* (Vol. IV, No. 1, April 2002), published by the National Association for Gifted Children, Washington, DC. www.nagc.org.

Over the last four years, we continued to engage in conversations about the nature of curriculum models and how they can be used to create rigorous learning opportunities for students. As before, these conversations ultimately led us to two additional projects. The first was to create an updated version of the original publication. This second edition of PCM was completed in spring, 2008, and is called *The Parallel Curriculum: A Design to Develop Leaner Potential and Challenge Advanced Learners*. The second edition extends our understanding of how this framework for curriculum development can be used to create, revise, or adapt curriculum to the needs of all students. In addition, it explores the concept of ascending intellectual demand for all learners in today's heterogeneous classrooms.

The second project was the creation of a series of curriculum units, based on PCM, for practitioners' use. To address the varying needs of teachers spanning Grades K–12—as well as different content areas—we decided to create a series of five publications. The first publication is dedicated to the elementary grades, K–5. It features lessons and curriculum units that have been designed to address the needs of primary and elementary learners.

The last four publications span the secondary grades, Grades 6–12. Each of the four publications focuses on a different content area: English/language arts, social studies/history, science, and mathematics. It is our hope that the lessons in each not only underscore important and discipline-specific content, but also illuminate the four parallels in unique and enduring ways.

Cindy Strickland and Marcia B. Imbeau joined the original PCM authors and contributed to 2nd edition publication in 2009, and Strickland also created *The Parallel Curriculum Multimedia Kit.* Imbeau is also a longtime user and trainer in PCM.

## THE PARALLEL CURRICULUM MODEL (PCM): A BRIEF OVERVIEW

A wonderfully illuminating fable exists about seven blind men who encountered an elephant. Because each man felt a different part of the beast, none was able to figure out the true nature of the gigantic creature.

Did you ever stop to think that students' perceptions about their learning experiences might be as limited as the perceptions the blind men had about the nature of the elephant? Perhaps, like the blind men, students learn only bits and pieces of the curriculum over time, never seeing, let alone understanding, the larger whole that is humankind's accumulated knowledge.

What if we were able to design curriculum in a multifaceted way to ensure that all learners understand: (1) the nature of knowledge, (2) the connections that link humankind's knowledge, (3) the methodology of the practitioner who creates knowledge, and (4) the "fit" between the learner's values and goals and those that characterize practicing professionals? How would classrooms be different if the focus of curriculum was *qualitatively differentiated curriculum* that prompts learners not only to accumulate information, but also to experience the power of knowledge and their potential role within it?

The Parallel Curriculum Model suggests that all learners should have the opportunity to experience the elephant and benefit from "seeing the whole." Moreover, as students gain more expertise in their understanding of all the facets of knowledge, the curriculum should support this development through *ascending levels of intellectual demand.* The following overview of PCM provides readers with a very brief summary of the model and an opportunity to see how the sum of the model's component parts can be used to create qualitatively differentiated curriculum for *all* students.

## THE PARALLEL CURRICULUM: A UNIQUE CURRICULUM MODEL

What is a curriculum model? Why are there so many models to choose from? A curriculum model is a format for curriculum design developed to meet unique needs, contexts, goals, and purposes. To address specific goals and purposes, curriculum developers design or reconfigure one or more curriculum components (see Figure I.1) to create their models. The Parallel Curriculum Model is unique because it is a set of four interrelated, yet parallel, designs for organizing curriculum: core, connections, practice, and identity.

**Figure I.1**   Key Curriculum Components

| Curriculum Component | Definition |
|---|---|
| Content | The knowledge, essential understandings, and skills students are to acquire |
| Assessment | Tools used to determine the extent to which students have acquired the content |
| Introduction | A precursor or forward to a lesson or unit |
| Teaching Methods | Methods teachers use to introduce, explain, model, guide, or assess learning |
| Learning Activities | Cognitive experiences that help students acquire, rehearse, store, transfer, and apply new knowledge and skills |
| Grouping Strategies | The arrangement of students |
| Resources | Materials that support learning and teaching |
| Products | Performances or work samples that constitute evidence of student learning |
| Extension Activities | Enrichment experiences that emerge from representative topics and students' interests |
| Differentiation Based on Learner Need, Including Ascending Levels of Intellectual Demand | Curriculum modifications that attend to students' need for escalating levels of knowledge, skills, and understanding |
| Lesson and Unit Closure | Reflection on the lesson to ensure that the point of the learning experience was achieved or a connection to the unit's learning goal was made |

*Source:* Reprinted from *Teaching for High Potential* (Vol. IV, No. 1, April 2002), published by the National Association for Gifted Children, Washington, DC. www.nagc.org.

# THE FOUR CURRICULUM PARALLELS

Let's look at these parallel designs through the eyes of Lydia Janis, a Grade 5 teacher, who develops expertise in using the four parallels over several years. We will focus on one curriculum unit, Lydia's Civil War unit, in order to illuminate how it changes, or transforms, to accommodate the goals and purposes of each parallel. For the sake of our discussion, we treat each parallel as a separate unit. In reality, teachers use the parallels fluidly to address students' talent development needs. At the end of this summary, we will speak directly to when and how these parallels are used. Readers wishing a more detailed analysis of Lydia's work are referred to Chapters 4 through 7 in both editions of *The Parallel Curriculum Model*.

## The Core Curriculum

Lydia Janis sat at her kitchen table and looked over her textbook objectives for the Civil War unit as well as her state frameworks. She was troubled. She realized that the textbook objectives were low level; they simply called for students to identify and describe facts, such as "Describe how the Civil War began," and "Identify the differences between the North and South." Her frameworks, on the other hand, required different kinds of knowledge and understandings: "Explain reasons for conflicts and the ways conflicts have been resolved in history," and "Understand causal factors and appreciate change over time."

Lydia realized that the content embedded in her frameworks—concepts and principles—lay at the heart of history as a discipline. These key understandings were vastly more powerful, enduring, and essential to the discipline than the facts in the textbook objectives. She decided to keep her textbook and use it as a resource, however. After all, the information was right there on her shelf, she was familiar with the contents, and the topics covered were fairly well aligned with her state frameworks. But Lydia decided to replace the more simplistic objectives found in the text with the objectives found in the state frameworks.

Lydia realized that the change in *content* would necessitate changes in other curriculum components. Her *assessments* would need to match the content. Her assessment tools would need to measure—both pre and post—students' conceptual understanding in addition to basic facts about the time period. Her *introduction* would need to be retooled to prepare students for the various roles they would assume during the unit as analyzers of documents, data, maps, and events, and to lead them to the powerful understandings she had targeted.

Lydia's *teaching methods* would no longer be strictly didactic, such as lecture and direct instruction, but more inductive to support students as they constructed their own understanding of the time period. Her *learning activities* invited students to think about and draw conclusions about maps, documents, and related data. She supplemented the textbook with other *resources*, such as primary source documents, college textbooks, and a video series on the Civil War. She imagined that she would have students who wanted to pursue *extension activities*. She gathered a few books about the Underground Railroad, Abraham Lincoln, and strategic battles. Finally, because she knew already that her students were at different stages in their ability to understand materials and content, she gathered print materials that varied in complexity from song lyrics and easy-to-decipher documents to several "dense" primary-source documents so that *all* students could work at *ascending levels of intellectual demand.*

Lydia also altered the *products* that students created. In a variety of *grouping* arrangements, they completed document-analysis worksheets, ongoing concept maps, and timelines to chronicle their deepening understandings about conflict and the causal relationships of events that led up to the Civil War.

Lydia reflected on her work. She had made significant changes to her teaching and student learning, and she was confident in her improvements. She felt the power of the Core Curriculum as a foundational curriculum.

## The Curriculum of Connections

Later in Lydia's career, she became aware of initiatives for interdisciplinary teaching. She was puzzled by some of the units that were labeled "interdisciplinary." A unit on Mexico, completed recently by fourth graders, came to mind. Students learned and performed the Mexican hat dance, held a fiesta during which they broke a piñata and ate tacos, viewed a display of Mexican money, and drew maps of the migration route of monarch butterflies. "Yikes," she thought to herself, "this unit is an illusion. It *looks* integrated, but it lacks a powerful theme to tie the activities together."

Lydia sat looking at the Core Curriculum unit on the Civil War that she had created a few years before. She thought about the concept that earlier had focused her work—conflict. It reminded her that history repeats itself across people, time periods, and cultures: the Vietnam War, women's suffrage, the civil rights movement, and the civil war in Bosnia. This principle, "history repeats itself," held so much power. She realized that she could use the macroconcept—conflict—and the generalization—history repeats itself—as the content centerpiece to help students build authentic and powerful "bridges" between their understanding of the American Civil War and other times, events, cultures, and people.

Lydia made preliminary plans for her Curriculum of Connections unit. She prepared some assessment prompts, with accompanying rubrics, to assess students' understanding of conflict and the idea that history repeats itself. She developed a preassessment and essential questions for the introduction to clarify the focus for this unit: "What is a war? Do all conflicts have a resolution? Does history repeat itself?" She knew that her teaching strategies would need to help students make their own "bridges" for the connections among the American Civil War and other events and time periods. She decided to emphasize synectics, metaphorical thinking, Socratic questioning, problem-based learning, and debriefing. Her learning activities emphasized analytic thinking skills to help students with the comparisons and contrasts they needed to make and to encourage analogy making. Her supplemental resources were more varied and covered more events, cultures, and time periods than the resources she had used in her old core unit, and the materials that she developed to scaffold student thinking included many more graphic organizers, such as Venn diagrams and reader response questions. She was pleased when she realized that the products, grouping strategies, and extension activities would remain similar to those she had used in the Core Curriculum.

For students needing support with this unit, she developed more detailed graphic organizers; for those needing increasing levels of ascending intellectual demand, she thought of several unfamiliar contexts to which students could apply their new learning, such as the Irish conflict and additional revolutionaries like Nelson Mandela and Elizabeth Cady Stanton. She tucked away these ideas for later use.

Lydia reflected on the modifications she had made. "This unit will benefit all my students, especially my abstract thinkers, students who value the 'big picture,' and my scholars," she thought. "It holds so much promise . . . much different than the Mexican hat dance unit," she mused.

## The Curriculum of Practice

That summer, Lydia realized she could polish the same unit even more. Even though she had seen her students engaged and learning deeply about the Civil War, she began thinking more about how talent develops, specifically how students become acquainted with and skillful in the use of methodologies. "Now that students have the important ideas within and across disciplines, they need to learn how to act like a practitioner," she thought to herself.

So began Lydia's journey through the Curriculum of Practice. She sought out her state and national frameworks to identify the standards related to the role of the historian. To address these, she decided to invite students to read historical novels set during the mid-1800s and record the characters' feelings, images, and perspectives, as well as note how they changed throughout the story. Second, she would deepen students' understandings of these historical perspectives by asking them to read related primary source documents and find evidence to support the characters' feelings and attitudes.

In order for students to complete these tasks, she decided to focus her teaching on the skills of the historian: the steps of historical research, taking notes, determining bias, and analyzing point of view, to name a few. She decided to demonstrate or model these skills for students and then use more indirect teaching methods, such as Socratic questioning, to help students construct their own analyses of primary source material. To help students focus on the methodology of the field, she decided to invite a local museum curator to take part in the introduction of the unit.

Lydia subsequently decided to scaffold students' work with a learning contract. The learning contract required specific learning activities and also asked students to complete several short-term products as well as a culminating project, their historical research. Lydia provided them with a rubric to guide and assess their final work. Lydia knew her grouping formats needed to be fluid to honor students' interests and acknowledge that there were times when students needed to work alone or in pairs. This fluidity would be especially important if students elected to complete extension activities around self-selected research questions.

To accommodate students with sophisticated knowledge about the historical research process, Lydia prepared a list of more complex research topics that required ascending levels of intellectual demand, such as inviting advancing students to conduct oral histories on a topic of their choice.

Lydia reviewed the lessons that now reflected the Curriculum of Practice. "Wow," she thought. "So far, I have three ways to optimize learning." Lydia compared and contrasted the three sets of revisions to the Civil War unit: core, connections, and practice. "Each approach is unique and powerful," she thought. And, she understood why teaching artful curriculum was a satisfying, career-long journey. "What will I discover next?" she wondered.

## The Curriculum of Identity

It was a student who set Lydia on her next journey through the PCM. His name was Jacob, and she was amazed at his knowledge of American history. She envisioned this boy as a history professor, immersed in his own research about historical topics and mentoring others as they investigated questions not yet answered.

She spent time thinking about how she could "morph" her curriculum once more. The content for any identity unit has a triple focus: her already rich Core Curriculum; the ideas, attitudes, beliefs, dispositions, and life outlooks of a professional; and the learning profile of each student, including his or her interests, learning style preferences, values, and goals. Her task, she thought, would be to increase students' awareness about the degree of "fit" between their own emerging sense of self and the profile of practitioners in the field.

Lydia developed a survey of her students' abilities, interests, grouping preferences, goals, and cocurricular activities. Next, she sketched out the stages that students might go through as they went from an early awareness of and interest in history to self-actualization *through* the discipline. "This tool will help me identify where each student currently is on this continuum so I can support his or her progress," she thought.

Now familiar with the many teaching strategies available, Lydia selected visualization as an important method because each student would have to move back and forth between past self, current self, and future self. She also knew that she would use problem-based learning, simulations, and coaching to help students come to understand their place in the Civil War unit as they acted as historians, authors of historical fiction, or war correspondents.

She envisioned her students in varied grouping formats as they spent time with learning activities that required self-analysis and reflection, prediction, and goal setting, among others. Ideas for products came easily to Lydia: completed learning profiles, prompts that asked students to reflect upon and note patterns in their changing profiles, and prompts that invited students to reflect upon the fit between themselves and those of the guest speakers (i.e., a local historian and journalist), who would take part in the introduction to the unit.

Lydia anticipated several extension activities including explorations about notable leaders from the 1860s, as well as less well-known figures, such as the girls who dressed and fought as soldiers during the Civil War. As she gathered resources to support this unit and its potential extensions, she made sure that her collection featured a variety of introspective materials that would help students understand the beliefs, values, goals, achievements, and sacrifices made by practitioners and enable students' comparisons between their own emerging beliefs and attitudes and those of the professionals.

Lydia reflected on her continuing journey with the Parallel Curriculum Model. Her journey elicited a clarity that comes only with time and persistence. She now understood deeply the model's power and promise. It held the power to awaken and support a teacher's passion and focused creativity. Equally important, it held such promise for uncovering and supporting the gifts and talents of *all* students.

Lydia imagined each of her students as a diamond (see Figure I.2). The model's four parallels—core, connections, practice, and identity—served as unique polishing tools to reveal the brilliance in each young person. The core fostered deep understanding in a discipline, while connections elicited the metaphoric thinking required to span the breadth of human knowledge. Practice advanced the methodological skills required to contribute in a field, and identity cultivated the attitudes, values, and life outlook that are prerequisites to self-actualization in a field.

**Figure I.2** Lydia's View of the PCM

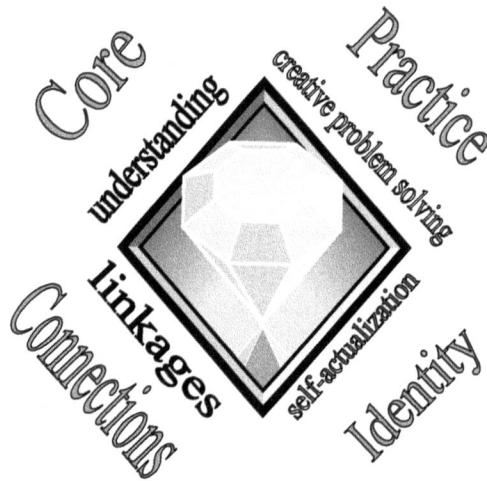

*Source:* Reprinted from *Teaching for High Potential* (Vol. IV, No. 1, April 2002), published by the National Association for Gifted Children, Washington, DC. www.nagc.org.

## THE FOUR PARALLELS: WHEN AND HOW

We began by talking about seven blind men, their limited perceptions about an elephant, and their ultimate realization that "knowing in part may make a fine tale, but wisdom comes from seeing the whole." Lydia's work with each of the parallels illustrates how different curriculum components can be modified to help students gain an understanding and appreciation for the whole of a particular discipline.

There are an infinite number of ways to draw upon the parallels. They can be used to *revise* or *design* tasks, lessons, or units. With a revised or designed unit "in hand," a teacher can move back and forth across one, some, or all parallels in a single unit. Equally attractive, a teacher might use just one parallel to extend a core unit.

Various individuals within a school can use the parallels differently. A classroom teacher can use the parallels separately for different purposes, or teachers can work collectively—within grade levels, or across grade levels and subjects—to use the parallels to support the learning for all, some, or a few students. Furthermore, classroom teachers can use the parallels to modify learning opportunities for students who need something beyond the grade-level curriculum.

What is the driving force behind decisions about when and how to use the parallels? Decisions stem from teacher expertise, the learning goals, and, most important, the students themselves. We draw upon the parallels to make curriculum more meaningful, emotive, powerful, engaging, and more likely to energetically advance the abilities and talents of students.

The PCM holds the power to help students and teachers "see the whole" of what they are learning. It is our hope that curriculum based upon this model will optimize student learning and enhance the likelihood that all students will lead productive and fulfilling lives. We invite practitioners to read more about this model and join us on a professional journey that we believe will yield that joy and wisdom that comes from seeing the whole. The possibilities are limitless.

## THE FORMAT

The curriculum books that are part of our latest initiative share four features that will provide common threads to readers as they transition among the publications. First, each unit contains background information that provides readers with a snapshot of the lessons or unit. If a series of lessons are provided—instead of a whole unit of study—the author may suggest ways to incorporate the subset of lessons into a larger unit. The parallel(s) that the author has elected to emphasize may also be identified, along with the rationale for highlighting the Core Curriculum, Curriculum of Connections, Curriculum of Practice, or Curriculum of Identity. Authors may share their experiences regarding the best time to teach the unit, such as the beginning of the year or well into the last half of the year. Finally, the author may share what students are expected to know before the unit is taught, as well as resources that support the teaching and learning activities.

The second common element is the content framework. One of the "nonnegotiables" of PCM units is that they lead students explicitly to a conceptual understanding of the topics and disciplines on which they are based. Thus, each set of lessons or unit contains a list of concepts, skills, and principles that drive the teaching and learning activities. We also included the national standards addressed in each unit and lesson.

The unit assessments are the third common feature. Within this section, authors have the opportunity to describe the assessments that are included within their lessons. Some authors, especially those who supplied an entire unit of study, included preassessments that align with a performance-based postassessment. All authors have included formative assessments. Naturally, scoring rubrics are included with these assessments. In many cases, authors describe the nature of students' misconception that surface when these performance measures are used, as well as some tips on how to address students' mistaken beliefs.

The final common element is the two-column format for organizing the lessons. In the left-hand column, authors sequence the instruction in a step-by-step manner. In the right-hand column, readers will hear the author's voice, thinking "out loud" about the introduction, teaching and learning activities, and closure. Authors provide many different kinds of information in the right-hand column including, for example, teaching tips, information about student misconceptions, and suggestions on how to differentiate for above-grade-level or below-grade-level students.

## OUR INVITATION . . .

We invite you to peruse and implement these curriculum lessons and units. We believe the use of these lessons will be enhanced to the extent that you incorporate the following:

• *Study PCM.* Read the original book, as well as other companion volumes, including *The Parallel Curriculum in the Classroom: Units for Application Across the Content Areas, K–12* and *The Parallel Curriculum in the Classroom: Essays for Application Across the Content Areas, K–12,* and *The Parallel Curriculum Multimedia Kit.* By studying the model in depth, teachers and administrators will have a clear sense of its goals and purposes.

• *Join us on our continuing journey to refine these curriculum units.* We know better than to suggest that these units are scripts for total success in the classroom. They are, at best, our most thoughtful thinking to date. They are solid evidence that we need to persevere. In small collaborative and reflective teams of practitioners, we invite you to field test these units and make your own refinements.

• *Raise questions about curriculum materials.* Provocative, compelling, and pioneering questions about the quality of curriculum material—and their incumbent learning opportunities—are absolutely essential. Persistent and thoughtful questioning will lead us to the development of strenuous learning opportunities that will contribute to our students' life-long success in the twenty-first century.

• *Compare the units with material developed using other curriculum models.* Through such comparisons, we are better able to make decisions about the use of the model and its related curriculum materials for addressing the unique needs of diverse learners.

## THE K–5 UNIT BOOK

This volume contains six units and sets of lessons. The first is a primary-grade science unit, Plants Alive. Christy McGee designed this ten-lesson unit to help young students "think like scientists." They explore the world of seeds and plants and keep a detailed record of their findings and observations in their science notebooks. Learning how to use technical writing allows them to understand that writers write for many purposes and that writing styles change to support these purposes. Students are exposed to a variety of science skills including observation, inference, measurement, communication, description, prediction, experimental techniques, and research design. Within the ten lessons, she highlights the Core Curriculum and the Curriculum of Practice, and briefly touches on the Curriculum of Connections and the Curriculum of Identity.

Laurie Boen created the second unit, Point of View Under Transition: Using the Work of Chris Van Allsburg for students in Grades 3–5. This unit emphasizes students using the tools of budding writers in the Curriculum of Practice. The unit has its roots as part of the Core Curriculum; however, students are expected to identify and use story elements in their own writing, moving the unit predominantly into the practice parallel. Students are exposed to the Curriculum of Identity when they examine themselves as writers, and the Curriculum of Connections is briefly addressed when students make connections to the arts by using artwork (pictures) to portray their perceptions of beauty.

Leighann Pennington designed the third unit, Experience Poetry, for students in Grades 2–5. Experience Poetry has six lessons designed primarily as a way for students to engage deeply in the discipline of creative writing. Her unit is primarily located in the Core Curriculum, because the unit explores the heart of a discipline, exemplified by the "big understandings" in the discipline of creative writing. Related to the Curriculum of Practice, students learn what a practitioner thinks about and does in daily life, through exploring how practitioners apply the skills and understandings of the creative writing discipline. The unit also touches on the Curriculum of Identity, inherent in how writing poetry helps poets to develop, refine, and express their sense of identity. Students identify their interests and what they love at the beginning of the unit and throughout, using their interests to write original poetry.

Linda Eilers presents Getting to the Heart of Mathematical Numbers and Operations, the fourth unit for students in Grades 2–5. The unit is designed to foster students' conceptual understandings of numbers and operations and might be best used as a companion to other elementary mathematics units to highlight or review important concepts and principles. The eight lessons contained in the unit prompt students to use important mathematic principles, and build new understandings based on prior knowledge. The lessons also provide opportunities for students to demonstrate and explain their reasoning when choosing computational methods. Acting as mathematicians, students produce accurate answers, but more important, explain and represent their thinking and work. The unit focuses on the Core Curriculum with brief lessons in the parallels of connections, practice, and identity.

Jennifer Beasley designed the fifth unit, Preserving Our Identity: Learning About the History of Our State, for students in the intermediate grades. This unit includes six lessons asking students to delve into the "famous faces and facts" of their state, using the methods and practices of someone who really does work with this information—a public historian. While all four parallels are used in this unit, the unit predominantly features the Curriculum of Practice and the Curriculum of Identity, focusing on students' lives and then moving to the history of a state.

Lisa DaVia Rubenstein designed the sixth and final unit, Conundrums in Criminalistics: Clues, Culprits and Conclusions, for students in Grades 4 and 5. This unit includes nine lessons that focus on the topic of forensics, looking at the skills and tools that forensic scientists use, how forensics ties to other disciplines, and what aspects of the field students can relate to most. The unit incorporates all four parallels but it is anchored in the Core Curriculum and the Curriculum of Practice. Since several experiments are included in the unit, the unit provides a detailed list of materials teachers need to complete the learning experiences. Additionally, many resources and suggestions are included for teachers who may want more information on the topic of forensics or have students who would like more advanced sources.

# 1

# Plants Alive

*Christy D. McGee*

## INTRODUCTION TO THE UNIT

### Overview of Unit

This plant unit emphasizes the importance of allowing students to discover scientific concepts and principles through hands-on exploration. In science, it is important to emphasize the concept of thinking like scientists. In this unit, students conduct experiments, create hypotheses, and record results just as scientists do in their laboratories. To encourage students to think like scientists, they wear lab coats and carry clipboards to record their observations of plants under a variety of circumstances.

In each of the lessons, students explore the basic concepts of living and nonliving things, seed germination, plant requirements for living, plant growth, seed dispersal, and plant parts. This unit culminates with a plant fair, allowing students to demonstrate what they learned throughout the unit. They create displays for each lesson that include a demonstration and a poster explaining their research. For the display, they also create a small, room-size plastic "bubble" (Resource 1.15) that serves as a greenhouse. The students fill the greenhouse with a variety of plants that they have categorized.

The purpose of this unit is to teach children how to think like scientists. Students explore the world of seeds and plants, and keep a detailed record of their findings and observations in their science notebooks. Learning how to use technical writing allows them to understand that they write for many purposes and that writing styles change to support these purposes. Students are exposed to a variety of science skills including observation, inference, measurement, communication, description, prediction, experimental techniques, and research design.

In this unit, students explore plant life through the use of the Parallel Curriculum Model (PCM). The Core Curriculum is dominant in that students work with key concepts and principles of science. Students also learn the importance of investigations in science. Keeping a precise account of the protocol used during their experiments teaches them the fundamentals of science inquiry. Posing questions and conducting experiments are essentials in the field of science. This unit is also closely aligned to the state standards of Kentucky. Those standards were developed using the national science standards as their model.

Because science and math are closely correlated, the Curriculum of Practice is also of key interest. Science and math both depend on systematic procedures and precise language to examine the world around us. Students use mathematical concepts when they use measurement to describe the growth of their plants and when they precisely measure the soil and water used when planting.

Language arts is another strong component in this unit. Scientific writing is technical in nature. Throughout the unit students are required to write about their observations, inferences, and predictions, recognizing that technical writing requires clear, concise, and detailed descriptions of events and observations.

The Curriculum of Practice is central in any investigative science unit. Students in this unit conduct experiments, record and follow protocol, learn the importance of a control in an experiment, and write down precise descriptions of observations. These activities emphasize that science is about doing, and the practice parallel is key to learning the scientific concepts and principles that practicing professionals use in a study of plants.

The Curriculum of Identity is also set forth in this unit, assisting students in finding their place in the world. Change, growth, and the importance of systems are central to understanding themselves and the world in which they live. In this unit, students begin to make the connection that the plant system is similar to their own system, in that growth and change are a part of all living things.

## Guiding Questions for the Parallels

### Core Curriculum

1. How do seeds differ in size, shape, color, and texture?

2. What are the various ways that seeds are dispersed?

3. What do plants need to grow?

4. What is the function of the parts of the plants?

5. How does a seed turn into a plant?

6. Can seeds sprout without soil?

7. What's inside fruit?

8. How are vegetables and fruits different?

### Curriculum of Practice

1. What do we know about plants?

2. How do scientists do their work?

3. How does experimental design work?

4. Why do scientists have to be so precise when recording their findings?

### Curriculum of Connections

1. Can writing solidify scientific understanding?

2. What role does mathematics play in the study of plants?

3. How does reading assist scientists in their work?

### Curriculum of Identity

1. What are the effects of people traveling to different places?

2. Do people share some of the same needs as plants?

3. What characteristics do living things share?

## Background for the Unit

The lessons in this unit assume that primary-aged children know very little technical information about seeds and plants. The use of the KWL (know, want to know, learned) as an introductory activity allows the teacher to assess student knowledge and understanding. It also allows the teacher to group students by readiness levels so that students who are budding horticulturists can move at a quicker pace than those who know very little about the plant world.

This unit is based on national and state standards for children at the primary level. It provides introductory activities that require students to explore the concept of living and nonliving matter, seeds, germination, plant growth, seed dispersal, seed classification, and, finally, the processes of organizing and delivering a plant fair for parents and other students at school.

A critical component of this unit is the classroom community. Students should be used to working together cooperatively to solve problems. Students should also be empowered in their classroom to be in control of their learning environment and themselves. Empowered students flourish in an inquiry-based classroom, and inquiry-based science demands that students explore the materials they work with and make decisions about how to use those materials. Students subsequently are responsible, focused, and intent in exploring the lessons.

# CONTENT FRAMEWORK

## Organizing Concepts

### Macroconcepts

M1: Cycles

M2: Systems

M3: Change

*Discipline-Specific Concepts*

C1: Patterns

C2: Production

C3: Survival

## Principles

1. Things in the environment are classified as living, nonliving, and once living.

2. Living things differ from nonliving things.

3. Organisms are classified into groups by using various characteristics (e.g., body coverings, body structures).

4. Plants grow from seeds and need water, soil, air, and nutrients to grow.

5. Seeds differ in size, shape, color, and texture and are dispersed in a variety of ways.

6. Each plant or animal has observable structures that serve different functions in growth, survival, and reproduction.

7. The details of a life cycle are different for different organisms. Observations of different life cycles are made in order to identify patterns and recognize similarities and differences.

## National Science Education Standards

*Content Standard A*

As a result of activities in Grades K–4, all students should develop

1. Abilities necessary to do scientific inquiry

2. Understanding about scientific inquiry

*Content Standard C*

As a result of activities in Grades K–4, all students should develop understanding of

1. The characteristics of organisms

2. Life cycles of organisms

3. Organisms and environments

## Kentucky State Standards

*Key to Standards*

Each content standard is preceded by a code. The code begins with SC for science followed by a grade-level designation and then a three-digit number that indicates subdomain, organizer, and sequential standard, respectively. The codes are deciphered in the first set of standards. The codes used for the rest of the standards are listed as follows.

| Grade-Level Codes | Subdomain | Organizer |
|---|---|---|
| EP = End of primary | 1 = Physical science | 1 = Structure and transformation of matter |
| 04 = Fourth grade | 2 = Earth/space science | 2 = Motion and forces |
| 05 = Fifth grade | 3 = Biological science | 3 = Earth and the universe |
| 06 = Sixth grade | 4 = Unifying concepts | 4 = Unity and diversity |
| 07 = Seventh grade | | 5 = Biological change |
| 08 = Eighth grade | | 6 = Energy transformations |

| Program of Studies: Understandings | Program of Studies: Skills and Concepts | Related Core Content for Assessment |
|---|---|---|
| **SC-P-UD-U-1 (Science-Primary-Unity & Diversity-Understanding-1st Standard)** <br><br> Students will understand that most living things need water, food, and air while nonliving things can continue to exist without any requirements. | **SC-P-UD-S-1 (Science-Primary-Unity & Diversity-Skills-1st Standard)** <br><br> Students will describe the basic needs of organisms and explain how these survival needs can be met only in certain environments. <br><br> **SC-P-UD-S-7** <br><br> Students will ask questions that can be investigated, plan and conduct "fair tests," and communicate (e.g., write, draw, speak, use multimedia) findings to others. | **SC-EP-3.4.1 (Science-End of Primary-Biology-Unity & Diversity-1st Standard)** <br><br> Students will explain the basic needs of organisms. <br><br> For example, organisms have basic needs. Animals need air, water, and food; plants need air, water, nutrients, and light. Organisms can survive only in environments in which their needs can be met. <br><br> **DOK 2** <br> **SC-EP-3.4.2** <br><br> Students will understand that things in the environment are classified as living, nonliving, and once living. For example, living things differ from nonliving things. Organisms are classified into groups by using various characteristics (e.g., body coverings, body structures). |
| **SC-P-UD-U-2** <br><br> Students will understand that plants and animals have features that help them live in different environments. | **SC-P-UD-S-1** <br><br> Students will describe the basic needs of organisms and explain how these survival needs can be met only in certain environments. <br><br> **SC-P-UD-S-2** <br><br> Students will identify the characteristics that define a habitat. | **SC-EP-3.4.3** <br><br> Students will describe the basic structures and related functions of plants and animals that contribute to growth, reproduction, and survival. <br><br> For example, each plant or animal has observable structures that serve different functions in growth, survival, and reproduction. Humans have |

*(Continued)*

(Continued)

| Program of Studies: Understandings | Program of Studies: Skills and Concepts | Related Core Content for Assessment |
|---|---|---|
| | **SC-P-UD-S-3**<br>Students will investigate adaptations that enable animals and plants to grow, reproduce and survive (e.g., movements, body coverings, method of reproduction).<br><br>**SC-P-UD-S-4**<br>Students will analyze structures of plants and animals to make inferences about the types of environments for which they are suited.<br><br>**SC-P-UD-S-7**<br>Students will ask questions that can be investigated, plan and conduct "fair tests," and communicate (e.g., write, draw, speak, use multimedia) findings to others. | distinct body structures for walking, holding, seeing, and talking. These observable structures are explored to sort, classify, compare, and describe organisms. |
| **SC-P-UD-U-3**<br>Students will understand that the offspring of living things are very much like their parents, but not exactly alike. | **SC-P-UD-S-5**<br>Students will use scientific tools (e.g., hand lens/magnifier, metric rule, balance) to observe, make comparisons of organisms, and to classify organisms using one or more of their external characteristics (e.g., body coverings, body structures). | **SC-EP-3.4.4**<br>Students will describe a variety of plant and animal life cycles to understand patterns of the growth, development, reproduction, and death of an organism.<br><br>For example, plants and animals have life cycles that include the beginning of life, growth and development, reproduction, and death. The details of a life cycle are different for different organisms. Observations of different life cycles are made in order to identify patterns and recognize similarities and differences. |
| **SC-P-UD-U-5**<br>Students will understand that organisms may not be able to survive if some of their parts are missing. | **SC-P-UD-S-3**<br>Students will investigate adaptations that enable animals and plants to grow, reproduce, and survive (e.g., movements, body coverings, method of reproduction).<br><br>**SC-P-UD-S-4**<br>Students will analyze structures of plants and animals to make inferences about the types of environments for which they are suited.<br><br>**SC-P-UD-S-7**<br>Students will ask questions that can be investigated, plan and conduct "fair tests," and communicate (e.g., write, draw, speak, use multimedia) findings to others. | |

## UNIT ASSESSMENTS

| | |
|---|---|
| *Preassessment* | Classification activity and KWL chart |
| *Formative Assessments* | Science journal entries (in 1-inch binders so lab reports can be added) |
| | Lab reports for each of the experiments conducted |
| | Observation checklists |
| | Discussion checklists |
| *Summative Assessments* | Plant fair and science notebooks |
| *Self-Assessments* | Daily checklist on group work |
| | Overall assessment of each summative assessment |
| *Unit Assessment by Students* | Completion of *W* and *L* on KWL chart |

## UNIT SEQUENCE AND TEACHER REFLECTION

### LESSON 1.1: WHAT DO WE KNOW ABOUT PLANTS?

**Length:** One 45–50-minute session

| Unit Sequence | Reflection |
|---|---|
| **Principles**<br><br>• Plants grow from seeds and need water, soil, air, and nutrients to grow.<br>• Seeds differ in size, shape, color, and texture and are dispersed in a variety of ways.<br>• Each plant or animal has observable structures that serve different functions in growth, survival, and reproduction. | KWL helps the teacher assess what students already know about plants. Putting the students' initials by their contributions serves as a checklist for a preassessment. |
| **Skills**<br><br>Communication, prediction, and inference | |
| **Guiding Questions**<br><br>• What do we know about plants?<br>• How do scientists do their work? | Developing two KWLs—one that explores student knowledge of plants and one that explores their understanding of how scientists work—sets the stage for this unit of study. |

*(Continued)*

(Continued)

| Unit Sequence | Reflection |
|---|---|
| **Materials Needed**<br><br>• Paper and pencils<br>• White "lab coats" and clipboards for each student | *Author's note:* I go to thrift stores and buy men's white dress shirts to serve as lab coats. I write each child's name on the shirt above the pocket in permanent marker. The students love wearing their lab coats and using clipboards to hold their lab reports. |
| **Introduction**<br><br>The teacher explains KWL if students have not used this organizer before. | |
| **Teaching Strategies and Learning Experiences**<br><br>The teacher introduces this unit by talking about the work of scientists, noting the importance of lab protocol, accuracy, and details. Students brainstorm what they know and what they want to know about plants.<br><br>This can be a whole-class activity or students can work in teams and make one KWL chart per group.<br><br>Students record this activity using the KWL chart with the *K* and *W* columns completed for their science notebooks. | For lab coats, the teacher can request that students bring an old, white dress shirt from home. (Extras can be purchased at Goodwill stores for a minimal amount of money.) With help, students then print their names over the left pockets in fabric pen. Students also have an individual clipboard to hold their lab reports. Donning the lab coat and using a clipboard adds to the seriousness of their work and helps to eliminate behavior problems. The teacher can empower students by allowing them to run the brainstorming session while the teacher scribes.<br><br>The team's KWL serves as a preassessment and allows for a variety of grouping practices. For example, the teacher can group students by readiness level or interest.<br><br>An excellent resource for the KWL strategy is an article found at www.accessmylibrary.com/coms2/ summary_0286–92503_ITM. The article describes using this reading strategy in a content area. |
| **Closure**<br><br>Students complete a lab sheet for their science notebooks that states three things they already knew and three things they still want to know about plants. | |

## LESSON 1.2: IS IT ALIVE?

**Length:** Two 45–50-minute sessions

| Unit Sequence | Reflection |
|---|---|
| **Concepts**<br><br>• Systems<br>• Cycles<br>• Change | |

| Unit Sequence | Reflection |
|---|---|
| **Principles**<br><br>• Things in the environment are classified as living, nonliving, and once living.<br>• Living things differ from nonliving things. | |
| **Skills**<br><br>Observation, description, communication, and prediction | |
| **Standards**<br><br>*KY State Standards*<br><br>SC-P-UD-U-1<br><br>*NSES Standards*<br><br>C1 | |
| **Guiding Question**<br><br>What characteristics do living things share? | Allowing the students to discover the different types of classification systems allows the teacher to assess the depth of student understanding and creativity. |
| **Materials Needed**<br><br>Rocks, buttons, soil, sand, empty seashells, and plant life (flowers or a small container of plants) Leaves, animals (meal worms, ants, or flies), and a variety of manmade objects | |
| **Introduction**<br><br>Each group has a variety of animate and inanimate objects. Through observation and classification, students think about the differences. By creating four to six stations in the room where students can compare and contrast these objects, the teacher allows students to discover the purpose of this lesson. Objects include inanimate ones such as rocks, soil, sand, and seashells (empty), and animate ones such as growing grass, leaves, animals, and insects. | By observing the students during this activity, the teacher gains insight into the children's knowledge of classification and identifies which students are already able to distinguish between living and nonliving things. |
| **Teaching Strategies and Learning Experiences**<br><br>In this opening lesson using discovery learning, students "mess around" with materials that promote their thinking and understanding of what it means to be alive.<br><br>An important scientific process is the ability to classify. | Jerome Bruner introduced the discovery method of learning. He encouraged teachers to allow children to discover scientific concepts by using the science processes to learn them.<br><br>In this lesson, students use the science processes of observation and classification to make predictions about the characteristics of the things they observe. |

*(Continued)*

(Continued)

| Unit Sequence | Reflection |
|---|---|
| *Observation/Classification*<br><br>The teacher guides students through the following steps:<br><br>• Ask the students to observe the selection of objects and record them on their lab report. They are to complete their work on this part of the lesson individually.<br>• Once this step is accomplished, have the students work together in groups of four (arranged by readiness levels) to discuss the various ways they made their classifications.<br>• Instruct students to compile their various categories into one list that they prioritize by the number of times they use each classification scheme.<br><br>*Class Discussion*<br><br>The students share their ideas with the whole class. If they have not made the connection of inanimate and animate objects, the teacher can assist them in doing so by asking,<br><br>*What makes the animals, insects, and plants different from the other things you observed?*<br><br>Students then complete a lab report (Resource 1.1). | Teachers can differentiate this lesson by providing the students with lab reports that vary in depth and the number of steps required to complete them.<br><br>*Author's note:* I have provided one type of report, but teachers should differentiate these reports by student readiness level and need.<br><br>The teacher provides each group with six to eight objects to classify. The lab report (Resource 1.1) serves as a formative assessment for student understanding of the classification of objects as living or nonliving.<br><br>Students' lists should generate that the plants and animals (this includes the insects) differ from the other objects they observe.<br><br>Websites with worksheets for living and nonliving things may be found at www.teachervision.fen.com/childrens-science-activities/printable/31997.html. |
| **Closure**<br><br>Students respond to the following question in their science journals:<br><br>What do the living things need in order to survive?<br><br>An extension for this activity can be a schoolyard walk with students continuing to explore the concept of living and nonliving things. Students note what they see in their science journals and then think-pair-share on commonalities of the plants and animals around them. | It is important not to rush this part of the lesson. Students need to know that what they put in their science notebook is important. Scientists keep detailed notes of their work and since the students are scientists, they must do the same thing. This entry will solidify what the students know about the needs of living things. Most students will be able to describe those needs in their journals after their observation and classification of the objects. Students who have more difficulty writing can draw what those needs are or the teacher can provide them with a more definitive worksheet that includes more opportunities to think about those classifications.<br><br>The schoolyard walk is a day-two activity for this concept. The amount of time needed to teach the concept of living and nonliving characteristics varies with the age and readiness levels of the students involved. |

## LESSON 1.3: WHAT'S IN A SEED?

**Length:** Two 45–60-minute sessions

| Unit Sequence | Reflection |
|---|---|
| **Concepts**<br><br>• Growth<br>• Change<br>• Systems | |
| **Principle**<br><br>Each plant or animal has observable structures that serve different functions in growth, survival, and reproduction. | |
| **Skills**<br><br>Conducting an experiment, measuring, informative writing, and research techniques | |
| **Standards**<br><br>*KY State Standards*<br>SC-P-UD-U-1, SC-P-UD-S-1, and SC-EP-3.4.1; SC-P-UD-U-2, SC-P-UD-S-1, and SC-EP-3.4.3; SC-P-UD-U-4, SC-P-UD-S-5, and SC-EP-3.4.4<br><br>*NSES Standards*<br>A1, A2, C1, C2 | |
| **Guiding Question**<br><br>What is inside a seed? | |
| **Materials Needed**<br><br>• Lima bean seeds soaked overnight<br>• A toothpick to help pry the seed open<br>• Lab report<br>• Handheld microscope or magnifying glass | |
| **Introductory Activity**<br><br>After reminding the students that they are scientists in search of answers about plant life, the teacher holds up a lima bean seed and prompts,<br><br>*What do you think is inside this seed? Once you have taken some time to answer that question, draw what you think you would find in the seed.* | This activity makes students think about the inside of a seed. By encouraging them to think like scientists, the teacher motivates them to take their work on this unit more seriously. |
| **Teaching Strategies and Learning Experiences**<br><br>Students work in cooperative groups, heterogeneous or differentiated by readiness level. | |

(Continued)

| Unit Sequence | Reflection |
|---|---|
| The teacher guides students through the following steps:<br><br>• Model how to open the seed, stressing the need for handling it gently.<br>• Ask the students to look for separate parts of the seed that they can see.<br>• Withhold the names of the parts until the students have time to observe what they see.<br>• During the observation time (10 minutes), check with each group, using probing questions to assist student understanding.<br>• At the end of the observation time, ask the students to discuss what they found within their group.<br>• Ask the group recorder to list the group findings.<br>• Follow this protocol:<br><br>  o *Provide at least one handheld microscope for each group of students.*<br>  o *Pass out lima beans that have been soaked overnight.*<br>  o *Instruct students to open the seed with their thumbnail or carefully use a toothpick.*<br><br>• Tell students to describe the inside of the seed and write those descriptions in their science notebooks, using the following prompts:<br><br>  o *What do you notice about your seed?*<br>  o *How does the inside feel?*<br>  o *Is there a smell? How would you describe it?*<br>  o *Does it look like the picture you just drew of a seed?*<br><br>• Ask students to draw a second picture of what they now see in their seeds.<br>• On the board, draw a diagram of the open seed (these are easily found on the Internet).<br><br>  o *Label the three parts: seed coat (outside protective tissue), cotyledon (food supply), and plant embryo.* | Seeds come in a variety of shapes and sizes, but they all share three things: (1) seed cover or coat, (2) plant embryo, and (3) food supply. The seed coat protects the seed. In lima beans and other plants, the seed food comes in the form of two seed leaves or cotyledons. Other seeds, such as corn and rice, have a single cotyledon. The baby plant has embryonic leaves and a root.<br><br>    Useful resources found on the Internet include a lesson plan and diagram of bean and corn seed found at www.herbsociety .org/fhc/fseeds2.php.<br><br>    Other helpful resources are *How a Seed Grows (Let's-Read-and-Find . . . Science 1)* by Helene J. Jordan and Loretta Krupinski and *From Seed to Plant (Rookie Read-About Science)* by Allan Fowler. |
| **Closure**<br><br>Students complete a lab report (Resource 1.2).<br><br>    Students review the questions provided in the teacher strategies and learning experiences section and respond in their science notebooks.<br><br>    On the second day of the activity, students examine a variety of seeds (corn, pea, mustard, grass, sunflower, etc.) and make predictions about the type of plant it is and how large it will grow (and add these predictions to the science notebook). Students research the other seeds so they can see if their predictions are correct. They can also explain the different lengths of germination. | The teacher ensures that students have the parts labeled correctly and reteaches if they have not labeled the parts correctly. It is important for students to understand the importance of their work and to be as detailed and precise as possible.<br><br>    Their research findings go into their science notebooks and are used as a reference when they make predictions about growth rate in subsequent lessons in this unit.<br><br>    As with the previous lesson, this takes more than one day to complete. |

## LESSON 1.4: WHAT DO SEEDS NEED TO GROW?

**Length:** One 45–50-minute session

| Unit Sequence | Reflection |
|---|---|
| **Concepts**<br><br>• Cycles<br>• Change<br>• Systems | |
| **Principles**<br><br>Plants grow from seeds and need water, soil, air, and nutrients to grow. | |
| **Skills**<br><br>Measurement, prediction, and communication | Students precisely measure the appropriate amount of soil for their container and add a measured amount of water. |
| **Guiding Questions**<br><br>• How does a seed turn into a plant?<br>• Can seeds sprout without soil? | Students understand that when a seed germinates it sprouts. |
| **Materials Needed**<br><br>• A small bag of lima bean seeds soaked overnight<br>• Grass seed<br>• A variety of seeds to plant (alfalfa seeds, sunflower seeds, millet, buckwheat, etc.)<br>• Clear plastic 8 to 12 ounce cups (two per child) to serve as containers<br>• One egg carton per group<br>• Potting soil: ¾ cup for each student's cup and approximately 2 cups of soil for each egg carton planter<br>• Water: ½ cup of water per clear plastic container, and ¾ cup of water for the egg carton planter<br>• Measuring cylinders<br>• Brown paper towels (the ones most schools supply work best)<br>• 1-quart ziplock bag for each student | Students make a natural connection to math by measuring the soil and water. |
| **Standards**<br><br>*KY State Standards*<br><br>SC-P-UD-U-1, SC-P-UD-S-1, and SC-EP-3.4.1; SC-P-UD-U-2, SC-P-UD-S-1, and SC-EP-3.4.3; SC-P-UD-U-4, SC-P-UD-S-5, and SC-EP-3.4.4<br><br>*NSES Standards*<br><br>A1, A2, C1, C2 | |

(Continued)

| Unit Sequence | Reflection |
|---|---|
| **Introductory Activity**<br><br>The teacher asks students,<br><br>*Do you remember when we looked at the inside of a lima bean seed? What did we find?*<br><br>After students answer the question, the teacher focuses on the baby plant and introduces the word *germinate*. Students should infer how they think the seed will become a plant. They can discuss this in their small groups and write down their inferences in their science notebooks. | This is a review for the students. |
| **Teaching Strategies and Learning Experiences**<br><br>Working in small groups, the teacher prompts students to complete the following tasks:<br><br>• Plant two containers of lima bean seeds per group.<br>• Plant a variety of seeds in an egg carton.<br>   o *Once the seeds are planted, label them by placing three of the seeds on a piece of tape and placing the tape over the area where you planted that type of seed. Repeat this for each of the two remaining areas.*<br>• Plant a bean seed and an alfalfa seed in ziplock bags to observe how the seeds begin to germinate.<br>   o *Predict which seed you think will sprout first (the one in the bag or the one in the soil).*<br>   o *Record your predictions in your science notebooks.*<br><br>The teacher gives students precise directions as to the amount of soil and water used in their experiments (Resource 1.3). They record all of their protocol in their science notebooks.<br><br>The teacher specifies planting in the egg carton, containers, and ziplock bags as follows:<br><br>• Place three different types of seeds in the egg carton (four sections per seed).<br>   o *Place about 2 centimeters of soil in each section.*<br>   o *Place the seeds over each area.*<br>   o *Cover with soil.*<br>   o *Water to moisten soil and keep soil moist throughout the experiment.*<br>   o *To identify the new plants, place three of each type of seed used on a piece of tape and place it on the lid of the egg carton above the same type of planted seeds in the egg carton. Do this with each type of seed.*<br>• In the containers (plastic cups), plant two bean plants per group.<br>   o *Measure ¾ cup of potting soil and put it in the container.* | This activity empowers students to take charge of their learning environment. Each group has the following jobs: lead scientist, materials handler, assistant materials handler, and recorder. Well-organized materials for the handlers assist in this activity. Task cards with the directions clearly and simply stated are also helpful. Additionally, it is important for students to realize that there isn't one right way to do something. Mistakes are an important part of a scientist's work. In fully assuming the role of scientists, students focus on their experiments and really act like scientists.<br><br>By making predictions about the time it will take their seeds to germinate, students begin to see the need for predictions based on evidence. It is illogical to think that the seed may take months to germinate. By discussing with the students ways scientists make hypotheses, the teacher allows them to see the need to base their predictions on prior knowledge and research. By reflecting on what they see in the spring when plants begin to germinate and grow, students make more accurate predictions.<br><br>*Author's note:* I use the strategy of thinking out loud to let them hear how I reason through problems so they have something on which to model their thinking.<br><br>The following books are excellent resources: *From Seed to Sunflower* and *How It Works: The World of Plant Life* by Gerald Legg; *What Is a Plant? The Science of Living Things, Introducing Living Things* by Bobbie Kalman; and *All About Plants* by Lisa V. Matthews. |

| Unit Sequence | Reflection |
|---|---|
|     o *Place the unopened presoaked bean seed in a ½-inch hole.*<br>    o *Cover gently with dirt—don't pack it.*<br>    o *Use a graduated cylinder to measure and pour ⅓ cup of water into the container.*<br>    o *Place it in a warm sunny area.*<br>    o *Water as necessary.*<br>• In the ziplock bags, plant seeds as follows:<br>    o *Fold the paper towel so there is a pocket for the seed to sit in.*<br>    o *Poke a hole in the bottom of the fold with a pencil.*<br>    o *Wet the paper towel so it is saturated, but not dripping.*<br>    o *Place the seed in the fold.*<br>    o *Zip the bag leaving a 1-inch opening at the top and hang it where it will get sunlight.*<br><br>Upon completion of the planting, students predict the number of days it will take for their plants to germinate and record their predictions in their science notebooks (Resource 1.4). | |
| **Closure**<br><br>Students share their predictions with others in their group, explaining why they chose the number of days they did for each seed. They record their explanations in their science notebooks along with their predictions.<br>    The teacher asks,<br><br>*What other things grow and change?*<br><br>As a follow-up, students can bring in pictures of a pet growing up, themselves as they grow, and so on. This discussion emphasizes the connection between students' own growth cycles and those of plants. | This reinforces the concept of accuracy in the scientific world.<br>    It is important to offer students a choice regarding the charts they use. Some students will be able to create their own chart, while others will need templates to follow. |

## LESSON 1.5: OBSERVING GERMINATING PLANTS

**Daily Observation and Notation of Growth:** 10 minutes

**Length:** One 45–50-minute session

| Unit Sequence | Reflection |
|---|---|
| **Concepts**<br><br>• Growth<br>• Systems | |

(Continued)

| Unit Sequence | Reflection |
|---|---|
| **Principles**<br><br>• Plants grow from seeds and need water, soil, air, and nutrients to grow.<br>• The details of a life cycle are different for different organisms. Observations of different life cycles are made in order to identify patterns and recognize similarities and differences. | |
| **Skills**<br><br>Investigative inquiry | |
| **Guiding Questions**<br><br>• What do plants need to grow?<br>• How does experimental design work?<br>• How do scientists do their work?<br>• Do people share some of the same needs as plants?<br>• What role does mathematics play in the study of plants? | |
| **Materials Needed**<br><br>• Six of the bean plants previously planted by the students to serve as a control<br>• Plastic pellets or packing pellets<br>• A dark place to keep the plants | |
| **Standards**<br><br>SC-P-UD-U-1, SC-P-UD-S-1, and SC-EP-3.4.1; SC-P-UD-U-2, SC-P-UD-S-1, and SC-EP-3.4.3; SC-P-UD-U-4, SC-P-UD-S-5, and SC-EP-3.4.4 | |
| **Introductory Activity**<br><br>The teacher asks students,<br><br>*How are your plants doing? Why do you think they are growing so well?*<br><br>A discussion follows explaining that to find out the needs of plants, scientists conduct experiments that test the conditions in which the plants live. In scientific terms, these requirements are known as *variables.* In order to test a variable, the conditions must remain exactly the same for everything else that affects the plant.<br>The teacher then asks students,<br><br>*What would happen if we changed some of the conditions in which the plants are growing? What conditions could we change? How do you think we could test these conditions?* | During this discussion, students review the growth of their plants. By discussing what conditions the plants are growing under, they are encouraged to think about what the plant needs to grow. Once they have named some of the conditions, the discussion about what to change gleans that light, water, soil, and nutrients have helped them grow.<br>Students brainstorm ways they might test the variables guiding them to reasonable tests. |

| Unit Sequence | Reflection |
|---|---|
| **Teaching Strategies and Learning Experiences**<br><br>In groups arranged by readiness levels, students use brainstorming and inquiry-based learning.<br>    The teacher brainstorms with students about what conditions to change for their plants. (Students should mention light, water, and soil.) The students conduct the following experiments:<br><br>1. Two groups place one of their plants in a dark place.<br><br>2. Two groups withhold water from one of their plants.<br><br>3. Two groups repot one of their plants in plastic pellets.<br><br>4. All groups ensure that every other condition remains exactly the same.<br><br>5. The remaining plants serve as the control group and continue to receive light and water.<br><br>6. Students predict what they think will happen to each of the plants.<br><br>7. Students observe their plants daily and note any changes taking place in their science notebooks.<br><br>Students complete lab reports (Resources 1.5 through 1.8) over the test period. | It is important to make sure the students understand that all other variables remain constant during this experiment. For example, the plant placed in the dark should continue to be watered and the plant receiving no water should continue to receive sunlight.<br>    This activity takes at least two weeks of observations. When the plants begin to change, the teacher leads a discussion about what they found and what they can infer from their findings. Students should also infer that soil provides more than a medium in which to anchor plants; it also provides nutrients to the plants. Students record their thoughts in their science notebooks by drawing what they see happening to each of the experimental plants and inferring why they think the plant reacts as it does. |

## LESSON 1.6: PLANT PARTS!

**Daily Observation:** 10 minutes

**Length:** Three 45–50-minute sessions

| Unit Sequence | Reflection |
|---|---|
| **Concepts**<br><br>• Systems<br>• Cycles | |
| **Principle**<br><br>Each plant or animal has observable structures that serve different functions in growth, survival, and reproduction. | Not all plants have stems, leaves, or roots, but students can explore this later or it can be an independent project for a student who excels in plant study. |
| **Skills**<br><br>Observation, classification, and measurement | |
| **Guiding Questions**<br><br>• What is the function of the parts of the plants?<br>• What characteristics do living things share? | |

*(Continued)*

(Continued)

| Unit Sequence | Reflection |
|---|---|
| **Materials Needed**<br><br>• Twelve different healthy potted plants<br>• Books about plants for students to use for research<br>• Websites for students to visit to learn more about plants<br>• Handheld microscopes or magnifying glasses for each pair of students | It is essential to use a plant that has easily distinguishable leaves and stems.<br>Handheld microscopes can be expensive. By procuring six handhelds (one for each group), students each have the opportunity to use one. The less expensive magnifying glass allows for each student to continue observing their plant while others use the handhelds. |
| **Standards**<br><br>SC-P-UD-U-1, SC-P-UD-S-1, and SC-EP-3.4.1; SC-P-UD-U-2, SC-P-UD-S-1, and SC-EP-3.4.3; SC-P-UD-U-4, SC-P-UD-S-5, and SC-EP-3.4.4 | |
| **Introductory Activity**<br><br>The teacher displays the twelve different plants for the students to observe, explaining that they will be paired and given one of the types of plants to thoroughly examine. Discussion focuses on what the students should be looking for during their examination. Students record what they will look for in their science notebooks. | Students describe what they see and mention the stem, leaves, soil, container, and so on. |
| **Teaching Strategies and Learning Experiences**<br><br>Students learn about the parts of plants through discovery learning and a jigsaw activity.<br>    The teacher gives each pair of students a healthy potted plant, asking them to observe what they see and to make sure they use the points they recorded in their science notebooks.<br>    After an appropriate amount of time, the teacher invites the students to share what they notice about the plants. If no one mentions roots, the teacher asks,<br><br>*Is there more to the plant than what you see?*<br><br>The teacher then shows students how to remove their potted plants from the containers and gently shake off the soil to allow examination of the roots of the plant using a handheld microscope or magnifying glass. | It helps if the soil surrounding the plants is semidry, and to remind the students to treat the plants as gently as possible because they are going to replant them to see if they will continue to grow after being disturbed.<br>    Once the roots are exposed, it is helpful to spray them lightly with water so they do not dry out.<br>    Some of the plants may not survive this examination, which can lead to a discussion about the need to carefully transplant plants.<br>    With a reminder, students gently remove the plants from the containers and observe the root system, the stem, and the leaves of the plant. They use handheld microscopes to examine the plant parts and note what they see in their science notebooks.<br>    After examining the plant, they gently replant it and give it sufficient water. In their science notebooks, students draw the parts of the plants and label them.<br>    Some good resources include the University of Illinois Extension, www.urbanext.uiuc.edu/gpe/case1/c1facts2a.html and the Enchanted Learning website, www.enchantedlearning.com/subjects/plants/label/plantsimple/. |

| Unit Sequence | Reflection |
|---|---|
| **Closure**<br><br>Students repot the plant and complete their drawings (Resource 1.9). They also record reflections about the activity in their science notebooks.<br><br>**Day 2 and Day 3 Activity**<br><br>In the jigsaw activity, the teacher divides the class into groups of four. One person from each group becomes an expert on one plant part (stem, leaf, root, and flower). After researching, the student returns to the group and explains each plant part's function. The students then complete their research log. | Depending on the age of the students and their readiness levels, this part of the lesson can be as easy or as complex as the teacher sees fit. A variety of plant reference books varying in complexity provide helpful resources for the students. If computers are available, students can use the Internet resources provided here. A simple search of the Internet also reveals many additional student-friendly resources for teachers. |

## LESSON 1.7: THE NEEDS OF EVERY LIVING THING

**Length:** One 45–50-minute session

| Unit Sequence | Reflection |
|---|---|
| **Concepts**<br><br>• Growth<br>• Systems | |
| **Principles**<br><br>• Plants grow from seeds and need water, soil, air, and nutrients to grow.<br>• The details of a life cycle are different for different organisms. Observations of different life cycles are made in order to identify patterns and recognize similarities and differences. | |
| **Skill**<br><br>Investigative inquiry | |
| **Guiding Questions**<br><br>• What do plants need to grow?<br>• How does experimental design work?<br>• How do scientists do their work?<br>• Do people share some of the same needs as plants?<br>• What role does mathematics play in the study of plants? | |

(Continued)

| Unit Sequence | Reflection |
|---|---|
| **Materials Needed**<br><br>• Six of the bean plants previously planted by the students to serve as a control<br>• Plastic pellets or packing pellets<br>• A dark place to keep the plants | |
| **Standards**<br><br>SC-P-UD-U-1, SC-P-UD-S-1, and SC-EP-3.4.1; SC-P-UD-U-2, SC-P-UD-S-1, and SC-EP-3.4.3; SC-P-UD-U-4, SC-P-UD-S-5, and SC-EP-3.4.4 | |
| **Introductory Activity**<br><br>The teacher asks students,<br><br>*How are your plants doing? Why do you think they are growing so well?*<br><br>A discussion follows explaining that to find out the needs of plants, scientists conduct experiments that test the conditions in which the plants live. In scientific terms, these requirements are known as *variables*. In order to test a variable, the conditions must remain exactly the same for everything else that affects the plant. The teacher then asks,<br><br>*What would happen if we changed some of the conditions in which the plants are growing? What conditions could we change? How do you think we could test these conditions?* | During this discussion, students review the growth of their plants. By asking what conditions the plants are growing under, the teacher encourages them to think about what the plant needs to grow. Once they have named some of the conditions, the discussion about what to change gleans that light, water, soil, and nutrients have helped them grow.<br><br>Students brainstorm ways they might test the variables guiding them to reasonable tests. |
| **Teaching Strategies and Learning Experiences**<br><br>In groups arranged by readiness levels, students use brainstorming and inquiry-based learning.<br><br>The teacher brainstorms with students about what conditions they want to change for their plants. (Students should mention light, water, and soil.) The students then conduct the following experiments:<br><br>1. Two groups place one of their plants in a dark place.<br><br>2. Two groups withhold water from one of their plants.<br><br>3. Two groups repot one of their plants in plastic pellets.<br><br>4. All groups ensure that every other condition remains exactly the same. | It is important to make sure the students understand that all other variables remain constant during this experiment. For example, the plant placed in the dark should continue to be watered and the plant receiving no water should continue to receive sunlight.<br><br>This activity takes at least two weeks of observations. When the plants begin to change, the teacher leads a discussion about what they found and what they can infer from their findings. Students should also infer that soil provided more than a medium in which to anchor plants; it also provides nutrients to the plants. Students record their thoughts in their science notebooks by drawing what they see happening to each of |

| Unit Sequence | Reflection |
|---|---|
| 5. The remaining plants serve as the control group and continue to receive light and water.<br><br>6. Students predict what they think will happen to each of the plants.<br><br>7. Students observe their plants daily and note any changes taking place in their science notebooks.<br><br>Students complete lab reports (Resource 1.10) over the test period. | the experimental plants and inferring why they think the plant reacts as it does. |

## LESSON 1.8: THE ADVENTURES OF A SEED

**Length:** Two 45–50-minute sessions

| Unit Sequence | Reflection |
|---|---|
| **Concepts**<br><br>• Change<br>• Systems<br>• Cycles | |
| **Principle**<br><br>Seeds differ in size, shape, color, and texture and are dispersed in a variety of ways. | |
| **Skills**<br><br>Investigative inquiry, classification, and observation | |
| **Guiding Questions**<br><br>• Why do seeds need to disperse?<br>• What are the effects of people traveling to different places? | |
| **Materials Needed**<br><br>• Seeds that disperse by wind<br>   o *Helicopters (maple, ash, sycamore)*<br>   o *Parachutes (dandelions, milkweed, cottonwood)*<br>• Seeds that disperse by water<br>   o *Boats (coconut, walnut, water lily, milkweed, pussy willow)* | This unit is best done in early spring or late fall when seeds are dispersing. It is important to tell students to be mindful that flowering plants should not be disturbed, and also to caution students not to strip a plant of all of its seeds. |

*(Continued)*

(Continued)

| Unit Sequence | Reflection |
|---|---|
| • Seeds that disperse by explosion<br>　○ *Bombs (pea, bean, lupine, gorse)*<br>• Seeds that disperse by animals<br>　○ *Tummy express (blackberry, cherry, apple, acorn, elderberry)*<br>　○ *Hitchhikers (cocklebur, tick seed, burdock)*<br>• A wooly mitten, scarf, or sock for each group<br>• Velcro<br>• Paper bag for each student | |
| **Standards**<br><br>SC-P-UD-U-1, SC-P-UD-S-1, and SC-EP-3.4.1; SC-P-UD-U-2, SC-P-UD-S-1, and SC-EP-3.4.3; SC-P-UD-U-4, SC-P-UD-S-5, and SC-EP-3.4.4 | |
| **Introductory Activity**<br><br>The class walks outside, preferably through a weedy area. As the children walk, the teacher asks them to look for dandelions and other types of plants in the area that have several examples within the area but aren't close together, asking,<br><br>*How did the dandelions spread from one area to another?*<br><br>Students then gather as many types of seeds that they can find. | This activity is tailored to the area around the school. It is important to use an area where there are examples of a variety of plants that represent seed dispersal. |
| **Teaching Strategies and Learning Experiences**<br><br>When students return to the classroom, they carefully remove the seeds from the bags they used for collection. They then begin to hypothesize as to how the seeds they collected might travel.<br>　Passing out cherries and blackberries for students to examine, the teacher asks,<br><br>*When animals eat these fruits, do they spit out the seed? If not, what might happen?*<br><br>Students then conduct a simple experiment to test their seeds by gently blowing on them to see if they stick to a woolen object or if they float. | Students complete a lab report (Resource 1.11) classifying the seeds under each of the main headings listed under the materials section.<br>　Students sanitize their hands before handling the edible seeds.<br>　Some helpful resources include *Tiny Seeds* by Eric Carle; *How Seeds Travel* by Cynthia Overbeck, Shabo Hani, and Cynthia Bix; and the websites www.countrysideinfo.co.uk/seed_dispersl/competit.htm and http://theseedsite.co.uk/dispersal.html. |
| **Closure**<br><br>Students complete a lab report (Resource 1.11)<br><br>**Day 2**<br><br>Students compare and contrast how movement to different places relates to seed travel. | Connecting literature and writing with science is powerful. Students learn informational writing when compiling their science notebooks, but it is also important to note that scientific information can be the basis for creative writing. |

## LESSON 1.9: WHAT'S INSIDE OUR FRUIT?

**Length:** Two to three 45–50-minute sessions

| Unit Sequence | Reflection |
|---|---|
| **Concepts**<br><br>• Growth<br>• Cycles<br>• Systems | |
| **Principles**<br><br>Seeds differ in size, shape, color, and texture and are dispersed in a variety of ways. | |
| **Skills**<br><br>Investigative inquiry, observation, and communication | |
| **Guiding Questions**<br><br>• What is inside a fruit?<br>• Can writing solidify scientific understanding? | Writing about what they know helps students remember key facts and understandings if they enjoy what they are writing about. The concept of thinking like a scientist reinforces student understanding and the need to be specific concerning details and observations. |
| **Materials Needed**<br><br>• Fruits (pears, oranges, apples, bananas, tomatoes, cucumbers, grapefruit, peanuts, avocados, pea and bean pods, etc.)<br>• Handheld microscopes<br>• Lab report | |
| **Introductory Activity**<br><br>The teacher holds up several types of fruits and asks,<br><br>*What are these? How do you know?*<br><br>Once students have established that all of the examples are fruits, the teacher explains that they are going to try and discover what makes each of the examples a fruit. | A fruit contains seeds; so technically, anything with seeds is a fruit including peas, beans, peppers, cucumbers, avocados, peanuts, and so forth. Fruits come from the flowers of plants. Vegetables are the roots, tubers, or stems of plants and do not contain seeds; examples include radishes, carrots, lettuce, celery, potatoes, and sweet potatoes. |
| **Standards**<br><br>SC-P-UD-U-1, SC-P-UD-S-1, and SC-EP-3.4.1; SC-P-UD-U-2, SC-P-UD-S-1, and SC-EP-3.4.3; SC-P-UD-U-4, SC-P-UD-S-5, and SC-EP-3.4.4 | |
| **Teaching Strategies and Learning Experiences**<br><br>Each pair of students receives three types of fruits, halved. Each group is then paired with another who has three different types of fruit so that each group has six different types of fruit. Their task is to observe | This activity is especially enjoyable for students because they get to eat and try the different types of fruit they examine. Students sanitize their hands and desks before and after completing this activity. |

*(Continued)*

(Continued)

| Unit Sequence | Reflection |
|---|---|
| their examples and discover what makes each of them a fruit. | Interesting resources are *It's a Fruit, It's a Vegetable, It's a Pumpkin* by Allan Fowler and *Fruits and Vegetables* by Susan Derkazarian. |
| **Closure**<br><br>Students complete a lab report (Resource 1.12). In addition, the teacher assigns one the following (Resource 1.13):<br><br>1. Write a newspaper article explaining that fruits contain seeds, which include several food items people mistakenly refer to as vegetables.<br><br>2. Take the role of a fruit that is normally called a vegetable and share how you think it might feel being misnamed.<br><br>3. Set up a vegetable and fruit market that correctly categorizes the items and advertise your fruits and vegetables. | These three activities can be differentiated by using Sternberg's intelligence preferences (analytical, creative, and practical). |

## LESSON 1.10: WHAT DO WE KNOW ABOUT PLANTS? REVISITED

**Length:** One 45–50-minute session

| Unit Sequence | Reflection |
|---|---|
| **Concepts**<br><br>• Systems<br>• Growth<br>• Change | |
| **Principles**<br><br>• Things in the environment are classified as living, nonliving, and once living.<br>• Living things differ from nonliving things.<br>• Organisms are classified into groups by using various characteristics (e.g., body coverings and body structures).<br>• Plants grow from seeds and need water, soil, air, and nutrients to grow.<br>• Seeds differ in size, shape, color, and texture and are dispersed in a variety of ways.<br>• Each plant or animal has observable structures that serve different functions in growth, survival, and reproduction. | |
| **Skills**<br><br>Summarizing and drawing conclusions | |

| Unit Sequence | Reflection |
|---|---|
| **Guiding Questions**<br><br>• Is what we thought we knew different from what we know now?<br>• Did we learn what we wanted to learn?<br>• What key ideas did we learn about plants? | Students discuss what they have learned during the plant unit.<br><br>*Author's note:* My students always enjoyed filling out the *L* column in the KWL charts. |
| **Materials Needed**<br><br>• Original KWL chart<br>• Marker | |
| **Standards**<br><br>SC-P-UD-U-1, SC-P-UD-S-1, and SC-EP-3.4.1; SC-P-UD-U-2, SC-P-UD-S-1, SC-EP-3.4.3; SC-P-UD-U-4, SC-P-UD-S-5, and SC-EP-3.4.4 | |
| **Introductory Activity**<br><br>The teacher reintroduces the students to the KWL chart they worked on at the beginning of this unit, asking why they think this strategy might have been important to use in the unit. | When using the KWL strategy, it is important to remember to complete the *L* portion at the end of the unit. This portion becomes an assessment tool for the students to evaluate not only what they learned, but also whether or not they learned what they wanted to learn in the *W* section.<br><br>This assists students in pulling together what they learned throughout the unit. It is also an excellent record for them of their accomplishments. |
| **Teaching Strategies and Learning Experiences**<br><br>Students are grouped in pairs or in their original KWL groups. Groups complete the *L* column, using their science notebooks and correcting any misunderstandings they might have listed in the *K* column. | Students review their notebooks to be sure that all of their lab reports and observations have been included. The teacher reviews with students the rubric (Resource 1.14) so that all students know what the teacher will look for when reviewing their work. If students have not had much experience with rubrics, the teacher might conduct a discussion to show how they are used to provide students feedback. |
| **Closure**<br><br>Students post their charts and use them during the plant fair to show visitors what they learned throughout the unit. | |

## CONCLUSION: PLANT FAIR

This is the concluding event for the unit on plants. Students prepare an exhibit to share, with their parents and other students in the building, what they have learned about plants in an all-day plant fair. Students prepare invitations for their parents and every class in their school. They develop a schedule for classroom visits that is completed by the classroom teachers. Each class is invited for a 15 to 30 minute session with an opportunity to visit each display.

Each experiment is displayed with a poster explaining what the students did and what happened. Students demonstrate the following: planting techniques, the importance of proper care, how to transplant a plant from one container to another, seeds found in fruits and vegetables, how seeds disperse, plant parts, and the use of a control for experiments. Students also create a greenhouse by building an inflatable structure with 25-milliliter plastic sheets that inflate using a 20-inch box fan (Resource 1.15).

Students create a guide to the tour using notes from their science notebooks. Each visitor receives a copy of the guide, condensed to two pages front and back. This is a student-directed project, so creating work teams to plan each section works well. Since parents are invited, they can also serve as volunteers. Students rotate the positions of tour guides and experts throughout the day.

*Author's note:* I used the language arts block of my day to work on this plant unit because it requires the students to use their skills in reading and writing. I have also done this activity with other units and it is a huge hit with classroom teachers and students.

# Plants Alive!

My Science Notebook

## RESOURCE 1.1: LESSON 2 LAB REPORT

*Living or Nonliving*

|  | Living | Nonliving |
|---|---|---|
| I can move. |  |  |
| I take up space. |  |  |
| I breathe. |  |  |
| I can be touched. |  |  |
| I grow. |  |  |
| I change. |  |  |
| I need food and water. |  |  |
| I reproduce. |  |  |
| I have weight. |  |  |

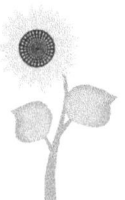

| Draw a picture of a non-living thing. | Draw a picture of a living thing. |
|---|---|
|  |  |

## RESOURCE 1.2: LESSON 3 LAB REPORT

*Seed Dissection*

In the box below predict what you think is inside a seed. Draw a picture of what you think you might find inside the seed.

I think a seed contains _____

_____

_____

and looks like this.

In the box below, draw a picture of what you saw inside your seed.

My seed looked like this!

Did your pictures look alike? Why or why not? _____

_____

_____

## RESOURCE 1.3: LESSON 4 LAB REPORT

### *My Plant Grows Up!*

Draw a picture of your lima bean and alfalfa seed each day you observe it. Write the date by the day.

**Lima Bean Seed**

Day 1 _____    Day 2 _____    Day 3 _____    Day 4 _____    Day 5 _____

Day 6 _____    Day 7 _____    Day 8 _____    Day 9 _____    Day 10 _____

**Alfalfa Seed**

Day 1 _____    Day 2 _____    Day 3 _____    Day 4 _____    Day 5 _____

Day 6 _____    Day 7 _____    Day 8 _____    Day 9 _____    Day 10 _____

## RESOURCE 1.4: LESSON 4 LAB REPORT

### *My Baggie Garden*

Scientists make careful notes of how they conduct experiments. This is called a *protocol.* Create your own protocol on how to make a baggie garden.

What materials do you need?

What steps did you take to make your garden?

## RESOURCE 1.5: LESSON 5 LAB REPORT

*My Plant Grows Up!*

Check your potted plant every other day after your seed germinates. Draw what you see. Using a ruler, measure the height of your plant and record it on your lab report. Make sure to include the date. On the back of your paper, describe your plant on each of your observation days.

| | | |
|---|---|---|
| Height: _____ in. | Height: _____ in. | Height: _____ in. |
| Day 1 _____ | Day 3 _____ | Day 5 _____ |
| Height: _____ in. | Height: _____ in. | Height: _____ in. |
| Day 7 _____ | Day 9 _____ | Day 11 _____ |
| Height: _____ in. | Height: _____ in. | Height: _____ in. |
| Day 13 _____ | Day 15 _____ | Day 17 _____ |

## RESOURCE 1.6: LESSON 5 LAB REPORT

*Writing About My Potted Plant*

Describe what you see on each day that you observe your plant.

Day 1

Day 2

Day 3

Day 4

## RESOURCE 1.7: LESSON 5 LAB REPORT

*Egg Carton Observations*

In what order did your seeds germinate?

1. _____

2. _____

3. _____

When your plants grow bigger, transplant one of each kind to a bigger container. How long do you think it will take for the one that germinated first to be ready to transplant?

Draw a picture of each of your plants.

## RESOURCE 1.8: LESSON 5 LAB REPORT

*Graphing My Plants' Growth*

Scientists keep accurate data. List the plants in your group and choose a color to represent each one. Carefully measure each daily and graph your results. Each square = ½ inch growth.

| 15 | | | | | | | | | | | | | | | |
|----|--|--|--|--|--|--|--|--|--|--|--|--|--|--|--|
| 14 | | | | | | | | | | | | | | | |
| 13 | | | | | | | | | | | | | | | |
| 12 | | | | | | | | | | | | | | | |
| 11 | | | | | | | | | | | | | | | |
| 10 | | | | | | | | | | | | | | | |
| 9 | | | | | | | | | | | | | | | |
| 8 | | | | | | | | | | | | | | | |
| 7 | | | | | | | | | | | | | | | |
| 6 | | | | | | | | | | | | | | | |
| 5 | | | | | | | | | | | | | | | |
| 4 | | | | | | | | | | | | | | | |
| 3 | | | | | | | | | | | | | | | |
| 2 | | | | | | | | | | | | | | | |
| 1 | | | | | | | | | | | | | | | |

Plant _____  ☐

Plant _____  ☐

Plant _____  ☐

Plant _____  ☐

Plant _____  ☐

## RESOURCE 1.9: LESSON 6 LAB REPORT

*Plant Parts: Labeling the Parts of a Plant*

After observing your plant, draw what you saw and label the parts.

## RESOURCE 1.10: LESSON 7 LAB REPORT

*Experimenting With the Basic Needs of Plants*

My prediction for the experimental plants:

| No soil | No light | No water |
|---|---|---|
| | | |

Draw what happened to each plant after one week.

| No soil | No light | No water |
|---|---|---|
| | | |

## RESOURCE 1.11: LESSON 8 LAB REPORT

*The Adventures of a Seed*

Glue each type of seed you found on the schoolyard walk in the space below. Underneath the seed, label it as a helicopter, parachute, boat, bomb, or tummy express.

_____

_____

_____

_____

_____

_____

_____

_____

_____

## RESOURCE 1.12: LESSON 9 LAB REPORT

*What's Inside Fruit?*

I explored these fruits (draw a picture of the inside of each). What did they have in common?

Check your partner pair's fruit drawing. What did they have in common?

## RESOURCE 1.13: LESSON 9 LAB REPORT

*Connecting Writing to Science*

Use the following writing prompts to encourage students to solidify their conceptual understanding of fruits in a literary venue.

### Sternberg's Analytical Intelligence

☐ Write a newspaper article explaining that fruits contain seeds, which include several food items people refer to as vegetables.

### Sternberg's Practical Intelligence

☐ Set up a vegetable and fruit market that correctly categorizes the items and advertise your fruits and vegetables.

### Sternberg's Creative Intelligence

☐ Take the role of a fruit that is normally called a vegetable and share how you feel being misnamed.

## RESOURCE 1.14: RUBRIC FOR SCIENCE NOTEBOOK

| Criteria | Developing | Proficient | Exemplary |
|---|---|---|---|
| Organization | Some work is missing or it is in disorder. | All work is complete. Entries are orderly. | All work is complete and extra work is evident. Entries are in excellent order. |
| Science Understanding | Some areas show a grasp of the science concepts and principles while some entries are inaccurate or unclear. | Entries are accurate and clear. A basic understanding of the principles and concepts is evident. | Entries are accurate and clear and contain additional information revealing an in-depth understanding of the concepts and principles. |
| Creativity | There is some evidence of creativity throughout the notebook. | Creativity is shown in some areas of the notebook while others remain basic. | Creativity is shown throughout the notebook. |

## RESOURCE 1.15: CREATING A PLASTIC BUBBLE GREENHOUSE

Using a plastic inflated bubble as a classroom "greenhouse" is a great project that emphasizes cooperation and mathematical skills to create. The "greenhouse" becomes a focal point for the plant fair.

The greenhouse is created using at least 6-milliliter-thick translucent plastic and duct tape; it is inflated by a 20-inch box fan.

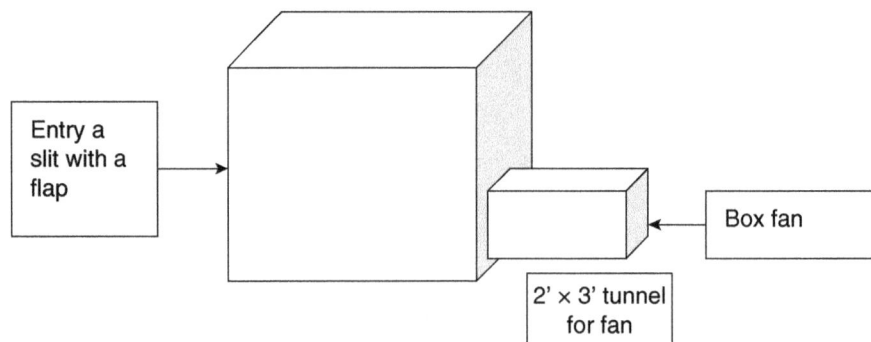

At least a 10′ × 10′ cube (using a 10′ × 10′ structure) is recommended.

### Materials Needed

70 feet of 6-milliliter clear plastic, 10 feet wide

A large roll of duct tape

20-inch box fan

Benches or tables for plants

*Author's note:* Students in my first-to-third-grade multiage class did all of the measuring, cutting, and taping.

1. Cut six 10′ × 10′ pieces of plastic.
2. Tape the pieces together to form a cube.
3. Cut a hole for the tunnel for the fan.
4. Tape the tunnel together and attach to the main cube.
5. Tape the fan to the tunnel so that it blows inward.
6. Cut a slit for an entry and tape a 2.5-foot strip over it to serve as a door.

The advantage of this bubble for the classroom is that it can be used for many activities. It can be converted to a planetarium when studying space, a rainforest when studying habitats, and also used as a book nook for students' reading.

# Point of View Under Transition

## Using the Work of Chris Van Allsburg

*Laurie Boen*

## INTRODUCTION TO THE UNIT

### Overview of the Unit

In the Point of View Under Transition unit, students review their understanding of common story elements such as character, conflict, setting, climax, and point of view; they then focus specifically on the point of view. Language arts, reading, and writing come together in this unit with the emphasis on using the tools of budding writers in the practice parallel of the Parallel Curriculum Model (PCM). The unit has roots in the core parallel; however, students identify and use story elements in their own writing, moving the unit predominantly into the practice parallel. Students are also exposed to the parallel of identity when they examine themselves as writers, and the parallel of connections is addressed as well, when students make connections to the arts by noting artwork that portrays their perceptions of beauty.

Students examine what point of view is and how it affects the plot of a story while implementing a fresh new point of view—their own. Students use a variety of thinking skills in this unit. They identify characteristics, make observations, identify points of view, compare and contrast viewpoints, classify, and formulate questions. Students also use the creative thinking skills of originality and elaboration, along with idea/product modification techniques, while formulating their own point of view. A variety of grouping strategies allow students to work with others to share ideas and push each other's thinking.

This unit could replace the popular fractured fairy tale unit. The fractured fairy tale tells a story from an alternative point of view much like students are asked to do here, but the Point of View Under Transition unit achieves this in a new and fresh way. The goal of this unit is for students to examine a different point of view while formulating their own, in order to have a deeper understanding of the concept.

Point of View Under Transition is a ten- to twelve-day unit starting with the What Is My Point of View? lesson, sparking students' initial engagements through connections to art. Students then use literature to identify the point of view in a core parallel lesson, titled What Is Point of View? Students next consider an alternative point of view in the Changing Point of View lesson. As students continue to write, they take time to examine their identity through the writing process in the lesson, Look . . . I Am an Author! The last lesson is Wrapping Up That Changing Point of View, taking students back to the practice parallel to complete the unit.

This unit can be taught in its entirety, allowing students to become writers themselves and incorporating the writing standards; or it can be completely literature based, asking students to make inferences to identify the point of view in a variety of literature sources.

## Background Information for the Unit

Point of View Under Transition begins much like a fractured fairy tale unit, but focuses primarily on a creative writing unit. The unit can be modified to meet the needs of the students as well as the state standards. Point of View Under Transition allows students to form their individual point of view and see themselves as writers, allowing for a deeper understanding of the concept.

Students will need background information about story elements to be successful in this unit. They will need to understand that the plot of a story takes the reader through a rising action up to the climax of the story, and then brings the reader to the ultimate solution for the problem. A quick preassessment is administered at the beginning to determine students' prior knowledge and understanding of story elements.

Teachers should gather resources on the story elements as well as point of view, along with books authored by Chris Van Allsburg. Some of his works include *The Wreck of the Zephyr, Two Bad Ants, The Polar Express, The Stranger, Jumanji, The Widow's Broom, The Sweetest Fig,* and *Just a Dream.* Van Allsburg's books have some great similarities in that they are all written from the point of view of a narrator who is not necessarily a character in the story; they are also fantasy based, so students generally respond well.

# CONTENT FRAMEWORK

## Organizing Concepts

### Macroconcepts

M1: Point of view/perspective

### Discipline-Specific Concepts

C1: Conflict

C2: Interactions

C3: Culture

C4: Stereotypes

C5: Perceptions

C6: Beliefs/values

C7: Mood

## Principles

P1: Beliefs and values affect point of view and one's perceptions, culture, and stereotypes influence one's beliefs and values.

P2: Authors manipulate various story elements when creating their stories for particular purposes and specific audiences.

P3: Authors often use the element of point of view to influence the interactions of the characters, the plot, the theme, and the conflict in a story.

P5: An individual's beliefs and values reflect a perception of one's self and therefore determine one's personal outlook on the world.

P6: An individual's point of view determines beauty.

## National or State Standards

### Missouri Grade-Level Expectations

Reading 2

SD 1: Develop and apply skills and strategies to comprehend, analyze, and evaluate fiction, poetry, and drama from a variety of cultures and times:

- o Analyze the influence of setting on characters, plot, and resolution (conflict and climax).
- o Identify the narrator.
- o Identify point of view and mood.
- o Make basic inferences about setting, characters, and problem.

Writing 3

SD 2: Write effectively in various forms and types of writing; write a narrative text that contains the following features:

- o A beginning, middle, and end.
- o Relevant details to develop main idea.
- o A clear controlling idea.
- o Precise and descriptive language.

### National Council of Teachers of English and the International Reading Association (NCTE/IRA) Standards

SD 3: Students read a wide range of print and nonprint texts to build an understanding of texts, of themselves, and of the cultures of the United States and the world; to acquire new information; to respond to the needs and demands of society and the workplace; and for personal fulfillment. Among these texts are fiction and nonfiction, classic and contemporary works.

SD 4: Students apply a wide range of strategies to comprehend, interpret, evaluate, and appreciate texts. They draw on their prior experience, their interactions with other readers and writers, their knowledge of word meaning and of other texts, their word identification strategies, and their understanding of textual features (e.g., sound-letter correspondence, sentence structure, context, and graphics).

SD 5: Students adjust their use of spoken, written, and visual language (e.g., conventions, style, and vocabulary) to communicate effectively with a variety of audiences and for different purposes.

SD 6: Students employ a wide range of strategies as they write and use different writing- process elements appropriately to communicate with different audiences for a variety of purposes.

SD 7: Students apply knowledge of language structure, language conventions (e.g., spelling and punctuation), media techniques, figurative language, and genre to create, critique, and discuss print and nonprint texts.

SD 8: Students use a variety of technological and information resources (e.g., libraries, databases, computer networks, and video) to gather and synthesize information and to create and communicate knowledge.

SD 9: Students develop an understanding of and respect for diversity in language use, patterns, and dialects across cultures, ethnic groups, geographic regions, and social roles.

SD 10: Students participate as knowledgeable, reflective, creative, and critical members of a variety of literacy communities.

SD 11: Students use spoken, written, and visual language to accomplish their own purposes (e.g., for learning, enjoyment, persuasion, and the exchange of information).

## Skills

S1: Identifying characteristics

S2: Making observations

S3: Identifying points of view

S4: Comparing and contrasting

S5: Identifying points of view

S6: Originality

S7: Elaborating

S8: Classifying

S9: Formulating questions

S10: Brainstorming

S11: Inferring

S12: Using ideas/product modification techniques

## UNIT ASSESSMENTS

### Preassessment

Preassessment allows the teacher to determine the readiness levels of the students, and includes basic story elements such as character, conflict, plot, setting, climax, and point of view. This can be done in a very informal setting with students answering questions on index cards or in their journals.

### *Suggested Preassessment Questions*

- Explain the basic story elements for the following terms:
  - o Character
  - o Conflict
  - o Plot
  - o Setting
  - o Climax
- What does *point of view* mean?
- Name three things that can affect point of view.

### Formative Assessments

Formative assessments include journal responses throughout the unit for students to reflect on their reactions to text and their progress. Students' drafts of stories also allow the teacher to assess their ongoing understanding of how to use point of view in their own writing. Story maps (Resource 2.1) are used for formative assessments.

### Postassessment

Postassessment focuses on the students' stories told from an alternative point of view. The assessment is evaluated using the writing rubric (Resource 2.3).

## UNIT SEQUENCE AND TEACHER REFLECTION

### LESSON 2.1: WHAT IS MY POINT OF VIEW?

*Parallel of Connections*

**Length:** Two to three 50-minute sessions

Students will have an opportunity to look at an object or person from afar or by using a "magnifying lens" while evaluating their own personal point of view.

| Unit Sequence | Reflection |
|---|---|
| **Concepts**<br><br>• Beliefs and values<br>• Motivation<br>• Perceptions | This lesson is designed to be a hook for the unit, focusing on individual students' points of view. |
| **Principles**<br><br>• Beliefs and values affect point of view and one's perceptions, culture, and stereotypes influence one's beliefs and values.<br>• An individual's beliefs and values reflect a perception of one's self and therefore determine one's personal outlook on the world.<br>• An individual's point of view determines beauty. | |
| **Skills**<br><br>• Identifying characteristics<br>• Making observations<br>• Identifying points of view<br>• Comparing and contrasting<br>• Classifying<br>• Formulating questions | Students identify relevant details of a piece of art and determine what they believe is the particular point of view of the artist. Students find similarities among their points of view while sorting them in small groups and then later as a whole class. Students may have to ask each other questions to explain or support what they believe is the point of view of the artist. |
| **Standards**<br><br>SD 1, SD 4, SD 10 | |
| **Guiding Questions**<br><br>• How does a picture depict beauty? Why do you think so?<br>• What makes something beautiful?<br>• How are point of view and beauty related?<br>• How does your perspective change your point of view? | These questions set the tone for the unit. Students are engaged and thinking about point of view and what affects it. |
| **Introduction**<br><br>The teacher first evaluates students' ability to use a camera.<br><br>For the hook, the teacher shows an interesting piece of art and uses Socratic questioning in order to gain interest. For example, the teacher might ask students the following questions:<br><br>*What do you think this piece of art is trying to communicate and why do you think so? What do you believe was the artist's point of view when creating this work? Why do you think so?*<br><br>The teacher also asks students to provide evidence for what they see in the artwork or for what they can connect to past experiences with regard to art or the artist.<br><br>Students receive firsthand experience at connecting point of view to another discipline by evaluating what they see as beautiful. | The class views the artwork via an online tour of a museum, actual artwork, or photographs. The teacher does not show the title of the piece so as to not clue students into the artist's point of view. The teacher may want to have several examples from different mediums as well as a variety of objects. Multiple viewpoints of a piece of art are valuable for allowing students to determine that perspective changes point of view. The teacher may give the students a camera to take home, reminding them to be careful to review the procedures for appropriate camera care. It is also possible that students share a camera, being mindful that if one of the pair loses it then the other person's pictures can be lost.<br><br>The teacher can explore possible sources for camera donations to the class or, if there are a limited number of cameras available, confine the camera use to the school grounds or building. |

| Unit Sequence | Reflection |
|---|---|
| Students are expected to make the connection that art and beauty are dependent on one's point of view. They will need to be able to infer why they think a picture is a representation of beauty.<br><br>Since students choose their own representation of beauty, they work within their own interests. | |
| **Teaching Strategies and Learning Experiences**<br><br>• Strategy-based instruction<br>• Demonstrating and modeling<br>• Socratic questioning<br><br>By using Socratic questioning, students connect the discipline of art and language arts while also using their logical reasoning and critical thinking skills about their point of view as they recognize attributes.<br><br>The teacher may model for the students what point of view is, and perhaps how that point of view was established so that students can follow the teacher's example.<br><br>In order to demonstrate their understanding, students produce a journal entry that includes their picture with a reflection of their point of view of the picture and the questions. | Strategy-based instruction is used because point of view is discovered and modeled for students and they then have an opportunity to take a look at their own point of view.<br><br>*Examples for Socratic Questions*<br><br>• Why are you saying that (example of beauty) is beautiful from your point of view?<br>• Explain your point of view about (example of beauty).<br>• Is there any way someone could argue that (example of beauty) is beautiful? Why? Or why not?<br>• Why did you choose this picture over others you have?<br><br>If students have multiple pictures, they rank the one they feel represents their point of view of something beautiful.<br><br>Students work alone so that they each can determine an individual point of view.<br><br>The reflection portion is very important for the students to justify their point of view while gaining an understanding of the concept.<br><br>Disposable cameras can be purchased and pictures put onto CDs if students are allowed to take the camera home.<br><br>Students who already have an understanding of point of view can make connections between other genres of literature and points of view; for example, students use music and determine the point of view of the author of the lyrics or the melody; plays or poems can also be used. |
| **Closure**<br><br>*Journal: Double-Entry Journal*<br><br>With a copy of the picture on one side of the journal, students reflect on what it is about the picture that they see as beautiful.<br><br>• How do perceptions, culture, and stereotypes change point of view?<br>• In what ways do beliefs and values affect point of view? | The journal entry at the conclusion of each day works best in a double-entry journal with a question from the principles of the unit on the left side, and a response concerning their thoughts about the picture and what they would like to change, or what they learned, on the right side.<br><br>The journal can also be completed as a blog to incorporate technology into the classroom. Students can respond to the questions on the Internet on a teacher's blog, or older students can produce their own blogs. |

## LESSON 2.2: WHAT IS POINT OF VIEW?

*Core Parallel*

**Length:** Two 50-minute sessions

Students will determine point of view in literature.

| Unit Sequence | Reflection |
|---|---|
| **Concepts**<br><br>• Conflict<br>• Point of view<br>• Perceptions<br>• Culture<br>• Stereotypes | Students need to know that conflict and point of view are important elements of stories. The teacher emphasizes that perceptions, culture, and stereotypes affect the point of view of the narrator as well as the conflict. |
| **Principles**<br><br>• Beliefs and values affect point of view and one's perceptions, culture, and stereotypes influence one's beliefs and values.<br>• An individual's beliefs and values reflect a perception of one's self and therefore determine one's personal outlook on the world. | |
| **Skills**<br><br>• Identifying characteristics<br>• Making observations<br>• Identifying points of view<br>• Comparing and contrasting | Students infer logical conclusions of relevant details that characterize point of view while selecting attributes of the story to determine that individuals and groups may have beliefs that influence perspective. |
| **Standards**<br><br>SD 1, SD 3, SD 7, SD 8, SD 9 | |
| **Guiding Questions**<br><br>• From whose point of view is the story told?<br>• In what ways does culture affect the point of view?<br>• In what ways do stereotypes affect the point of view?<br>• What is the time period of the story?<br>• What is the setting?<br>• Who are the main characters?<br>• What is the conflict (problem) in the story?<br>• What is the plot (storyline)?<br>• What is the theme (the author's purpose)?<br>• What is the influence of the setting on the characters? The problem?<br>• In what ways are you able to infer from what point of view the story is told? | If there are students who have difficulty inferring, it may be necessary to teach a mini-lesson on the skill to those who need it. |

| Unit Sequence | Reflection |
|---|---|
| **Introduction**<br><br>Student's verbal and written responses from the story map (Resource 2.1) serve as an assessment. The teacher completes the following steps.<br><br>• Ask students how point of view affects the plot of a book.<br>• Do a read-aloud using one of Chris Van Allsburg's books such as *The Wreck of the Zephyr*. Using the story map, ask students to identify each of the story elements: character(s), setting, plot, conflict, main idea, and point of view.<br>• Determine from whose point of view the story is told. Discuss what would happen if the story were told from an alternate point of view.<br>• Check story maps to ensure student understandings of story elements as well as point of view. | This is a beginning lesson for students to infer what point of view is told in a story. Students will use a graphic organizer (Resource 2.1) to organize information from the story and form a new version of the story. If there are enough copies of the book, students can take turns reading. |
| **Teaching Strategies and Learning Experiences**<br><br>• Strategy-based instruction<br>• Graphic organizer<br>• Cooperative learning<br><br>As a whole class, the teacher completes a mini-lesson on how to use the graphic organizer of the story map (Resource 2.1), and then partners students according to readiness and interest so they can complete their story maps and journal reflections.<br><br>The teacher provides books with the various reading levels represented in the class. Other resources include http://hrsbstaff.ednet.ns.ca/ engramja/elements.html and http://users.aber.ac .uk/jpm/ellsa/ellsa_elements.html.<br><br>To extend the lesson, students can analyze the motives of the character(s) from the point of view of the narrator using same literature.<br><br>To provide ascending intellectual demand, students can answer the following questions:<br><br>In what ways do perceptions, culture and stereotypes affect the news that is reported? What differences in the news might you find in different areas? | Students first explore the concept of point of view as a whole class and then move on to their own creations. The graphic organizer is a way for students to record their ideas on paper after they have inferred from whose point of view the story is told. In small groups, students have an opportunity to interact in ways that will help them to gain the concept of point of view while discussing the elements of the story.<br><br>Readiness levels are determined by using data obtained from observations, review of students' work, or particular assessments.<br><br>Students can work with a partner at their particular readiness level, as well as interest.<br><br>After identifying the story elements and determining point of view, students reflect on the guiding principles of the unit.<br><br>Students determine the motives of the characters in the story from the narrator's point of view.<br><br>Students examine how the reporting of the news, either from television or in print, is affected by perceptions, culture, and stereotypes.<br><br>Students make inferences of the culture of the community for which the news is intended. |
| **Closure**<br><br>*Journal: Double-Entry Journal*<br><br>• In what ways do people's beliefs and values reflect how they see themselves and the world?<br>• How do perceptions, culture, and stereotypes change point of view? | Teachers should reserve quality time for students to write.<br><br>In place of a journal entry for this lesson, an exit card can be implemented. For example, "three things I now know about point of view"; "two ways a reader's culture can affect his/her perception of the author's point of view"; and "one thing that I still want to learn about point of view." |

## LESSON 2.3: CHANGING POINT OF VIEW

*Parallel of Practice*

**Length:** Two 50-minute sessions

Students will write their own fractured story.

| Unit Sequence | Reflection |
|---|---|
| **Concepts**<br><br>• Point of view<br>• Interactions<br>• Conflict<br>• Perceptions | |
| **Principles**<br><br>• Beliefs and values affect point of view and one's perceptions, culture, and stereotypes influence one's beliefs and values.<br>• An individual's beliefs and values reflect a perception of one's self and therefore determine one's personal outlook on the world.<br>• Authors often use the element of point of view to influence the interactions of the characters, plot, theme, and conflict in a story. | |
| **Skills**<br><br>• Identifying characteristics<br>• Making observations<br>• Identifying points of view<br>• Comparing and contrasting<br>• Brainstorming<br>• Originality<br>• Elaborating<br>• Using ideas/product modification techniques | Students determine what the point of view of the story is by identifying the elements of the stories. They compare and contrast their ideas to decide on the point of view that they believe is the best. They use the skills of originality and elaboration in their writing, as well as ideas/product modification, which includes substituting, combining, adapting, modifying, making larger or smaller, putting to new uses, eliminating, reversing, or rearranging. Students are encouraged to use these thought processes to write their own versions of the story. |
| **Standards**<br><br>SD 1, SD 2, SD 4, SD 6, SD 7, SD 8, SD 10, SD 11 | |
| **Guiding Questions**<br><br>• How is point of view changed by time, place, culture, events, and circumstances?<br>• What are the strengths and weaknesses of different points of view?<br>• Why do different people have different points of view? | These questions are very important for guiding students' thinking. |

| Unit Sequence | Reflection |
|---|---|
| **Introduction**<br><br>After assessing students' previous journal entries to determine their needs for more practice, the teacher leads a roundtable discussion to provide *what if* questions about another of Chris Van Allsburg's books (such as *The Stranger*), changing the point of view each time.<br><br>The teacher demonstrates a story being told from an alternate point of view using *The True Story of the Three Little Pigs!* and the traditional version of *The Three Little Pigs*. Students then complete a story map (Resource 2.1) for both stories and then a T-chart or Venn diagram to compare and contrast the stories.<br><br>In groups of two or three, students brainstorm different possible points of view that could be told from their chosen book and then rewrite the story map. | A roundtable discussion is an open-ended discussion format.<br><br>Modeling with students using a fairy tale may assist students in seeing how a point of view can alter a story. Guiding questions focus on the change of the plot due to the new point of view.<br><br>Using a familiar fairy tale helps students make the connections of the differences in point of view.<br><br>Students consult their point-of-view story map (Resource 2.1) to see how the elements are used in the different fairy tale versions.<br><br>At this point, students begin to work on their own new version of a story.<br><br>Students who wish to do so should be given the opportunity to publish their work online. |
| **Teaching Strategies and Learning Experiences**<br><br>• Coaching<br>• Demonstrating and modeling<br>• Cooperative learning<br>• Shadowing<br><br>Moving from group to group, the teacher uses coaching strategies by giving feedback to students on their progress while they apply the methodologies and concepts of the language arts discipline to their individual story maps to create another story map for a new story from a different point of view.<br><br>All students need exposure to the techniques of writing and points of view within a small group, or their readiness groups, while they are prewriting and completing their story maps and beginning their new stories. | The teacher evaluates students' understanding of the concept of point of view while checking on the various groups. Asking students to share their ideas and from whose point of view they believe a story is told reveals who has a strong grasp of the concept.<br><br>Students' story maps must be detailed enough for them to use in their writing.<br><br>The teacher decides on the cooperative learning groups by using a variety of criteria; however, it may be wise to use readiness groups at this stage of the unit so that students who have similar skills in reading and writing can push each other's progress.<br><br>The prewriting comes from brainstorming that the students do, or from the story map.<br><br>Some resources to find information about publishing student's work may be useful for the adept writers:<br><br>• http://eduscapes.com/tap/topic113.htm<br>• http://weblogg-ed.com/2006/great-example-of-elementary-school-publishing-and-kids-teaching/<br>• www.monash.com/writers.html<br><br>Other genres of literature can provide a more in-depth experience for some students by determining how events in the life of an author can affect the point of view in the writing. For example, a student can determine if the life events in a songwriter's life affected the lyrics of the songs written during a certain time frame. |

*(Continued)*

(Continued)

| Unit Sequence | Reflection |
|---|---|
| **Closure**<br><br>*Journal: Double-Entry Journal*<br><br>• In what ways did your perceptions, culture, and stereotypes change point of view in the story?<br>• How did the author use the element of point of view to influence the interactions of the characters, plot, theme, and conflict in the story?<br>• How did you change point of view with the interactions of the characters, plot, theme, and conflict in your story? | Students love to share what they are writing, so this is a good time to allow students to share in a class meeting or in cooperative groups. |

## LESSON 2.4: LOOK . . . I AM AN AUTHOR!

*Parallel of Identity*

**Length:** Two to three 50-minute sessions

Students will reflect on themselves as writers.

| Unit Sequence | Reflection |
|---|---|
| **Concepts**<br><br>• Beliefs and values<br>• Motivation<br>• Perception | |
| **Principles**<br><br>• Beliefs and values affect point of view and one's perceptions, culture, and stereotypes influence one's beliefs and values.<br>• An individual's beliefs and values reflect a perception of one's self and therefore determine one's personal outlook on the world. | |
| **Skills**<br><br>• Identifying characteristics<br>• Making observations<br>• Comparing and contrasting<br>• Classifying<br>• Formulating questions | Students identify characteristics of themselves as well as traits of favorite authors and make observations as to whether or not those match up to themselves while comparing, contrasting, and classifying those characteristics. Students can ask questions of themselves and of guest author(s). |
| **Standards**<br><br>SD 1, SD 3, SD 11 | |

| Unit Sequence | Reflection |
|---|---|
| **Guiding Questions**<br><br>• Why do people write?<br>• Who are some writers with whom you are familiar?<br>• How do they spend their days?<br>• What, do you suppose, are some characteristics of writers?<br>• How are these characteristics like your own?<br>• How are they different? | These can be asked in a Socratic format so that students think about how their identity compares to that of an author. |
| **Introduction**<br><br>Inventories about students' preferences regarding their learning may be important to highlight at this point in the unit.<br><br>The teacher hooks the students by asking how they think it feels to be an author. Students think of the answer by using the think-pair-share method, discuss it with a friend, and then share aloud with the class.<br><br>Another fractured fairy tale can be used to continue students' interest.<br><br>Students are now engaged in the writing process, and this lesson is designed to determine if their personal identity meshes with that of being an author.<br><br>Students complete a self-evaluation using the How Is This Like Me chart (Resource 2.2).<br><br>Students continue work within their readiness and interest groups. | As students continue in their writing process, the teacher asks them to evaluate how they are feeling about their authorship.<br><br>Learning profile inventories can include multiple intelligences, modality, and so forth.<br><br>A fractured fairy tale such as *Cinderella's Stepsister*, and *Cinderella: The Untold Story*, as told by Russell Shorto, are good examples to use.<br><br>Bringing in a local guest author for the students to question is also effective. |
| **Teaching Strategies and Learning Experiences**<br><br>• Socratic questioning<br>• Graphic organizer<br><br>The teacher leads the group with questions that allow students to evaluate their personal skills and compare their skills to those of authors by filling in the graphic organizer, How Is This Like Me chart (Resource 2.2). | The Socratic format is one where questions are asked of students for clarification, to probe assumptions, for explaining their rationale, for discussing their perspective, for sense making, and to question the question at hand.<br><br>Providing the graphic organizer allows students the opportunity to organize their thoughts about their identity as an author.<br><br>Students use introspection to determine if the skills an author needs matches those they have or skills that they have an interest in developing.<br><br>The grouping needs to be flexible and allow students to communicate with others in a nonjudgmental and supportive way.<br><br>These products may not need a grade; however, feedback is very important as students see themselves as authors.<br><br>The intent is for students to think about how writing relates to their view of themselves. |

*(Continued)*

(Continued)

| Unit Sequence | Reflection |
|---|---|
| | Students can read autobiographies or biographies about authors for an extension and then follow up with a teacher or class discussion.<br><br>Students who are interested and need the opportunity to immerse themselves in the field of writing perhaps can participate in a mentorship program with a local author. |
| **Closure**<br><br>*Journal: Double-Entry Journal*<br><br>• How do your beliefs and values affect your point of view about you being an author?<br>• What kind of skills does a writer/author need or use?<br>• What are your strengths?<br>• How do your strengths and the skills of a writer relate to those you have read about? In what ways?<br>• In what ways do you think you need to grow as an author?<br>• Ask yourself: As I complete my new version of a book, what is one thing I can do to become a better writer? | Students reflect on the learning profile (information that they know about themselves) as they record their thoughts in response to the journal questions. The teacher reminds students to provide examples that support their answers from their past experiences as well as their hopes and dreams. |

## LESSON 2.5: WRAPPING UP THAT CHANGING POINT OF VIEW

*Parallel of Practice*

**Length:** Two 50-minute sessions

Students will complete their writing after they have discovered they are indeed authors.

| Unit Sequence | Reflection |
|---|---|
| **Concepts**<br><br>• Point of view<br>• Interactions<br>• Conflict<br>• Perceptions | |
| **Principles**<br><br>• Beliefs and values affect point of view and one's perceptions, culture, and stereotypes influence one's beliefs and values.<br>• An individual's beliefs and values reflect a perception of one's self and therefore determine one's personal outlook on the world. | |

| Unit Sequence | Reflection |
|---|---|
| • Authors often use the element of point of view to influence the interactions of the characters, plot, theme, and conflict in a story. | |
| **Skills**<br><br>• Identifying characteristics<br>• Making observations<br>• Identifying points of view<br>• Comparing and contrasting<br>• Brainstorming<br>• Originality<br>• Elaborating<br>• Using ideas/product modification techniques<br>• Comparing and contrasting | Students generate ideas about their stories to decide how the plot of their story will evolve. They make observations about their writing and edit them appropriately. They use skills of originality and elaboration in their writing, as well as ideas/product modification that includes substituting, combining, adapting, modifying, making larger or smaller, putting to new uses, eliminating, reversing, or rearranging. Students then use these thought processes to write their own version of the story. |
| **Standards**<br><br>SD 1, SD 2, SD 4, SD 5, SD 6, SD 7, SD 10, SD 11 | |
| **Guiding Questions**<br><br>• How is point of view changed by time, place, culture, events, and circumstances?<br>• What are the strengths and weaknesses of different points of view?<br>• Why do different people have different points of view? | These questions are very important to guiding student thinking. |
| **Introduction**<br><br>The teacher continues to focus students on their writing by having them share what they have thus far with the class.<br><br>Information from each student's previous journal entries determines their needs while the teacher checks on their progress in small groups.<br><br>Students work with their new point of view while completing their stories.<br><br>Students have a final product of a new version of a book and use the writing rubric (Resource 2.3) to evaluate it. | The teacher continues to monitor students and provide feedback in small-group or one-on-one settings.<br><br>It is important to remind students of the quality elements that will be used to evaluate their work. One way to demonstrate the use of the rubric (Resource 2.3) is through a whole-class lesson using one of the published books with which the students are already familiar.<br><br>Asking students to identify examples of particular elements of the rubric they believe are reflected in their work is also a means to ensure that they are very clear on each element, and thereby elevate the quality of their finished products. |
| **Teaching Strategies and Learning Experiences**<br><br>• Coaching<br>• Synectics<br>• Demonstrating and modeling<br>• Cooperative learning<br>• Shadowing<br><br>Practicing as authors in readiness and interest groups but working individually, some students | Coaching, again, occurs during teacher conferences about point of view and other story elements. Modeling correct grammar and story elements occurs in the conferences as well. Students can peer edit in their cooperative groups. The teacher shadows students by bringing in the guest author again, or in the readiness groups.<br><br>Students' groups change somewhat depending on their writing needs. If a student needs more |

(Continued)

| Unit Sequence | Reflection |
|---|---|
| may need assistance from the teacher in different ways depending on their readiness levels.<br><br>Students use the story map (Resource 2.1) they created previously and brainstorm to create another alternate story map from a different point of view, which allows them to continue writing their new version of the book. | scaffolding, the teacher moves to a group where this can be provided.<br><br>Students who are interested in other fields of study can determine how point of view is used in that particular discipline; for example, a student determines how detectives use point of view in solving crimes.<br><br>College professors, local authors, and retired English teachers are just a few examples of those who may be able to work with more skilled writers for a more in-depth learning experience; with e-mail as an option, distance is not a concern. |
| **Closure**<br><br>*Journal: Double-Entry Journal*<br><br>• How did perceptions, culture, and stereotypes change point of view?<br>• How did you make the point of view influence the interactions of the characters, plot, theme, and conflict in your story?<br>• What accomplishments did you make as an author?<br>• What was the most challenging experience? Why? | This journal entry should reflect that students have a strong understanding of how point of view affects a story. If there are students who do not have that understanding, reteaching activities will need to be planned. |

# RESOURCE 2.1: STORY MAP

Name _____ Date _____

Title of the book or story _____

## Original Version

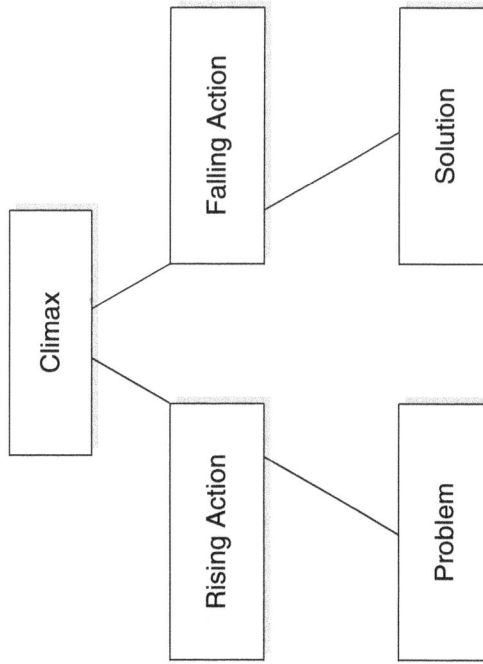

```
        ┌─────────┐
        │ Climax  │
        └─────────┘
       ╱           ╲
┌──────────────┐   ┌────────────────┐
│ Rising Action│   │ Falling Action │
└──────────────┘   └────────────────┘
       │                   │
┌──────────────┐   ┌────────────────┐
│   Problem    │   │   Solution     │
└──────────────┘   └────────────────┘
```

## New Version

```
        ┌─────────┐
        │ Climax  │
        └─────────┘
       ╱           ╲
┌──────────────┐   ┌────────────────┐
│ Rising Action│   │ Falling Action │
└──────────────┘   └────────────────┘
       │                   │
┌──────────────┐   ┌────────────────┐
│   Problem    │   │   Solution     │
└──────────────┘   └────────────────┘
```

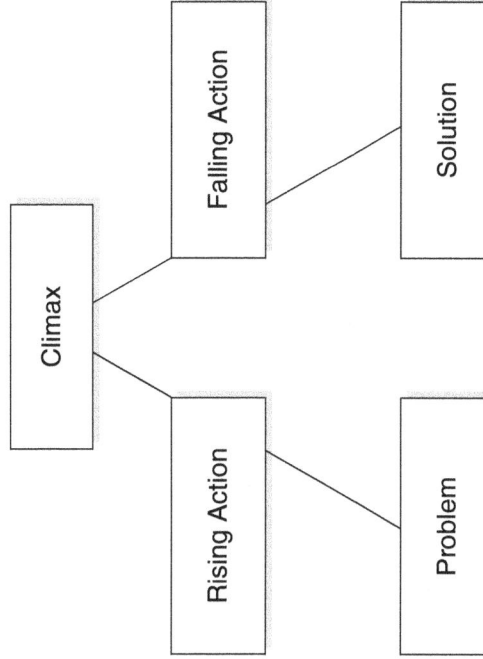

*Source:* Modified from *Five Elements of a Story* from Teacher Vision website, http://www.teachervision.fen.com/reading/graphic-organizers/2277.html.

## RESOURCE 2.2: HOW IS THIS LIKE ME?

Name _____ Date _____

| Like Me | Not Like Me | Maybe Like Me |
|---------|-------------|---------------|
|         |             |               |

## RESOURCE 2.3: WRITING RUBRIC

### Content

| | |
|---|---|
| 5 | Rich understanding of the topic with logical reasoning and insight. Focus on audience and purpose is exemplary. |
| 4 | Proficient understanding of the topic and effective response. Shows good insight and reasoning. Focuses on the audience and purpose. |
| 3 | Keeps to the topic. |
| 2 | Exhibits partial understanding the topic. |
| 1 | Does not address the topic. |

### Mechanics

| | |
|---|---|
| 5 | 0–1 mechanical errors |
| 4 | 2–3 mechanical errors |
| 3 | 4–5 mechanical errors |
| 2 | 6–7 mechanical errors |
| 1 | More than 7 mechanical errors |

### Sentence Structure

| | |
|---|---|
| 5 | Variety of sentence structures used correctly |
| 4 | Sentence structures used correctly |
| 3 | 0–1 sentence structure errors |
| 2 | 2–4 sentence structure errors |
| 1 | More than 4 sentence structure errors |

### Spelling

| | |
|---|---|
| 5 | 0–1 spelling errors |
| 4 | 2–3 spelling errors |
| 3 | 4–5 spelling errors |
| 2 | 6–7 spelling errors |
| 1 | More than 7 spelling errors |

# 3

# Experience Poetry

## (Grades 2–5)

*Leighann Pennington*

## INTRODUCTION TO THE UNIT

### Overview of the Unit

The Experience Poetry unit introduces students to the literary devices of poetry and applies this knowledge to writing original poetry. The foundation of this unit is for students to have the *experience* of being a writer—to think like a writer. Students learn about where creative people find inspiration. They learn the importance of closely observing the world around them, along with reading and examining high-quality poetry. The experience of poetry requires students to use their thinking skills as they analyze, synthesize, use inductive reasoning, create, imagine, and apply.

The instructional strategies are experiential, hands-on, and interactive. Complex instruction is enhanced through small- and large-group discussions, presentations, inductive-reasoning activities, and graphic organizers. Unit assessment differs for each teacher and student, depending on the students' previous knowledge of poetry as the preassessment determines. Poetry assignments are not graded—they are often students' first attempts at poetry writing and this creativity and joy in learning should not be stifled. Instead, the teacher evaluates students' growth on an individual basis, as well as their ability to apply the "big understandings" of the unit.

The sequence of the unit and lessons within is significant. Students begin their experience through engagement, interest, interaction, and foundational knowledge. This sequence then leads to application and creation. For example, the introductory activities, "What I Know" Interest Inventory and "What I Love" and the Five Senses, engage students because they are fun and they help students identify the inspiration for writing along with the practice of thinking like a writer. The Elements of Poetry lesson introduces students to the language and conventions of poetry to prepare them for writing and discussing poetry. The Junk Festival lesson helps students hone their close observation skills and artistic eye. These activities engage students at the very beginning and they don't even realize they are studying poetry and developing a poetic sensibility. The William Carlos Williams Poem Imitation portion of the lesson provides models for the structure of poetry and sources of inspiration. Roller 'Roo Story and Poem Differentiation and Found Poems subsequently assists students in moving away from writing stories instead of poems, and to focus more on the structure of poems, such as line breaks. The Interactive Poetry Museum lesson asks students to combine all larger concepts in an in-depth study of a particular poet, Mary Oliver. Students are then assigned activities that require them to creatively communicate their insights and knowledge.

The goal of the Experience Poetry unit is for students to understand poetry and begin thinking like writers to find inspiration for writing poems. Students learn to write poems as they analyze the elements of poetry. They create "found sculpture" and relate this activity to finding art and poetic inspiration in everyday life— examining the world in a fresh way. Students also create presentations, poems, and other creative products to share what they know about poets through the interactive poetry museum. The products created for the museum are authentic and modeled after what real poets do. When creating the museum exhibit, students choose among roles that appeal to each child's multiple intelligences and learning styles, including visual, auditory, linguistic, and artistic. Many hands-on materials are employed, especially with the Five Senses and the Junk Festival activities.

Experience Poetry began primarily as a way for upper elementary (Grades 2–5) students to engage deeply in the discipline of creative writing and as support for their exploration of high-level, literary quality poetry, usually reserved for older students and adults. This unit has been taught, in expanded or modified versions, to nine different classes of students, in public and private schools and in enrichment and summer programs for gifted students. Participating grades ranged from second grade through sixth grade. The goal is to make the advanced content engaging and fun and support students in their exploration. Students learn about the lives of poets and are inspired by them. They learn about the real lives and career paths of poets and explore what a real poet's life is like in the real world. Through this experience, students develop the skills for writing, drawing inspiration for poetry and communicating to others what poets do and why people write poetry.

The unit is primarily located in the Core Curriculum, because the unit explores the heart of a discipline, exemplified by the greater concepts (big understandings) in the discipline of creative writing. The representative topic of poetry focuses on these understandings in the context of the discipline. Reading and writing poetry and studying the lives of poets helps students understand why writers write. Related to the Curriculum of Practice, students learn what a practitioner thinks about and does in daily life. Students learn how practitioners apply the skills and understandings of the creative writing discipline. In this unit, a practitioner is a writer. The class learns about why writers write, what writers think about, and where they find their inspiration.

At the same time, Experience Poetry focuses on the core because it introduces students to the understandings of the discipline. To focus more deeply in the practice parallel, the teacher may talk about the structure of the discipline and the problems that writers more explicitly consider. The Curriculum of Identity is particularly engaging because students include real-life experiences, relate their sense of self to their learning, and grow in self-awareness.

When writing poetry, a student's identity is inherently included, because real poets use identity to fuel their poetry. The act of writing poetry helps poets to develop, refine, and express their sense of identity. Students identify their interests and what they love at the beginning of the unit and throughout, using their interests to write original poetry. The unit asks students to understand why writers write and consider why they too might like to write. However, the unit is not primarily rooted in the Curriculum of Identity. It does not ask students to reflect on their engagement in the discipline and how they can shape the discipline in the future. For the most part, the unit focuses on understanding poetry, how to write poetry, and the lives of writers.

## Background Information for the Unit

The Experience Poetry unit does not require students to have prior experience with poetry. The "What I Know" Interest Inventory preassessment informs teachers about what students know and when administered as a postassessment, shows their growth. The preassessment may also point out misconceptions students have about poetry; for example, "all poems rhyme." Some lessons, such as Roller 'Roo Story and Poem Differentiation, were chosen because students were unaware of the structural elements that define poetry, including line breaks and syntactical structure. Found Poems, a related activity, allows students to practice line breaks, which is a purposeful choice that poets make.

Several resources are useful when preparing to teach the unit. *A Poetry Handbook* by Mary Oliver (1994) is a refresher on poetic terms including the literary devices included in discussion. *Rose, Where Did You Get That Red? Teaching Great Poetry to Children,* by Kenneth Koch (1990), shows samples of student work and examples of poem imitation (drawing from Koch's work for designing the William Carlos Williams Poem Imitation activity). The book *Heart to Heart: New Poems Inspired by Twentieth Century American Art,* edited by Jan Greenberg (2001), is an example of the relationship between poetic inspiration, visual images, and art that is reinforced throughout the unit.

# CONTENT FRAMEWORK

## Organizing Concepts

### *Macroconcepts*

M1: Creativity

### *Discipline-Specific Concepts*

C1: Communication

C2: Rhythm

C3: Perception

C4: Inspiration

C5: Patterns

C6: Production

## Principles

P1: Poets observe and describe the world around them in detail using the five senses.

P2: Music and rhythm influence poets, and poets also pay attention to sound when writing poetry.

P3: Poets create their art from everyday life and observations. Poets share their unique view of the world with others through vivid description in their poetry.

P4: Whom and what poets love inspire them. The world around them and the work of other writers also inspire poets.

P5: Poets make artful choices to emphasize certain words and sounds to achieve certain rhythms.

P6: Poets create their art from everyday life and observations.

## National or State Standards

While the standards for a subject might not always be the most inspiring reason to teach, they can help guide and focus teaching. Standards are addressed here to show that the Parallel Curriculum Model (PCM) and standards are not mutually exclusive. Standards can be integrated into the larger (and sometimes more complex) network of a PCM unit.

Author's note: Because I have a clear picture of goals for the discipline of creative writing and the life of a writer, my disciplinary knowledge helped guide the larger concepts for the unit. I took note of the standards later.

Because this unit was taught several times in Virginia, the Virginia standards of learning (SOLs) for sixth-grade English are outlined subsequently. Since standards vary from state to state, the National Council for Teachers of English (NCTE) standards are also included. These standards assist in looking at the goals of modern literacy and creativity on a larger scale.

### Virginia Sixth-Grade Standards of Learning for English

No one unit will meet all of the standards, and it should not be expected to do this. With foresight and planning over the course of the school year, standards can be met through a variety of units. Because standards have very specific goals, they cannot all be met. The heart of the sixth-grade SOLs for Virginia focuses on writing essays, comparing and contrasting viewpoints (both in written and oral discussion), reading and writing, and understanding narrative and poetic structure. The following list includes some relevant standards and highlights those that pertain to the Experience Poetry unit. However, these standards are more mechanical and skim the surface of the larger concepts intended for this unit. This is why, when developing a unit, both the standards and a curriculum model like PCM can guide teachers.

Reading

6.4. The student will read and demonstrate comprehension of a variety of fiction, narrative nonfiction, and poetry.

   a. Identify the elements of narrative structure, including setting, character, plot, conflict, and theme.
   b. Use knowledge of narrative and poetic structures to aid comprehension and predict outcomes.
   c. Describe the images created by language.
   d. Describe how word choice and imagery contribute to the meaning of a text.
   e. Describe cause-effect relationships and their impact on plot.
   f. Use information stated explicitly in the text to draw conclusions and make inferences.
   g. Explain how character and plot development are used in a selection to support a central conflict or story line.
   h. Paraphrase and summarize the main points in the text.

Writing

6.6. The student will write narratives, descriptions, and explanations.

   a. Use a variety of planning strategies to generate and organize ideas.
   b. Establish central idea, organization, elaboration, and unity.
   c. Select vocabulary and information to enhance the central idea, tone, and voice.
   d. Expand and embed ideas by using modifiers, standard coordination, and subordination in complete sentences.
   e. Revise writing for clarity.

### National Council for Teachers of English (NCTE) Standards

All of the standards are included, with those most relevant to this unit in italics, along with comments related to the standards.

   1. *Students read a wide range of print and nonprint texts to build an understanding of texts, of themselves, and of the cultures of the United States and the world;* to acquire new information; to respond to the needs and demands of society and the workplace; and *for personal fulfillment.* Among these texts are fiction and nonfiction, classic and contemporary works.

   2. *Students read a wide range of literature from many periods in many genres to build an understanding of the many dimensions (e.g., philosophical, ethical, aesthetic) of human experience.* (This unit has both contemporary and historical poets. Students are only beginning to understand the structure and purpose of poetry. While they build a surface understanding of all the mentioned dimensions, their understanding might not be sophisticated enough at this time—for instance, in a unit intended as an introduction to the essence of poetry—to delve deeply into those areas.)

3. *Students apply a wide range of strategies to comprehend, interpret, evaluate, and appreciate texts. They draw on their prior experience, their interactions with other readers and writers, their knowledge of word meaning and of other texts, their word identification strategies, and their understanding of textual features (e.g., sound-letter correspondence, sentence structure, context, graphics).*

4. Students adjust their use of spoken, written, and visual language (e.g., conventions, style, vocabulary) to communicate effectively with a variety of audiences and for different purposes.

5. *Students employ a wide range of strategies as they write and use different writing process elements appropriately to communicate with different audiences for a variety of purposes (such as strategies about how to become inspired to write and how to revise poetry).*

6. *Students apply knowledge of language structure, language conventions (e.g., spelling and punctuation), media techniques, figurative language, and genre to create, critique, and discuss print and nonprint texts.*

7. Students conduct research on issues and interests by generating ideas and questions, and by posing problems. They gather, evaluate, and synthesize data from a variety of sources (e.g., print and nonprint texts, artifacts, people) to communicate their discoveries in ways that suit their purpose and audience.

8. *Students use a variety of technological and information resources (e.g., libraries, databases, computer networks, video) to gather and synthesize information and to create and communicate knowledge.*

9. *Students develop an understanding of and respect for diversity in language use, patterns, and dialects across cultures, ethnic groups, geographic regions, and social roles.* (For example, use of slang in Langston Hughes's poems for the Elements of Poetry lesson. Students benefit from a variety of poets from diverse backgrounds who write both in English and other languages, such as Spanish or German.)

10. *Students whose first language is not English make use of their first language to develop competency in the English language arts and to develop understanding of content across the curriculum.* (Throughout the unit, teachers can share bilingual poetry, both in the original language and in translation. Poet Julia Alvarez writes in Spanish and English and Pablo Neruda anthologies show Spanish and English poems side by side.)

11. *Students participate as knowledgeable, reflective, creative, and critical members of a variety of literacy communities.*

12. *Students use spoken, written, and visual language to accomplish their own purposes (e.g., for learning, enjoyment, persuasion, and the exchange of information).*

## Skills

S1: Analyze

S2: Synthesize

S3: Practice inductive reasoning

S4: Create

S5: Imagine

S6: Apply

# UNIT ASSESSMENTS

## Experience Poetry's Forms of Student Assessment

| | |
|---|---|
| *Preassessment* | What I Know |
| *Ongoing Assessment* | Journal entries, original poetry, letter to William Carlos Williams, and contributions to class discussions |
| *Summative Assessment* | Interactive Poetry Museum |
| *Self-Assessment* | Interactive Poetry Museum Graphic Organizer (identity questions), Goal Setting, What I Learned, returning to preassessment and correcting mistakes at end, and "What I Love" Interest Inventory |
| *Unit Assessment* | Ungraded student evaluation of the unit |

Assessing student work is basically *process oriented*—seeing where students begin in their poetry experience, looking at the progression of their work, and concluding their growth in applying poetic devices, attitudes about poetry, and awareness of the dynamic state of inspiration. The following chart shows the progression of a beginner of poetry to a more proficient writer.

| | |
|---|---|
| Student is scared of poetry or hates to write. | Student moves to "I like it and I like to write or I want to learn more." |
| Student latches onto a variety of things, depending on his or her interest. | Student uses pictures, sounds, touch, taste, smells all to inspire, as well as varied role models, frameworks of poem structure, and ideas. |

## Overview of Evidence of Student Growth and Criteria for Success

### The Students' Poetry

Students use the following poetic devices and demonstration of understandings to measure growth:

- Rhyme or slant rhyme
- Rhythm
- Free verse or any type of poetic structure
- Images
- Attention to sound of language

- Simile or metaphor
- Influences or examples of poets' work
- Evidence of methods of inspiration, such as five senses, visuals, or close observation

Students answer the following questions (return to preassessment, becoming a postassessment):

1. What is a poem?
2. How is a poem like a story?
3. How is a poem different from a story?
4. Why do writers write?
5. What do writers do when they are not writing?
6. Where do writers find their inspiration?

If students cannot verbalize answers to these questions, the teacher can note if they have shown evidence of understanding integrated into their work.

# UNIT SEQUENCE AND TEACHER REFLECTION

### LESSON 3.1: PREASSESSMENT: "WHAT I KNOW" INTEREST INVENTORY AND "WHAT I LOVE" AND THE FIVE SENSES

**Length:** One 60-minute session for stations and poem or one 90-minute session for extended version

| Unit Sequence | Reflection |
|---|---|
| **Concepts** <br><br> Communication | |
| **Principles** <br><br> • Poets observe and describe the world around them. <br> • Poets write in detail using the five senses. | The principles help students experience the worldview of writers. PCM discusses the powerful idea that each discipline has a particular way of looking at or understanding the world. These principles are the first steps by which students experience how creative writers understand and experience their world. |
| **Skills** <br><br> • Observe the world closely. <br> • Use words to describe tangible and seemingly intangible sensations. <br> • Cultivate a unique and creative perspective of the world, like that of an artist or poet. | Students gain opportunities to practice doing what writers do. <br><br> *Author's note:* This activity was the first one I designed, because it fully represents the PCM idea that students should be working like experts. |

| Unit Sequence | Reflection |
|---|---|
| **Standards**<br><br>*VA-SOL*<br><br>6.4c, 6.4d, 6.6a<br><br>*NCTE*<br><br>5, 11, 12 | |
| **Guiding Questions**<br><br>• What do you love?<br>• How do you observe the world (detailed observation)? | In this unit, the guiding questions are often a rephrasing of the principles. |
| Students complete the preassessment, What I Know worksheet (Resource 3.1). Each student shares at least one of their answers with the class.<br><br>    The Five Senses activity is a fun way to dive right into the poetry unit. Students begin to think and experience the world like writers. They practice describing the "hard-to-describe." They hone their senses and practice putting sensations into words. They notice how sensation is connected to the memory and scenes that give rise to poems.<br><br>    Students then apply what they have learned by writing a five-senses poem and share their products with classmates. | Writers experience the world using their five senses. They teach us to appreciate the world around us, with all its sensations and all its tiny details. Poet Naomi Shihab Nye (1990) describes how she absorbs the world with all her senses:<br><br>    Tiny things other people overlooked seemed like treasures and clues. I wrote them down so I would not forget them. I did not begin writing because I imagined a writing career . . . I started keeping my own notebooks because I wanted to remember everything. The quilt, the cherry tree, the creek. The neat whop of a baseball rammed perfectly with a bat. My father's funny Palestinian stories. The feeling of the breeze as my brother and I rode our bicycles down the hill. The blood-red stain of a ripe strawberry on my fingertips; the rich smell of earth at Mueller's Organic Farm a few blocks from our house. (p. 7) |
| **Introduction**<br><br>Students complete the following introductory activity:<br><br>*What I Love*<br><br>  My name:<br>  My favorite animal or pet:<br>  My favorite place or vacation spot:<br>  My favorite memory:<br>  My favorite smell:<br>  My favorite sound:<br>  My favorite food or candy or dessert:<br>  My favorite holiday or special occasion: | "Poets write about what they love" is an understanding principle of the unit. This brief introductory activity helps the teacher get to know the students and identify specifically things they love, which could lead to an inspiration for a poem. Reading each student's completed form assists in connecting their individual interests with interest-based activities. Students keep their What I Love form and return to it later when they need inspiration for a poem. It is important to tell them that, if they cannot think of their *very* favorite thing, they can write more than one response. Getting as many ideas as one can on paper is a key strategy for a writer. |

(Continued)

| Unit Sequence | Reflection |
|---|---|
| *Five Senses Introduction Speech*<br><br>*Today we are beginning our practice in "thinking like a poet." While this activity looks like a lot of fun (and it is!), it is not just about eating candy. Poets describe the world around them using their five senses. They also describe the "hard-to-describe" in words. Poets have a unique view of the world. They express their creative thoughts on paper and then share their products with others.*<br><br>*The five senses help us build a memorable scene that appeals to readers. Today we will practice using our five senses using this guided worksheet to help us form more distinct and interesting descriptions. We will use what we write on our worksheets (Resource 3.2) to inspire a Five Senses poem at the end of class.* | *Five Senses*<br><br>After each station is assembled, the students are typically abuzz with excitement, especially when they notice the laptop computer (with music playing), speakers, and snacks. Depending on the group and their attention spans, the students circulate from one station to the next every 5 to 10 minutes.<br><br>While this rotation occurs in a one-hour segment, the Five Senses activity is an hour-and-a-half time period with older students (fifth and sixth grade). The extra 20 to 30 minutes allows completion of the smell and touch stations outside in nature. About 30 minutes can also be reserved for the sound station (a real favorite) so students have time to discuss each song and share scenes the song inspired in their minds.<br><br>Distributing the taste station to a whole class at once allows closer supervision on the amounts eaten. Overall, shorter time periods may require stations while longer time periods are best used in a whole-class setting. |
| **Teaching Strategies and Learning Experiences**<br><br>• *Preassessment:* identifying what students know and misconceptions held about material<br>• *What I Love:* interest inventory<br>• *Five Senses:* interactive, experiential, hands-on practice<br><br>*A Peek Into the Classroom*<br><br>The following passage is on the board when students arrive:<br><br>Poets observe and describe the world around them using the five senses.<br><br>Then the stations are organized, setting up the music station first and (because it has candy) the taste station last. The following example provides a list of possible items for each station.<br><br>*Hear.* CDs of nature music or small musical instruments (e.g., a recorder or harmonica). CD ideas include *Of Wind and Water,* a nature sounds CD, and selections from the film soundtrack *The Motorcycle Diaries.* The film is about a journey and, like many popular film soundtracks, evokes a special scene. When visiting this station, students close their eyes and talk about how the music | As students take part in the Five Senses activity, they practice what writers do every day—closely observing the world and putting their sensations into words. Lush sensory description makes poetry stand out from other forms of writing. This attention to detail and close observation helps students when they move on to metaphor and analyze literature, and it also inspires poems. |

| Unit Sequence | Reflection |
|---|---|
| draws a picture in their minds. For example, a Christmas song might remind students of a family Christmas or drumbeats might remind them of horses galloping. (Students write down their specific responses on the worksheet.) Other favorites sounds include Caribbean steel drum music, which often reminds the class of the beach, and classical music, especially selections with a particular mood, like a *rondeau* by Mozart or *nocturne* by Chopin. As mentioned in the introduction, this works even better when more time is scheduled so students can discuss their mental scenes and the scenes music evoke.<br><br>*See.* Photos of nature from old calendars, photographs of people interacting, postcards with scenes of nature or artwork, and so on; photography, art, or picture books from the library; and personal photos. Photos that have a sense of story or that appeal to a diverse array of students work best. For describing the play of light, unique kinds of light-catchers can be used, such as sequins and a CD turned upside down.<br><br>*Touch.* Pine cones, crunchy leaves, a soft scarf or blanket (fleece), plastic cling wrap, marshmallows, and cold cooked spaghetti. Less messy options include a spongy paintbrush (without the paint) and hairbrush bristles. Other ideas include unique textured surface objects like suede, velvet, or cotton. If possible, the class can experience textures in nature outside.<br><br>*Taste.* Cinnamon red hots, salty pretzels or popcorn, mints, or mini-Mounds coconut and chocolate bars. Describing unique tastes that are distinct from one another is key in this activity. Choosing tastes that might remind students of something memorable in their lives is also important in inspiring poems. (It is necessary to find out before the lesson if any of the students have food allergies or are on special diets. It is also always crucial to remind students not to eat anything for which they have an allergy.)<br><br>*Smell.* Fragrant candles, tarts, incense sticks, and so on. Smell is the most nostalgic sense, so scents that go with the season or certain locations—such as lemonade, pumpkin, pine, lemon, coconut, and pineapple—are effective. If possible, it might be better to go outside and smell things like walnuts, | |

(Continued)

| Unit Sequence | Reflection |
|---|---|
| pine trees, dirt, grass, and flowers. Most important, students use their worksheets to guide them to not only pinpoint the scents, but also to convey the story different scents evoke. | |
| **Closure**<br><br>*Five Senses Poem Example*<br><br>The following example appears on the board and is shared with students before they write their own poem.<br><br>    *See* the waves come and go<br>    *Feel* the sand grains on your toes<br>    *Smell* the tangy, fishy scent<br>    *Hear* the rustling palm tree leaves<br>    *Taste* the sea salt on the breeze<br><br>*Reinforcing the Understanding: Journal Entry*<br><br>Students keep a poet's journal and record the poems they write during class and then take the journal home each night to share with their families.<br>    The concepts introduced in this activity are reinforced when students go home—or to a park or favorite or interesting place—and observe using their five senses. Students write their observations in their journals and then share them as a class before beginning the next poetry activity. | Whenever students write a poem in this unit, they have a sample poem to guide them. The teacher thus models expectations and provides the students with structure. Very young students have not encountered many poems, and therefore are unfamiliar with poetic structure.<br>    The simple structure of the five senses poem is a good place to begin. Students choose a scene from their worksheets and compose a poem about that scene, using all five senses. They can choose to use the format and phrasing of the sample poem or use a format of their own as long as all five senses are mentioned.<br>    Some students have a tendency to just list every sensation mentioned on the worksheet. This, of course, does not serve the goal of creating a fully realized scene. Referring to the sample poem about the beach allows the students to practice, as they pretend they are at the beach.<br>    As students write, the teacher helps with ideas or supervises lists of brainstorming ideas. Providing postcards, paintings, and other artwork, in case they need a scene to write about, is also beneficial. |

## LESSON 3.2: ELEMENTS OF POETRY

**Length:** One 45–60-minute session

| Unit Sequence | Reflection |
|---|---|
| **Concept**<br><br>Rhythm | |
| **Principles**<br><br>• Poets observe and describe the world around them in detail using the five senses.<br>• Music and rhythm influence poets, and they also pay attention to sound when writing poetry. | |

| Unit Sequence | Reflection |
|---|---|
| **Skills**<br><br>• Identify literary devices in context.<br>• Create definitions of elements of poetry.<br>• Apply knowledge to create metaphors, rhymes, and so on, and in the future, to create poems. | |
| **Standards**<br><br>*VA-SOL*<br><br>6.4b, 6.4c, 6.4d, 6.4h<br><br>*NCTE*<br><br>2, 3, 6, 9, 11, 12 | |
| **Guiding Questions**<br><br>• What makes poetry, poetry?<br>• What makes poetry different from other forms of writing?<br><br>The five ideas with sample poems attached to each provide a definition of poetry:<br><br>• Figurative language<br>• Sensory images<br>• Music<br>• Rhythm<br>• Sound | The Experience Poetry unit introduces students to the essence of poetry and to cultivating a love for poetry. Students experience what it means to be a poet. This is the central understanding of the unit.<br><br>    Honing in on big ideas and what exactly differentiates a poem from a story helps with choosing which elements of poetry to introduce. Many students who have little experience with poetry will automatically write a story rather than a poem. Their writing can be identified as a story by the idea sequence and sentence structure. |
| **Introduction**<br><br>*Elements of Poetry Introduction Speech*<br><br>   *We will be learning about literary devices and reading poems that will show us examples of the elements of poetry. We can use what we learned to talk about poetry in the way real writers do. This will also help us write poems.* | Figurative language and sensory images complement one another, while music, rhythm, and sound are a natural combination.<br><br>    Students are not given clear-cut definitions of the elements of poetry. They are given examples and then asked to help define each element based on what they understand. This is an inductive approach to learning. Students form their own understandings from the evidence at hand, and then move from examples to a generalization about the examples. |
| **Teaching Strategies and Learning Experiences**<br><br>• Whole-class and small-group discussion<br>• Inductive reasoning<br>• Close reading of poems<br>• Hands-on or movement-based learning (rhythm)<br><br>*The Three Poems*<br><br>1. "Fog" by Carl Sandburg<br>2. "It's Raining in Honolulu" by Joy Harjo<br>3. "Hope Is a Thing With Feathers" by Emily Dickinson | *Figurative Language*<br><br>Students learn about personification, metaphor, and simile. They are given three poems, as well as two examples, of symbol and simile.<br><br>• Symbol: dove = peace.<br>• Simile: "My love is like a red, red rose" (Burns, 2002, p. 197).<br><br>The most important part of the lesson is for students to understand and identify the uses of |

(Continued)

| Unit Sequence | Reflection |
|---|---|
| *"Fog" by Carl Sandburg.* "The fog comes on little cat feet" (2003, p. 33). This poem is an example of personification, which is a particular type of metaphor. The fog, an inanimate object, is compared to an animate object, a cat. Throughout the poem, the fog is characterized as a cat, moving on "little cat feet," then sitting back on its "silent haunches" before moving away from the city. | metaphor, simile, and symbols in poetry, and then use these literary devices in their own poems. |
| | After studying the selected poems, the teacher guides students in making up their own metaphors and similes. For example, with a picture of a wheat field, they describe the wind blowing through the wheat. ("Waves like the ocean" is a popular comparison.) Figurative language is the most difficult category for students to understand and for the teacher to explain. Guiding students closely allows them more freedom in arriving at their own conclusions as they begin to work with the other elements of poetry. |
| *"It's Raining in Honolulu" by Joy Harjo.* Some students see connections easily, think in analogous ways, and will see metaphors and similes in the poems easier than others. Metaphor can be spelled out and pinpointed in this poem using the phrase "rain opens up like flowers" (2007, p. 34). People are being compared to flowers. When it rains, the people open up to the world like a flower does when it blooms. | |
| | The figurative language provides an example before students divide into four groups. Each group works on a different element; then the class comes together to share their self-derived definitions. Students read a poem aloud as an example of their assigned element. |
| *"Hope Is a Thing With Feathers" by Emily Dickinson.* In this poem, hope is compared to a bird throughout, beginning with the first line, "Hope is a thing with feathers" (2003, p. 22). Students underline the ways in which Dickinson describes hope as a bird. They end up highlighting almost the entire poem, because this poem is comprised of an extended metaphor. | A chance to reinforce students' understandings arrives when students come back together to share information about each element. |
| | *Extension: Figurative Language* |
| | Some students will understand metaphors and similes quickly, while others will need continuous reinforcement during the entire unit. An "abstract to concrete" activity, where students write what the term *hope, peace,* or *love* is like supports understanding. (Students enjoy doing this activity on the board.) Then they can use Emily Dickinson's poem as a model for imitation or their own free form to write an extended metaphor poem. |
| *Sensory Images* | |
| The following poems provide a good introduction to the use of sensory images for students. The poems are simple and focus on a specific image: "The Red Wheelbarrow" by William Carlos Williams (1970); haikus by Bashō (Hass, 1995), the Japanese father of haiku; and "September Moon" by Joy Harjo (1983). Students identify which senses are used when describing the images in the poems. Students can draw a picture of what they see in their "mind's eye" to reinforce this idea. | |
| | *Extension: Sensory Images* |
| | This includes asking students to write several haikus, recalling that the format for a haiku is based on syllables per line: five for the first line, seven for the second, and five for the third. Going around the room and choosing favorite haikus to read aloud helps students isolate a very specific image, because the syllable requirements are limiting. |
| *Music.* Meena Alexander said that poetry is "dancing words" and "the music of survival." Students read the poems aloud in a musical way. Langston Hughes's poems describe scenes that involve music. His poems are influenced by jazz and blues, illustrated with reading "The Weary Blues," "Jazzonia," and "Blues Fantasy" by Langston Hughes. (A word that could be inappropriate to use in "The Weary Blues" may need to be edited.) | *Music* |
| | Before reading the Langston Hughes poems, the teacher assesses whether anyone has heard of the |

| Unit Sequence | Reflection |
|---|---|
| Students may also listen to a recording of Langston Hughes reading his poems so they can hear the music in his voice as he reads.<br><br>*Rhythm.* First, the students just listen for the rhythm (even closing their eyes) as the teacher reads the Robert Frost poem "Stopping by Woods on a Snowy Evening" aloud. Next, the teacher reads while tapping the table on the emphasized syllable, and then again, reading the poem slowly while the students emphasize each syllable with their "drumbeat." The teacher reads the poem two or three times until the students beat in time with the emphasized syllable. (The emphasis may need to be exaggerated as the teacher reads.) This kinesthetic approach in emphasizing rhythm helps many students better understand the rhythm in poetry.<br><br>*Sound.* Sound focuses on rhyme, repetition (repeating words or phrases in a poem or within lines of a poem), and alliteration. First, alliteration is explained using tongue twisters. Students practice their understanding of alliteration by creating their own tongue twisters. They can then include their classmates in the fun. A common tongue twister example is "Sally sells sea-shells by the sea-shore." Using students' names to make tongue twisters gets them more involved.<br><br>*Rhyme.* Students make up a rhyme. An easy example of a rhyme to share is as follows:<br><br>Jack and Jill went up the hill to fetch a pail of water. Jack fell down and broke his crown and Jill came tumbling after.<br><br>Students identify the rhymes: Jill/hill and down/crown rhyme. This may sound simple or obvious, but not all students have prior experience with poetry or the elements of poetry. A script for helping students find a rhyming word is as follows:<br><br>*When I am writing a poem and become stuck, looking for a rhyme, I write out the alphabet. Say to yourself, "I am looking for a word that rhymes with 'hill,' one that will go with my poem. I will start with A, no, B-bill, C-no, D-dill, E-no, F-fill, G-gill, and so on." You might find a rhyme and use it in your poem, decide to change the original word "hill" to something else, or decide not even to use rhyme in your poem!* | Harlem Renaissance, and if not, explains that Langston Hughes was a leader for a creative and artistic movement that took place in a neighborhood called Harlem in New York City where art, literature, and musical creation flourished.<br><br>Next, the teacher asks students if they have heard of jazz or blues, and after reading the poems, explains how the rhythms of the poems mirror the rhythm and structure of the music. For example, "Blues Fantasy" has the structure of a person singing, and the audience replying, urging the singer on; also, Hughes was inspired to write his poems by going out in his neighborhood and listening to the music.<br><br>*Rhythm*<br><br>While discussing rhythm requires mentioning the term *meter,* it is not necessary to emphasize, because it is technical and can be difficult to hear. Instead, students can understand that Robert Frost often wrote in a certain kind of meter in order to capture the rhythm that English speakers use in everyday conversation.<br><br>The discussion of rhythm concludes by pointing out a stanza and line break. A stanza or line break affects rhythm by bringing about a slight pause, depending on the punctuation at the end of a line or stanza. Line breaks are discussed further in a later lesson.<br><br>*Rhyme*<br><br>Sharing this strategy is another unit example of how poets think while they are writing. Students spontaneously apply this strategy later in the unit when they are freewriting poems. Depending on the students, they can work with a poem already underlined with examples of alliteration and rhyme or, for example, underline rhymes in blue and alliteration in yellow. Almost every poem has rhyme or internal rhyme, allowing much freedom in choosing a poem that students will like. |

*(Continued)*

(Continued)

| Unit Sequence | Reflection |
|---|---|
| **Closure**<br><br>*Reinforcing the Understanding: Journal Entry*<br><br>Students choose an image in a photo, picture, on TV, or anything they see, and write a poem using haikus as modeled by Basho, "The Red Wheelbarrow" by William Carlos Williams, or "September Moon" by Joy Harjo as a guide. The book *Heart to Heart: New Poems Inspired by Twentieth Century American Art*, edited by Jan Greenberg (2001), can be shared with students before or after asking them to write an art/visually inspired poem. | In the future, in all poems that are read, these literary devices are pointed out or students identify them. This especially helps students understand difficult terms like *metaphor* and *personification.* Because this unit focuses on the discipline of creative writing, if students cannot always identify these literary devices in context, they can still use them in their writing.<br><br>This activity is never "closed" because students must continue to apply their knowledge with each poem they read or write in the future. Students can also write definitions and examples of each trait (sound, music, or figurative language) on pieces of poster board to hang around the room, and add to the posters later in the unit when more examples arise or to revise the definitions. |

## LESSON 3.3: THE JUNK FESTIVAL AND WILLIAM CARLOS WILLIAMS POEM IMITATION

**Length:** Junk Festival, one 60-minute session (90-minute session if class goes outside to find "junk"); Williams Carlos Williams Poem Imitation, one 60-minute session

| Unit Sequence | Reflection |
|---|---|
| **Concepts**<br><br>Perception | |
| **Principles**<br><br>• Poets observe and describe the world around them in detail using the five senses.<br>• Whom and what they love inspire poets. The world around them and the work of other writers also inspire poets.<br>• Poets create their art from everyday life and observations.<br>• Poets share their unique view of the world with others through vivid description in their poetry. | |

| Unit Sequence | Reflection |
|---|---|
| **Skills**<br><br>• Practice inductive reasoning.<br>• Identify and imitate poetic structure. | |
| **Standards**<br><br>*VA-SOL*<br><br>6.4b, 6.4c, 6.4d, 6.6a, 6.6c<br><br>*NCTE*<br><br>2, 3, 5, 6, 9, 11, 12 | |
| **Guiding Questions**<br><br>• Why do writers write?<br>• Where do writers find inspiration?<br><br>This is a two-part lesson.<br>   Students create a "found sculpture." In William Carlos Williams's poem "Imitation," students relate Williams's poetic inspiration, "the beauty of the real," to the junk festival and use their new observation skills to imitate four of his poems. Finally, they write Williams a letter verbalizing their new understandings. | |
| **Introduction**<br><br>The teacher or a student reads "The Fish" by Elizabeth Bishop (2005). Students close their eyes and picture the images the poem conjures in their minds.<br>   If time, students write a poem to describe a pet or animal (or any object) with great detail as Bishop modeled. | Using copies of Bishop's poem, students point out any similes or metaphors they notice. By asking, "Why did the author let the fish go?" the teacher probes past the typical response that "she felt sorry for the fish" to how she admired the fish. The line "five-haired beard of wisdom" (2005, p. 174) illustrates this. The author also uses a description of the fishing lines in his chin as "like medals . . ." (p. 174). Students thus practice in-depth reading skills (reading like writers) and becoming detailed observers. |
| **Teaching Strategies and Learning Experiences**<br><br>• Inductive reasoning<br>• Hands-on experiential learning<br>• Artistic practice<br><br>The process of creating a *found sculpture* is parallel to that of creating a poem. | When students choose "junk," they look at the world with a fresh perspective—something poets do. They learn to see things in a new way.<br>   Two students explained the purpose of the Junk Festival activity especially well: "The point of the junk festival was to show that it was like poetry—taking raw ideas (junk) and turning them into |

*(Continued)*

(Continued)

| Unit Sequence | Reflection |
|---|---|
| *Part One: Junk Festival*<br><br>Students bring pieces of "junk" from home—items they think are interesting or beautiful that others might overlook or consider junk. Their final product is a "found sculpture." The class can also go outside on school grounds and look for litter, pebbles, fallen leaves and tree branches, and so forth.<br><br>*Author's note:* I always bring some empty water bottles and pieces of cardboard, which are good bases to stabilize the *found sculpture*. Once I brought a broken curling iron and two girls were inspired to make a sculpture symbolizing the "average American girl." The sculpture may take on an abstract or human form or even a symbolic form, such as "nature warrior" and "litter monster."<br><br>After completing their sculptures, students write something modeled after a placard in a museum, as though their sculpture is art on display. The written component includes the sculpture's title, artist, description of the work, and accompanying poem. Students then present their sculpture and description or poem to the class.<br><br>*Part Two: William Carlos Williams Poem Imitation*<br><br>The photos and visuals shown in Resources 3.3 through 3.6 exemplify how the surrounding world can inspire poetry. Reading a poem example assists students as they begin their own poems. Also, the collection of photos, postcards, and artwork from the Five Senses activity inspires students' poems. A guide follows for how to sequence students through this part of the lesson.<br><br>1. "Between Walls" (Resource 3.3). Find something that most people would consider ugly and describe it in a way that makes it beautiful. Observing trash or junk like this helps us attune our eyes and present things in a fresh light, forgoing the everyday eye, which misses much.<br><br>2. "The Red Wheelbarrow" (Resource 3.4). Zoom in on a specific image and describe it in a few yet power-packed words. Notice how Williams plays with line breaks and stanzas. Observe where he places words on the page. | beautiful poetry (sculptures)" and "It means that you can take simple things and make them more complex and beautiful."<br><br>After the junk festival, students explain why they did the activity. Through inductive reasoning, they share the big idea without any help from the teacher.<br><br>Students work on their sculptures individually or in groups of two or more, whichever they prefer.<br><br>*William Carlos Williams: Examining the World With a Fresh Eye*<br><br>William Carlos Williams's most famous poems have few words and zoom in on particular images. Students readily imitate his work, and this activity helps them engage deeply in the discipline of creative writing by thinking and viewing the world like a writer. By choosing a particular author, students' understanding becomes more concrete through the use of poems as specific examples.<br><br>The book *Rose, Where Did You Get That Red? Teaching Great Poetry to Children* by poet Kenneth Koch (1990) is a great resource to accompany this activity. Mirroring this lesson, Koch employs the work of master poets to teach children poetry. Students learn the structure of poetry by reading poems and imitating the style and structure of William Carlos Williams's poems. His poems work well because he observes nature with his five senses and his poems are simple enough on the surface that readers new to poetry can appreciate his poems and imitate his style. Williams focuses on an image and simply describes it. This is how students need to practice as they begin writing poetry. |

| Unit Sequence | Reflection |
|---|---|
| 3. "The Locust Tree in Flower" (Resource 3.5). Use one-word lines to write your poem. This can help you choose your words carefully. You might select a scene in nature, like the poet did, or something else entirely. | |
| 4. "This Is Just to Say" (Resource 3.6). Notice how the title flows into the poem—the title becomes part of the poem. Williams is apologizing for something he did that he is not really sorry for. This is a chance for you to experience how a poet's sense of humor can affect poetry. | |
| **Closure**<br><br>Students write a letter to William Carlos Williams, answering the following questions:<br><br>• What is your favorite Williams poem? Why?<br>• Share one of your imitation poems. Why is this one was your best?<br>• What Williams poem inspired you to write your poem?<br>• What is the meaning behind the junk festival? Why did we do it? | In writing this letter, students use inductive reasoning to present their ideas about the purpose of the junk festival. They raise self-awareness by assessing their poems and analyzing sources of inspiration. |

## LESSON 3.4: *LOVE THAT DOG* AND WHY WRITE POETRY?

**Length:** One 45–60-minute session

| Unit Sequence | Reflection |
|---|---|
| **Concepts**<br><br>Inspiration | |
| **Principles**<br><br>• Writers write about what they love.<br>• Other writers' works and words inspire poets.<br>• What we read can inspire us to write poetry. | |
| **Skills**<br><br>• Comprehend<br>• Analyze<br>• Create<br>• Apply | |

*(Continued)*

(Continued)

| Unit Sequence | Reflection |
|---|---|
| **Standards**<br><br>*VA-SOL*<br><br>6.4b, 6.4d<br><br>*NCTE*<br><br>3, 6, 11, 12 | |
| **Guiding Questions**<br><br>• Why do writers write?<br>• Where do writers find inspiration?<br><br>This lesson involves reading aloud *Love That Dog* by Sharon Creech (2003), a story about a boy named Jack who didn't want to write poetry. He also didn't believe he could write poetry. As Jack reads poems, his mind opens up to new types of poems including the poetry of Robert Frost, William Carlos Williams, and more. | *Love That Dog* is a starting point for a discussion about why poets, and students, write poetry and where they can find inspiration. Story time builds community; it is a shared experience that students can refer back to in later discussions. |
| **Introduction**<br><br>Love That Dog *Introduction Speech*<br><br>*Today we'll be reading* Love That Dog *by Sharon Creech. You may recognize some of the poems we have read so far—they're in the book. As we read, think about what inspires Jack to write, why he likes to write, and what poets do in their spare time. Even though this book is a novel, it is especially interesting because it's written in free-verse poem form.* | *Love That Dog* works well because students relate to the main character, Jack. Like Jack, they may have approached poetry reluctantly and hopefully will change their minds. During the unit, the class reads and imitates some of the poems Jack reads and writes. |
| **Teaching Strategies and Learning Experiences**<br><br>The following questions are written on the board:<br><br>• Why do writers write?<br>• Where do writers find their inspiration?<br><br>After reading the book, students write their answers on the board. | The greater concepts of the unit are inherent in the book. Through discussion while reading, students draw out these ideas.<br><br>These questions and answers remain on the board. The class adds more as students think of new ideas. |
| **Closure**<br><br>The class reviews the Why Write Poetry? handout (Resource 3.7). | The handout takes what students have written on the board and reinforces this knowledge, using quotes from poets to support the statements. The Why Write Poetry? lesson discusses the motivations of writers and refers back to previous activities to show how students have already applied these ideas in their work. |

## LESSON 3.5: ROLLER 'ROO STORY AND POEM DIFFERENTIATION AND FOUND POEMS

**Length:** One 45–60-minute session

| Unit Sequence | Reflection |
|---|---|
| **Concepts**<br><br>Patterns | |
| **Principles**<br><br>• A line break is an artful choice a poet makes to emphasize certain words or sounds or achieve a certain rhythm in the poem.<br>• Prose and poetry have a relationship but are different, and line break is one thing that makes them different.<br>• Other writers' works and words inspire poets, and what students read can inspire them to write their own poems. | |
| **Skills**<br><br>• Compare and contrast stories and poems.<br>• Analyze poetry based on literary devices.<br>• Apply knowledge of poetic structure.<br>• Create original poems.<br><br>**Terms to Know**<br><br>• Alliteration<br>• Rhyme<br>• Stanza<br>• Simile<br>• Repetition<br>• Rhythm<br>• Found poems<br>• Line breaks | |
| **Standards**<br><br>*VA-SOL*<br><br>6.4b, 6.4c, 6.4d, 6.4h<br><br>*NCTE*<br><br>3, 5, 6, 9, 12 | |
| **Guiding Questions**<br><br>• What is a story?<br>• What is a poem?<br>• How are stories and poems alike and different? | |

*(Continued)*

(Continued)

| Unit Sequence | Reflection |
|---|---|
| **Comparing and Contrasting Stories and Poems**<br><br>The Roller 'Roo and Found Poems activity makes explicit to students the differences between poems and stories and then asks them to apply what they have learned by writing a *found poem:* taking a prose or story passage and turning it into a poem. | Reading the What I Know worksheet results (Resource 3.1, poetry preassessment) often reveals that students are not always clear on how poems and stories are different and what they have in common. This confusion may show up when students try to write poems. |
| **Introduction**<br><br>Reading aloud the Roller 'Roo poem (Resource 3.8), the teacher emphasizes the poetic devices, such as repetition, rhythm, and so forth—taking note the alliteration in the first line: "Rolling, rolling round the rink." | This poem appeals to students, because it is rhythmic, humorous, and about a roller-skating kangaroo. |
| **Teaching Strategies and Learning Experiences**<br><br>Strategies include<br><br>• Whole-group instruction<br>• Discussion<br>• Venn diagram<br>• Group analysis<br>• Creating original poems<br><br>*Learning Experience*<br><br>The teacher completes the following steps:<br><br>• Read aloud the Roller 'Roo prose passage (Resource 3.9). Then on the board draw three columns or a Venn diagram.<br>• Ask students to describe the story and the poem, using the vocabulary of literary devices learned in the Elements of Poetry lesson.<br>• Write what is different and then what could be part of both a story *and* a poem in the middle area.<br>• After the students learn about poems using the Roller 'Roo annotated poem, return to the Venn diagram or columns and make any changes necessary to correct it.<br>• Examine the annotated version of the Roller 'Roo poem (Resource 3.10), which labels the poetic devices as they appear in the poem.<br>• Ask students to apply what they have learned about stories and poems by taking a story or memoir excerpt and turning it into a poem, just as you did with the Roller 'Roo poem and story. | Words for the three columns include rhythm, repetition, metaphor, simile, personification, stanzas, line breaks, slang language, dialogue, characters paragraphs, and sentences.<br><br>| Poetry | Both | Stories |<br>|---|---|---|<br>| rhythm | | |<br>| repetition | | |<br>| metaphor | | |<br>| simile | | |<br>| personification | | |<br>| stanza | | |<br>| line breaks, etc. | | |<br><br>This is a sample of what the columns include.<br><br>*Author's note:* Technically, many of the literary devices in the poetry column can also be used in a story, but I put them in the poetry category because we use them as the defining elements of poetry.<br><br>The Roller 'Roo poem points out certain poetic devices in context—as they occur in the poem. The poem highlights rhyme (slant and internal rhyme), line breaks, stanzas, repetition and rhythm, alliteration, allusions, simile, and the use of slang and dialogue. The poem also gives students a model to apply when writing their own found poem. |

| Unit Sequence | Reflection |
|---|---|
| *Found Poems*<br><br>Students read a prose passage with a marker in hand and highlight words they like (passage is from samples the teacher prepares from books students will find interesting). They then read over these words for help with writing their own unique poem. They can try to capture the essence of the prose passage in fewer words or choose a totally different subject, using some words from the original passages and others that they have added. They then volunteer to share what they have written and how they came up with their ideas.<br><br>Student Directions for Found Poems<br><br>1. Choose a passage.<br>2. Read a passage.<br>3. Highlight words you like from the passage.<br>4. Use the words you like to write a poem.<br>5. Add words of your own if you like. | |
| **Closure**<br><br>*Reinforcing the Understanding: Journal Entry*<br><br>Students write responses to the following questions in their journals:<br><br>• How did you go about moving from a poem to a story?<br>• What was difficult and what was easy?<br>• Why do you think the poem you've written is a poem?<br>• Which of your poems will shed light on the literary devices you understand so far? | This activity raises self-awareness and allows students to examine their poetic work, demonstrating knowledge of the literary devices that are the defining characteristics of poetry. |

## LESSON 3.6: INTERACTIVE POETRY MUSEUM

**Length:** One 2- to 3-hour session; this depends on student work time, and if presenting to another class, practice presentation may be done first.

| Unit Sequence | Reflection |
|---|---|
| **Concepts**<br><br>Production | |

(Continued)

| Unit Sequence | Reflection |
|---|---|
| **Principles**<br><br>• Poets observe and describe the world around them in detail using the five senses.<br>• Whom and what poets love, the world around them, and the work of other writers all inspire poets to write.<br>• Poets create their art from everyday life and observations. They share their unique view of the world with others through vivid description in their poetry. | |
| **Skills**<br><br>• Identify personal strengths or interests.<br>• Discover and comprehend "big understandings" from written material and poems.<br>• Communicate in an interesting way through a chosen medium.<br>• Create a poetry exhibit to share with others. | |
| **Standards**<br><br>*VA-SOL*<br><br>6.4b, 6.4c, 6.4d, 6.4h, 6.6a, 6.6b, 6.6c<br><br>*NCTE*<br><br>1, 3, 5, 6, 8, 11, 12 | |
| **Guiding Questions**<br><br>• Why do writers write?<br>• Where do writers find inspiration?<br>• What makes Mary Oliver's poetry unique or different from other poems? | |
| The Interactive Poetry Museum lesson emphasizes the understanding that poetry is meant to be shared and uses the complex instruction method. Students create an authentic interactive poetry exhibit that can be shared with other students at the school. Before creating the exhibit, students act out a poem, read a fictionalized Mary Oliver speech, fill out a note-taking guide that emphasizes the understandings of the unit, and read several of Mary Oliver's poems. | A focus on a particular poet, Mary Oliver, allows insight about why writers write. Her poetry is accessible yet contemplative, and the poetry's subjects—animals and nature—appeal to students. Students react to her poems on one level, that is, the descriptions of scenes in nature, or take it further to the more abstract and philosophical level. The resource material thus presents varying levels of challenge, which supports the PCM components of modification for individual learners and ascending intellectual demand (AID). |
| **Introduction**<br><br>The class acts out "The Summer Day" by Mary Oliver (2005), with the following prompt for students: | Integrating movement and a sense of drama or playacting is always appealing to children. Acting like a grasshopper or a bear is particularly fun. |

| Unit Sequence | Reflection |
|---|---|
| *Multiple abilities are required to craft an exhibit for the interactive poetry museum. Choose which of your abilities you would like to express and develop in this activity. Everyone's unique contributions and talents are equally needed to make this the most interesting and interactive poetry exhibit ever!*<br><br>*Have you ever been to a science museum?* [Students share experiences.] *We want our exhibit to be interactive in the same way. We want to entice students to learn more about poetry and read more of Mary Oliver's work. Some students think poetry is boring . . . that is because they haven't experienced poetry. It is up to you to build that experience for your classmates or class visitors.*<br><br>Students present and perform their museum contributions for their own class or other classes. | Explaining to students that "The Summer Day" is typical of Oliver's work, the teacher notes the following features:<br><br>• Close observations of nature<br>• Use of inspiration found in nature to ask a bigger questions<br>• Reflections on life<br><br>The class considers the last two lines: "Tell me, what is it you plan to do / with your one wild and precious life?" (2005, p. 94). |
| **Teaching Strategies and Learning Experiences**<br><br>• Complex instruction<br>• Graphic organizers<br>• Group and independent work<br>• Reading<br>• Roles differentiated by multiple intelligence<br><br>The teacher completes the following steps:<br><br>1. Read the fictionalized speech (Resource 3.11) aloud with students. Pause to reinforce the "big understandings" along the way through questions:<br><br>  • What inspires Mary Oliver?<br>  • What is her advice to writers?<br>  • How does Mary Oliver say we can learn to be a good poet?<br><br>2. Ask students to fill out graphic organizers and read Mary Oliver's poems. Depending on their reading level or speed, they can read at least three, but try to read all of them. The poems are "The Summer Day," "The Chance to Love Everything," "The Swan," "Wild Geese," "Peonies," "Why I Wake Early," and "Morning Poem."<br><br>3. Review the Interactive Poetry Museum: The Roles handout (Resource 3.13) with students. If some students are interested in the same role, those students can work together. They may need help choosing among the roles.<br><br>4. Provide time for students to create their products. | While reading the speech, a pause and emphasis on the following points highlight the greater concepts:<br><br>*The speech highlights where Mary Oliver finds her inspiration and her advice on how to become a poet. For example, on her long early morning walks, Oliver always carries a notebook and pencil with her and closely observes the scene around her. Her close study of other poets' work is a learning process that informs and inspires her poetry.*<br><br>The Interactive Poetry Museum Note-Taking Guide (Resource 3.12) reinforces the greater concepts and asks students to draw out relevant information from the text. It also asks students to self-reflect and choose favorite lines from a poem, which helps them read poems more attentively.<br><br>The roles allow students to work in a preferred area to communicate their knowledge or even to challenge themselves by choosing a new area. The multiple intelligences address an array of creative forms to communicate why Oliver likes to write, what inspires her, and what entices museum visitors to read more of her poetry. |

*(Continued)*

(Continued)

| Unit Sequence | Reflection |
|---|---|
| **Closure**<br><br>To truly emphasize the idea that poetry is meant to be shared, students present the poetry museum to another class. Students present to their own class if another class cannot meet with them, or for practice before the final presentation. | |

# REFERENCES

Alexander, M. (2005). *Poetry: The question of home.* Retrieved from http://www.poets.org/viewmedia.php/prmMID/19032

Assisi, F. (n.d.). *Meena Alexander: Poet and daughter of the Indian Diaspora.* Retrieved from http://www.indolink.com/displayArticleS.php?id=120105041513

Bishop, E. (2005). The fish. In G. Keillor (Ed.), *Good poems for hard times.* (p. 174). New York: Penguin Books.

Burns, R. (2002). A red, red rose. In *The complete poems and songs of Robert Burns* (pp. 197). London: Geddes & Grosset.

Creech, S. (2003). *Love that dog.* New York: Harper Trophy.

Dickinson, E. (2003). Hope is a thing with feathers. In G. Stade (Ed.), *The collected poems of Emily Dickinson* (p. 22). New York: Barnes and Noble Classics.

Dickinson, E. (2003). If I can stop one heart from breaking. In G. Stade (Ed.), *The collected poems of Emily Dickinson* (p. 8). New York: Barnes and Noble Classics.

Engelbrett, M. (2005). *Mother goose:* One hundred best-loved verses. New York: HarperCollins.

Greenberg, J. (Ed.) (2001). *Heart to heart: New poems inspired by twentieth century American art.* New York: Harry Abrams.

Frost, R. (1969). Stopping by woods on a snowy evening. In E. C. Lathem, *The Poetry of Robert Frost* (p. 224). New York: Henry Holt and Company. (original work published in 1951)

Harjo, J. (1983). September moon. In *She had some horses* (p. 60). New York: Thunder's Mouth Press.

Harjo, J. (2007). "It's raining in Honolulu" as part of four poems. *World Literature Today, 6,* 34.

Hass, R. (Ed.). (1995). *The essential haiku.* New York: Ecco.

Koch, K. (1990). *Rose, where did you get that red? Teaching great poetry to children.* New York: Vintage.

Nye, N. (1990). Naomi Shihab Nye. In P. Janeczko (Ed.), *The place my words are looking for: What poets say about and through their work* (pp. 6–7). New York: Simon and Schuster Children's Publishing.

Oliver, M. (1994). *A poetry handbook.* Wilmington, MA: Mariner.

Oliver, M. (2005). The summer day. In *New and selected poems* (Vol. 1) (p. 94). Boston: Beacon Press.

Ratiner, S. (1992, December 9). Mary Oliver: A solitary walk. *Christian Science Monitor,* p. 16.

Sandburg, C. (2003). Fog. In *The complete poems of Carl Sandburg* (p. 33). Boston: Houghton Mifflin Harcourt.

Williams, W. C. (1970). The red wheelbarrow. In *Imaginations* (p. 30). New York: New Directions Publishing.

## RESOURCE 3.1: WHAT I KNOW

Name _____

1. What is a poem?

2. How is a poem like a story?

3. How is a poem different from a story?

4. Why do writers write?

5. What do writers do when they are not writing poems?

6. Where do writers find their inspiration?

## RESOURCE 3.2: FIVE SENSES ACTIVITY

Do not eat anything unless you are at the **Taste** station! You do not have to eat, touch, or smell anything you do not want. Respond to the questions and prompts on this worksheet.

**Sight: I see** _____.

This reminds me of _____.

This picture looks _____ because _____.

**Taste: I taste** _____.

This tastes like _____.

I like this taste because _____.

This taste reminds me of a time when _____.

**Touch: I feel** _____.

This feels like _____.

**Sound: I hear** _____.

This sounds like _____.

When I hear this sound, I see or feel _____.

**Smell: I smell** _____.

This smell makes me think _____.

I describe this smell as _____ and the best word for this smell is _____.

## RESOURCE 3.3: "BETWEEN WALLS"

Find something that most people would consider ugly and describe it in a way that makes it beautiful.

**Between Walls**

By William Carlos Williams

the back wings
of the

hospital where
nothing

will grow lie
cinders

in which shine
the broken

pieces of a green
bottle

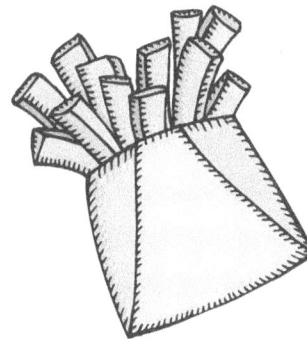

**Moldy Fries**

By Leighann Pennington

You were pretty
good, days ago

on some long-forgotten
lunch break,

you were loved
by some guy

and his tummy.
Now you're just

furry with green
moss, reminding me

of Ireland's emerald
hills.

"Between Walls," by William Carlos Williams, from *The Collected Poems: Volume I, 1909–1939,* copyright © 1938 by New Directions Publishing Corp. © 2000 by Carcanet Press Limited. Reprinted by permission.

## RESOURCE 3.4: "THE RED WHEELBARROW"

Zoom in on a specific image and describe it in few yet power-packed words. Notice how Williams plays with line breaks, stanzas, and where he places words on the page.

| | |
|---|---|
| **The Red Wheelbarrow** | **Tiny Frog Prince** |
| By William Carlos Williams | By Leighann Pennington |
| so much depends<br>upon | my heart revolves<br>around |
| a red wheel<br>barrow | you, tiny frog<br>swimming |
| glazed with rain<br>water | in your brown<br>paper pond |
| beside the white<br>chickens. | among the yellow<br>corn husks |
| | |

## RESOURCE 3.5: "THE LOCUST TREE IN FLOWER"

Use one-word lines to write your poem. This will help you choose your words carefully. You might select a scene from nature, like the poet did, or something else entirely.

In the foothills, Stanford, CA, 2003.

| The Locust Tree in Flower | Landscape Painting |
|---|---|
| By William Carlos Williams | By Leighann Pennington |
| Among | You |
| of | are |
| green | a |
|  | brush |
| stiff | dipped |
| old | in |
| bright | red |
|  | paint |
| broken | on a |
| branch | canvas |
| come | of |
|  | waving |
| white | yellow |
| sweet | grasses |
| May | and |
|  | windswept |
| again | clouds |

## RESOURCE 3.6: "THIS IS JUST TO SAY"

Notice how the title flows into the poem—it becomes part of the poem. This poem is a lot of fun, because Williams is apologizing for something he did that he is not really sorry for. This is a chance for you to experience how a poet's sense of humor affects poetry.

As you can see, the two poems are not exactly the same but similar, because Williams's poem inspired an idea for my original poem. Have you ever apologized for something you actually had fun doing? Write about it!

**This Is Just to Say**

by William Carlos Williams

I have eaten
the plums
that were in
the icebox

and which
you were probably
saving
for breakfast

Forgive me
they were delicious
so sweet
and so cold

After a pie in the face, clearly Ben needed to be washed off by a bucket of water.

**Dear Ben**

By Leighann Pennington

In case you're
wondering, I'm oh-
so sorry
my hand slipped—

Whoops!
Pie oozed on
your face.
so sweet
so creamy
melting in the sun

## RESOURCE 3.7: WHY WRITE POETRY?

### To Share My Unique View of the World

William Carlos Williams wanted to let other people see the world with the simplicity and beauty that he saw it. We showed people what *we* thought was beautiful by turning junk into art for the junk festival.

### To Remember

Naomi Shihab Nye (1990) answers the question "Why write?" when she remembers why she began writing as a child. She began writing when she was six because she didn't want the details she loved about the world to be lost:

> Tiny things other people overlooked seemed like treasures and clues. I wrote them down so I would not forget them. I did not begin writing because I imagined a writing career . . . I started keeping my own notebooks because I wanted to remember everything. The quilt, the cherry tree, the creek. The neat whop of a baseball rammed perfectly with a bat. My father's funny Palestinian stories. The feeling of the breeze as my brother and I rode our bicycles down the hill. The blood-red stain of a ripe strawberry on my fingertips; the rich smell of earth at Mueller's Organic Farm a few blocks from our house. (pp. 6–7)

### For Solace—Poetry Is Meant to Be Shared and It Comforts People

A poem titled "If I Can Stop One Heart From Breaking" by Emily Dickinson illustrates the solace poetry gives us, and how we can use it to touch other people:

If I can stop one heart from breaking

I shall not live in vain;

If I can ease one life the aching

Or cool one pain, or help one fainting robin

Unto his nest again,

I shall not live in vain

Remember Jack from *Love That Dog?* He wrote

- To *express emotions*
- About *"what I love!" (his yellow dog)*
- Because he was *inspired by other writers (like Mr. Walter Dean Myers).*

## RESOURCE 3.8: "ROLLIN' WITH MY PEEPS" POEM

**Rollin' With My Peeps**

By Leighann Pennington

Rolling, rolling round
the rink, and look!
There's Roller 'Roo!

Children are chirping
like chickens,
the chicken dance!

"I don't wanna be a chicken
I don't wanna be a duck
So I shake my butt!"

Behinds wiggle, except for
Maddie, who is wobbly on
Her roller skates, Wait!
Wait up, she shouts
to her ponytailed friends

Today she is eight.
Maddie's birthday party
on wheels, but she is
shy, so I lead her out
to dance the
Hokey Pokey!

And I think . . . the last time
I was on skates
I was eight . . .
Did it go out of style?
Or did I just grow up?

## RESOURCE 3.9: ROLLER 'ROO AT SKATETOWN, USA

*A Personal Narrative by Leighann Pennington*

After twelve years away from a roller skating rink, it feels good to be back. When I enter the blue-carpeted, gym-floor varnished world of Skatetown, USA, the lighting is low while parents and children struggle to skate gracefully in circles. Little girls run, red tickets streaming behind them, their mouths greasy after eating cheese pizza, toward the Claw, the game where no one wins the cheap stuffed animals they so desperately need. Among red and blue balloons, my mom and I spot my cousin Maddie, happy in her purple and silver glittery birthday shirt, chomping away on pizza and Coke with the other eight-year-olds. Her sister Hayden, age 10, several inches taller on her rollerblades, hugs me as I say, "Hey, birthday girl!"

"Come on, Maddie!"

She won't budge, so I lift her out of her seat and roll her limp, unwilling body onto the skating rink. The lights dim even more as Roller 'Roo (a roller-skating kangaroo) skates in the middle of the "Hokey Pokey" circle and children wiggle their limbs as the song dictates. After "Hokey Pokey," they move on to the chicken dance. "I don't wanna be a chicken, I don't wanna be a duck, so I shake my butt." I look around at Maddie's friends to make sure they all know the dance. For the next verse, Maddie sings, "I don't wanna be a chicken, I don't wanna be a duck, so kiss my butt." I look over at her—I must look shocked, because she quickly says, "Those are the words, that's how it goes."

Roller 'Roo skates by, shaking his heavy kangaroo tail, so I yell, "Hi, Roller 'Roo! We love you!" The girls laugh and they all start blushing. Am I becoming one of those embarrassing adult figures that kids cringe about? But they secretly like the attention the next time Roller 'Roo whooshes past and waves at us.

## RESOURCE 3.10: "ROLLIN' WITH MY PEEPS" DISSECTED

| | |
|---|---|
| **Rollin' With My Peeps**<br>By Leighann Pennington | A *free verse poem* varies—this one has no formal meter or rhyme pattern, although it includes rhyme.<br>The title is an *allusion*, refers to a song, and uses *slang language*. |
| *R*olling, *r*olling round<br>the *r*ink, and look!<br>There's *R*oller 'Roo! | Writer uses *repetition* and *rhythm*.<br>*Alliteration:* The words begin with the same letter or *R* sound. |
| *Ch*ildren are *ch*irping<br>like *ch*ickens,<br>the *ch*icken dance! | *Simile:* "Children are chirping like chickens."<br>*Alliteration:* The words begin with the same letter or *Ch* sound. |
| "I don't wanna be a chicken<br>I don't wanna be a duck<br>So I shake my butt!" | Writer uses *slang language*. Poems, like stories, can use *dialogue*. |
| Behinds *w*iggle, except for<br>Maddie, who is *w*obbly on<br>Her roller *skates, Wait!*<br>Wait up, she shouts<br>to her ponytailed friends<br><br>Today she is *eight*.<br>Maddie's birthday party<br>on *w*heels, but she is<br>shy, so I lead her out<br>to dance the<br>Hokey Pokey! | *Alliteration:* The words begin with the same letter or *W* sound.<br>This line includes *slant rhyme* (almost rhymes, but not exactly) and *internal rhyme* (rhyme within the same line) with "skates/Wait!"<br>There is also typical *rhyme* with "Wait!/eight" in the next stanza. |
| And I think . . . the last time<br>*I* was on skates<br>*I* was eight . . .<br>Did it go out of style?<br>Or did I just grow up? | A *stanza* is a poem's form of a paragraph. It is often used to separate thoughts or images within a poem.<br>*Line breaks* make a poem different from a story. One line of a poem can be a full sentence or break before the sentence ends. A line break is used to emphasize certain words or to use with certain meter or rhyme schemes. |

## RESOURCE 3.11: A FICTIONALIZED FIRST-PERSON SPEECH ABOUT MARY OLIVER

*Based on an Interview, Including Direct Quotes From Mary Oliver, by Leighann Pennington*

My name is Mary Oliver. I was born in Ohio and I still enjoy living among the woods, the meadows, and the ponds. One of my greatest pleasures is rising early in the morning and going for a walk to breathe in nature, and to see the first beads of morning dew before the sun dries them.

My poems arise from these journeys into nature: I can study a flower or an animal and I want to feel what it feels, to paint this being in a poem. On these solitary strolls, I am never really alone. Flora and fauna are company enough. "This is not a walk to arrive; this is a walk that's part of a process," (as cited in Ratiner, 1992, p. 16) and it is part of the poetry writing process for me.

"I decided very early on that I wanted to write. But I didn't think of it as a career . . . I didn't question if I should . . . I just kept sharpening pencils" (as cited in Ratiner, 1992, p. 16). On my walks, I always carry a pencil and paper with me so I don't miss a moment or let a thought float away like a leaf on a river. As a poet, sometimes people ask me, where do I get my inspiration? Do I have a muse? My reply is this: "The angel doesn't sit on your shoulder unless the pencil's in your hand" (as cited in Ratiner, p. 16).

Although I teach poetry now and some of my poems have been chosen for a Pulitzer Prize, I don't think of myself as principally a teacher or a poet. Before publishing my poems, I did not pursue an "interesting" job. If a job is too interesting, it possesses your time and your mind in a place that I could be using for poetry. I am a person interested in observing the world, absorbing the world with its many scents and sights. I am not sure that the sensibility of a poet can be taught, and I certainly do not think that one must go to college in order to learn how to be a poet. One must read poetry, must fall in love with poetry, its sounds, its structures, its nuances, and its rhythms. "My school was the great poets. I read, and I read, and I read" (as cited in Ratiner, 1992, p. 16). You must fall in love with the world and express it: that is poetry.

## RESOURCE 3.12: INTERACTIVE POETRY MUSEUM NOTE-TAKING GUIDE

Student name _____

| | |
|---|---|
| *Lines from poems that I like are . . .* | |
| *What/who/where inspires my poet's work?* | |
| *What do I have in common with my poet?* | |
| *How are we different?* | |
| *An interesting fact about my poet is . . .* | |
| *Why do I think my poet likes to write?* | |
| *Why do I write?* | |

## RESOURCE 3.13: INTERACTIVE POETRY MUSEUM: THE ROLES

The purpose of the museum exhibit is to raise awareness about Mary Oliver's poetry and why she writes poems. Each role assumed for the activity provides a different way to present this purpose. You may work individually or with a partner, but whatever part you choose is equally needed to make the most *interactive* poetry exhibit that other students will enjoy and learn from. Do you like words, music, or art? Do you love to move around, like working with people, or are you good at persuading people? Choose a role from below to share your talents!

### Drama Queen/Shakespeare-in-Training

You are responsible for a skit in which you can act out a scene from the author's life or dramatize a poem or scene from a poem. You may want to design a costume the poet might wear.

### Musical Director

You can choose to write a song inspired by the poet or the poet's life, or choose from the playlist certain songs to (1) play when students enter the room of the exhibit; (2) complement the actual display; (3) enhance the description of who the poet is; or (4) help set the mood, personality, or rhythm of her poetry.

### Art Expert

You can (1) illustrate a poem; (2) draw a portrait of the poet; (3) draw a picture that reflects a scene from the author's life; or (4) design posters or the artwork for the brochure. Whatever you choose to do, your task should focus on the purpose of the exhibit: raising awareness about Mary Oliver's poetry and why she writes poems.

### Interactive Tour Guide

You can (1) write an introductory speech about the exhibit or poet; (2) plan an interactive activity to introduce students to the exhibit; (3) prepare questions to lead a discussion as part of the exhibit or after students look at the exhibit.

### Public Relations Guru

You will formulate a brochure or plan a website and other aspects of the campaign to attract students to the exhibit. Will you need a commercial? An ad in the school newspaper? Posters or brochures to hand out? It's up to you to decide.

### The Poet[s]

Depending on your mood, you might want to (1) write a poem inspired by the author; (2) write a poem side-by-side imitating the style of the author; or (3) write a short piece to hang on the wall that tells about Mary Oliver's poems and why she writes.

### Journalist

You've been given a sneak peek behind the scenes. You are here to review the exhibit and tell people why they should visit, what they can learn, and whatever else you want to include in your article.

# 4

# Getting to the Heart of Mathematical Numbers and Operations

## (Grades 2–5)

*Linda H. Eilers*

## INTRODUCTION TO THE UNIT

### Overview and Background of the Unit

The ideas represented in this unit of study are important for helping students develop a strong mathematics foundation in the elementary grades. The unit is designed to focus on students developing conceptual understandings of numbers and operations. The success of all learners depends not only on their abilities to add, subtract, multiply, and divide, but also to understand the meanings of these operations and when to use them. These topics are explored in this curricular unit through authentic and meaningful learning activities that develop important number and operation concepts, as well as process standards and principles aligned with those of the National Council of Teachers of Mathematics (http://standards.nctm.org/).

This unit is designed to be a basic mathematics unit that teachers in Grades 2–5 might use when addressing the topic of numbers and operations. Since it spans a number of grade levels, the unit might best be used as a resource for teachers when teaching or reviewing these foundational concepts.

The lessons contained in the unit engage students in coherent activities—aimed toward important mathematic principles—and build new understandings based on prior knowledge. Opportunities to demonstrate and explain sound reasoning when choosing computational methods are provided. Acting as mathematicians, students produce accurate answers, but more important, explain and represent their thinking and work.

The assessments for this unit are ongoing and link to instruction. They take the form of questions, interviews, writing tasks, and other means. They focus on conceptual understanding as well as procedural skills and provide varied ways for students to show what they know.

## Parallels for the Unit

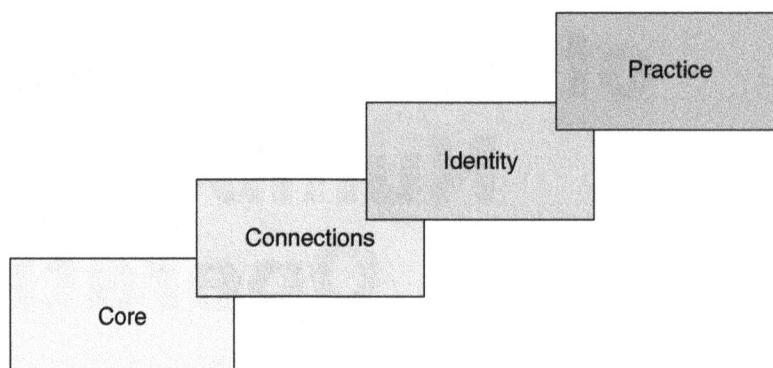

This unit incorporates all four parallels. Students must develop underlying conceptual understandings within the Core Curriculum as the foundation for all other parallels. The core concepts are the basis for making connections within and across mathematics and mathematical operations. The core is the mirror for reflecting identity and the window for viewing practice.

## Guiding Questions for Each Parallel

### Core Curriculum

- How are the properties of numbers used in operations?
- What are some algorithms for each operation?
- How do algorithms for an operation lead to correct answers?
- What is the relationship between addition and subtraction?
- What is the relationship between addition and multiplication?
- What is the relationship between multiplication and division?
- What is the relationship between subtraction and division?
- What is the language of mathematical communication?
- How do problem-solving strategies facilitate daily life?

### Curriculum of Practice

- How would the properties of numbers be developed for a numeration system other than base ten?
- What is the role of technology in mathematics?

- How do you know when to use each operation?
- How might a new operation for whole numbers be developed?

### Curriculum of Connections

- How are addition and multiplication similar?
- How are subtraction and division similar?
- How are addition and subtraction related?
- How are multiplication and division related?

### Curriculum of Identity

- What is a mathematician?
- What does a mathematician do?
- Which professions use mathematical operations?

# CONTENT FRAMEWORK

## Organizing Concepts

### Macroconcepts

M1: Systems

M2: Relationships

M3: Communication

### Discipline-Specific Concepts

C1: Whole numbers

C2: Operations

C3: Computation

C4: Estimation

## Principles

P1: Addition, subtraction, multiplication, and division are mathematical operations that have specific properties.

P2: While there may be alternate ways to obtain a right answer, knowing particular steps to follow, often called *algorithms,* when using specific mathematical operations increases the chances of obtaining a correct result.

P3: Mathematical ideas are related and build on one another.

P4: Communicating mathematical processes builds new mathematical knowledge.

P5: Real life requires applying and adapting a variety of problem-solving strategies.

P6: Numbers can be represented in different ways.

## National Council of Teachers of Mathematics Standards

SD 1: Students will be able to understand numbers, ways of representing numbers, relationships among numbers, and number systems.

SD 2: Students will be able to understand meanings of operations and how they relate to one another.

SD 3: Students will be able to compute fluently and make reasonable estimates.

SD 4: Students will be able to understand patterns, relations, and functions.

SD 5: Students will be able to represent and analyze mathematical situations and structures using algebraic symbols.

SD 6: Students will be able to use mathematical models to represent and understand quantitative relationships.

SD 7: Students will be able to analyze change in various contexts.

SD 8: Students will be able to apply appropriate techniques, tools, and formulas to determine measurements.

SD 9: Students will be able to formulate questions that can be addressed with data and collect, organize, and display relevant data to answer them.

SD 10: Students will be able to develop and evaluate inferences and predictions that are based on data.

SD 11: Students will be able to build new mathematical knowledge through problem solving.

SD 12: Students will be able to solve problems that arise in mathematics and in other contexts.

SD 13: Students will be able to make and investigate mathematical conjectures.

SD 14: Students will be able to organize and consolidate their mathematical thinking through communication.

SD 15: Students will be able to communicate their mathematical thinking coherently and clearly to peers, teachers, and others.

SD 16: Students will be able to analyze and evaluate mathematical thinking and strategies of others.

SD 17: Students will be able to use the language of mathematics to express mathematical ideas precisely.

SD 18: Students will be able to recognize and use connections among mathematical ideas.

SD 19: Students will be able to understand how mathematical ideas interconnect and build on one another to produce a coherent whole.

SD 20: Students will be able to recognize and apply mathematics in contexts outside of mathematics.

SD 21: Students will be able to create and use representations to organize, record, and communicate mathematical ideas.

SD 22: Students will be able to select, apply, and translate among mathematical representations to solve problems.

SD 23: Students will be able to use representations to model and interpret physical, social, and mathematical phenomena.

## Skills

S1: Use the properties of numbers to perform mathematical operations.

S2: Distinguish between situations that require different operations.

S3: Compute fluently.

S4: Solve problems in a real context.

S5: Articulate mathematical thinking.

## Ensuring That the Parallels Remain Central in Teaching and Learning

| Curriculum Component | Component Descriptions and Rationale |
| --- | --- |
| Content | Students develop conceptual understanding of the operations and algorithms for addition, subtraction, multiplication, and division as they come to understand how these concepts are connected and interrelated. |
| | *Core Curriculum.* The focus of this parallel is to discover how the properties of numbers facilitate addition, subtraction, multiplication, and division and to develop algorithms for each operation. The relationship between addition and subtraction, addition and multiplication, and multiplication and division are communicated and used to solve problems. |
| | *Curriculum of Connections.* Students compare and contrast operations using basic understanding of numbers and the numeration system. |
| | *Curriculum of Practice.* Students act as mathematicians to analyze number properties and operations to formulate rules and generalizations. They develop computational fluency as they distinguish among operations to solve problems using appropriate algorithms. |
| | *Curriculum of Identity.* Students identify and choose real-world problems to solve using appropriate number concepts and algorithms. |
| Assessments | Conceptual understanding is monitored through varied formats. The focus is on conceptual understanding rather than rote memory of isolated facts. Student choice allows selection from different ways of demonstrating individual understanding. |
| Introductory Activities | Introductory activities engage students by stimulating prior knowledge through tasks focusing on key concepts. |
| | *Core Curriculum.* The introductory activities focus on the meaning of mathematical operations (addition, subtraction, multiplication, and division), |

(Continued)

| Curriculum Component | Component Descriptions and Rationale |
|---|---|
| | algorithms for each operation, and how the properties of numbers facilitate the understanding of operations and algorithms. |
| | *Curriculum of Practice.* The introductory activity engages students in the importance of choosing the correct mathematical operation to solve a real-life problem. |
| | *Curriculum of Connections.* The introductory activity helps students discover the relationship between the operations and how one builds on and facilitates another. |
| | *Curriculum of Identify.* The introductory activity is designed to encourage students to consider their beliefs about what a mathematician is and help them come to understand that they *are* mathematicians as they use real mathematics to solve problems in their daily lives. |
| **Teaching Strategies** | Teaching strategies are intended to facilitate conceptual understanding rather than focus on rote memory of isolated facts and numbers. The intent is to lead students to discover the practicality of mathematics through activities they enjoy and find important. |
| **Learning Activities** | Whole-group, small-group, and individual activities stimulate active engagement in exploration of mathematical concepts. Students are given information and then guided through activities with support to develop important understandings of properties and number relationships. They then work independently as they acquire sensible strategies related to key concepts. |
| **Grouping Strategies** | Varied grouping strategies are used in this unit. Whole-group activities are used to stimulate and generate ideas from varied viewpoints. Small-group activities allow students with similar strengths and needs to work collaboratively to support their individual learning. Independent work builds and strengthens understandings through self- and teacher-selected activities that communicate high expectations and worthwhile opportunities for all. |
| **Products** | Various products allow students to demonstrate their understandings of key concepts. Students select or identify different ways to illustrate and provide evidence and support the learning of important mathematics. |
| **Resources** | The resources for this unit vary with each parallel and the specific needs of individual students. The resources are tools for learning important mathematics and include manipulatives such as tiles and cubes, calculators, computers, and web-based information. These are designed to help students visualize, represent, explore, organize, and analyze information to facilitate learning. |
| **Extension Activities** | Opportunities to extend mathematical thinking and explore ideas based on student interest and need are provided throughout the unit. |
| **Differentiation Based on Learner Needs, Including Ascending Intellectual Demand (AID)** | Students bring different experiences and levels of readiness to each learning opportunity. High expectations and worthwhile opportunities are provided based on specific needs through varied activities and resources designed to support all students.<br><br>AID for advanced students requires them to work at more advanced levels, to provide deeper analyses and richer explanations of mathematical thinking. |

## UNIT ASSESSMENTS

### Preassessments

A formal assessment that reveals what students know about using mathematics is administered before the beginning of the unit. The assessment may be given to a whole class, small group, or individually and may be completed independently or read aloud to students by the teacher.

### Formative Assessments

Short assignments tied to each lesson should be reviewed and used for a formative assessment so that any adjustments to subsequent lessons can be made. Several student-activity pages are provided for teachers to use and may be found in the resources for this unit. A problem-solving rubric is provided to accompany Lesson 4.5 (Resource 4.6).

### Summative Assessment

The summative assessment for this unit is left open for the user since it is likely that these lessons are tied to a larger unit of study. Teachers are cautioned, however, to design an assessment that checks for understanding in addition to basic computational skills. A written test using examples from some of the lessons in the unit is likely a helpful means to reveal the degree of students' understanding of the important mathematical principles addressed in this unit of study.

## UNIT SEQUENCE AND TEACHER REFLECTION

### PRIOR TO LESSON 4.1: PREASSESSMENT

**Length:** One 30-minute session

| Unit Sequence | Reflection |
| --- | --- |
| Before starting the unit, current understandings of numbers properties, operation algorithms, and perceptions of a mathematician are assessed. | The questions from the unit Preassessment (Resource 4.1) serve as a model for the format and concepts to be measured. The exact questions and numbers are tailored to meet the developmental levels and abilities of students. <br><br> The preassessment determines students' understandings of the specific number properties, how algorithms work, and what a mathematician is. <br><br> The preassessment is designed to provide information about students' level and depth of understanding. It may be that students work only with addition and subtraction and not all four operations. This assessment should be modified to meet the needs and abilities of the students. |

## LESSON 4.1: KNOW WHEN TO ADD, SUBTRACT, MULTIPLY, OR DIVIDE

**Length:** One 60-minute session

| Unit Sequence | Reflection |
|---|---|
| **Concepts**<br><br>• Operations<br>• Relationships | |
| **Principles**<br><br>• Addition, subtraction, multiplication, and division are mathematical operations that have specific properties.<br>• Mathematical ideas are related and build on one another.<br>• Communicating mathematical processes builds new mathematical knowledge.<br>• Real life requires applying and adapting a variety of problem-solving strategies. | |
| **Skills**<br><br>Distinguish between situations that require different operations. | |
| **Standards**<br><br>SD 2, SD 5, SD 6, SD 11 | |
| **Guiding Question**<br><br>How do you decide what mathematical operation to use when solving a problem? | The activities for this lesson provide experiences that establish a foundation for the meanings of operations and for the ability to distinguish among them (knowing when to add, subtract, multiply, or divide). Numbers, place value, and operations are adjusted to fit students' needs. |
| **Introduction**<br><br>The teacher poses a thought-provoking question that requires students to identify the mathematical operation(s) that are appropriate to answer the question.<br>    Manipulative materials (e.g., cubes) accompany a question such as,<br><br>Jack has $8.00. He wants to buy a trading card that costs $10.00. How much more money does Jack need to make the purchase?<br><br>The teacher then discusses how to answer this problem, accepting and testing all responses so that the focus is on the procedures and operation and not necessarily the answer to this question. | The lessons are created so that addition and subtraction, and then multiplication and division, are explored simultaneously. The properties for the operations are discussed when these operations are explored. |

| Unit Sequence | Reflection |
|---|---|
| **Teaching Strategies and Learning Experiences**<br><br>To explore this subtraction situation and answer the *what is needed* question, students work in small groups with ten cubes. They count and record the number of cubes that represent what the trading card costs. Next, they arrange the cubes into piles of what Jack has and what Jack needs, and record these responses. They then identify the operation needed to answer the question most efficiently. Through discussion, the teacher leads students to see that $10.00 (how much Jack needs) minus $8.00 (how much Jack has) equals $2.00 (how much more Jack needs) is a subtraction problem.<br>    Students then work with similar scenarios for other situations requiring subtraction other than simply "take away" or how many are left. These include *comparative* (who has more and how many more); *partitioning* (how many red, how many blue, which is more and how much more); and *incremental* (if the temperature is 40 degrees and it drops by 10 degrees, what is the temperature?). | |
| Using the same numbers helps students construct the meaning *of addition*. The first and most obvious meaning stems from combining sets, and evolves through a scenario where students find how many in all. (Tom has 8 pencils and Marty has 2. How many pencils do they have in all?) Cubes allow students to combine sets, write number sentences ($8 + 2 = [ \ ]$), and then record the responses ($8 + 2 = 10$). | It is helpful to use the same numbers and introduce addition and subtraction concepts together. This allows students to see the relationship and discover that for each addition fact, they can find two related subtraction facts ($8 + 2 = 10$; $10 - 2 = 8$; $10 - 8 = 2$). |
| Students continue to work with similar scenarios for *static* situations where they can't physically combine objects. (Tom has 4 pencils in his desk and 6 more at home. How many pencils does he have in all?) Another scenario called *incremental* involves situations related to growth or temperature change where there are no objects to count or manipulate. (Tom grew 8 inches in first grade and 2 inches in second grade. How much did Tom grow in first and second grade?) | Several examples might be needed to establish a base for these important ideas in the core parallel. The sample lesson examples provided in Resource 4.2 create more practice for learners.<br>    For students who are ready for multiplication and division, the teacher leads a discussion about those operations using similar ideas or problems that follow.<br>    Knowing when to multiply involves situations that are *additive*, or repeated addition. (Three sets of two is the same as $2 + 2 + 2$; each set has the same number in each set.)<br>    *Combination* also requires multiplication. This involves two sets of objects where one object from the first set is |

(Continued)

| Unit Sequence | Reflection |
|---|---|
| | combined with one from the second set. (Let's pretend you have a set of "pants" and a set of "shirts" as you pack for a trip. You have 3 pairs of pants and 4 shirts. If you combine each pair of pants with a different shirt, you have 12 different outfits for your trip because $3 \times 4 = 12$. You could be gone for 12 days and wear a different outfit each day.) |
| | Students should also be exposed to situations that require division. One situation is known as *subtractive*, or similar to additive multiplication; this is repeated subtraction. If students know how many in all (the total number of objects) and they know the number of objects in each set and need to figure out the number of sets, they can do this by repeatedly subtracting. For example, if there are a dozen (twelve) cookies and each child must get three cookies, repeatedly subtracting will determine how many children get three cookies ($12 - 3 = 9 - 3 = 6 - 3 = 3 - 3 = 0$), and counting the number of times three was subtracted (which is four); or dividing twelve by three to get four. |
| | Another similar situation that requires division is *distributive*. In this situation, as always with division, how many in all is known; there are twelve cookies; the number of sets is known (four children), and how many cookies each child will get must be determined. The twelve cookies can be distributed among the four sets and then the number that each set (child) got counted ($12 \div 4 = 3$). |
| **Closure**<br><br>The class discusses different scenarios for specific operations. Students write (or dictate as the teacher writes) a scenario for the different situations for the operations. Students illustrate a scenario and then solve it. The lesson concludes with students displaying their writing and explaining their mathematical thinking to the group. | Students who are advanced may work with larger numbers and even work with addition and subtraction that requires regrouping. These students write detailed explanations of their thinking. It may be helpful for them to pretend they are writing their explanation to a younger sibling or friend who is just learning this information. |

## LESSON 4.2: FACILITATING EASY RECALL OF MATHEMATICAL "FACTS"

**Length:** One 60-minute session

| Unit Sequence | Reflection |
|---|---|
| **Concepts**<br><br>• Operations<br>• Relationships<br>• Communication | |

| Unit Sequence | Reflection |
|---|---|
| **Principles**<br><br>• Addition, subtraction, multiplication, and division are mathematical operations that have specific properties.<br>• Numbers can be represented in different ways. | The activities for this lesson provide experiences that establish a foundation for the organization of addition/subtraction or multiplication/division facts. It is presented in this format only after students have been exposed to the facts and can make sense of how the tables are organized. |
| **Skills**<br><br>• Use the properties of numbers to perform mathematical operations.<br>• Articulate mathematical thinking. | Students should also be able to represent sums of numbers less than ten with objects before working with the table. They should also have had opportunities to organize facts into families and articulate why a number sentence (i.e., 2 + 8 = [ ] ) belongs to a particular family of facts.<br><br>It is important when discussing these concepts with students to remember that being able to memorize and recite the operations is not the goal, but instead to recognize how these properties facilitate understanding and remembering addition/subtraction and multiplication/division facts.<br><br>It further facilitates conceptual understanding to use the phrase "is the same as" when using the equal ( = ) sign. |
| **Standards**<br><br>SD 1, SD 3, SD 5, SD 6 | |
| **Guiding Question**<br><br>How is information organized? | |
| **Introduction**<br><br>The teacher leads a discussion asking students if they have ever noticed how airports or public transit systems organize the schedule of arrivals and departures. After encouraging students to articulate how they form rows and columns for specific information, the teachers shows them a TV schedule organized into a table with times going across (columns) and stations going down (rows). Discussing the purpose for this organization leads students to see that a random organization would be difficult to read. | The lessons are created so that addition and subtraction, and then multiplication and division, are explored simultaneously. The properties for the operations are discussed when these operations are explored. |
| **Teaching Strategies and Learning Experiences**<br><br>Students look at a table of basic facts to carefully identify and describe the organization of the table. Figure 4.1 provides an example of an addition and multiplication table. | Resource 4.3 provides sample activities for this lesson.<br><br>The first row represents sums for zero (0 + 0, 0 + 1 = 1, etc.). The first column represents sums for zero (0 + 0, 0 + 1 = 1, etc.). The diagonal from left to right represents doubles (0 + 0, 1 + 1, etc.). It is important for students to recognize the *identity element* for addition, which means that for any whole number, $a + 0 = a$. Any time a |

(Continued)

| Unit Sequence | Reflection |
|---|---|
| | number is added to zero, that number is the total. The bottom part of the table below the diagonal is a mirror image of the part above the diagonal $(2 + 3 = 3 + 2)$. Questioning students will lead them to the understanding that if they memorize one part of the table they can use the *commutative property* to remember the other facts. (For any whole numbers $a$ and $b$, $a + b = b + a$ because addition is a commutative operation). |

The table illustrates sums for numbers greater than ten. Any sum greater than ten can be represented and rewritten in a simple combination of ten: $(6 + 7 = 6 + (4 + 3) = (6 + 4) + 3 = 10 + 3 = 13$. This facilitates learning the facts and demonstrates the *associative property* of addition. The associative property means that for any whole numbers $a$, $b$, and $c$ $(a + b) + c = a + (b + c)$. Addition is an *associate* operation.

The teacher constructs a similar table to illustrate basic multiplication facts, and students examine the table and are questioned until they recognize that one is the *identity element* for multiplication: any time a number is multiplied by one, that number is the result $(n \times 1 = n$ and $1 \times n = n)$. Helping students contrast the functions of zero in addition and multiplication $(0 \times n = 0)$ leads them to see that when a number is multiplied by zero, the result is always zero.

Constructing multiplication sentences and rectangular models helps students understand that for all numbers, $a \times b = b \times a$.

Therefore, $3 \times 4 = 4 \times 3$. It may be important to show students using models like the following:

| $3 \times 4$ | is the same as | $4 \times 3$ |
|---|---|---|
| ☺ ☺ ☺ ☺ | | ☺ ☺ ☺ |
| ☺ ☺ ☺ ☺ | | ☺ ☺ ☺ |
| ☺ ☺ ☺ ☺ | | ☺ ☺ ☺ |
| | | ☺ ☺ ☺ |

This is the *commutative property* of multiplication.

After the teacher presents situations, students construct rectangle models and multiplication sentences to illustrate the *associate property* for multiplication.

| Unit Sequence | Reflection |
|---|---|
| | For example, |

| $3 \times 4$ | $=$ | $3 \times (2 + 2)$ |
|---|---|---|
| ☺ ☺ ☺ ☺ | | ☺ ☺ + ☺ ☺ |
| ☺ ☺ ☺ ☺ | | ☺ ☺ + ☺ ☺ |
| ☺ ☺ ☺ ☺ | | ☺ ☺ + ☺ ☺ |

The teacher presents situations using rectangular models and number sentences and students verify the *distributive property* of multiplication over addition.
For example,

| $3 \times (2 + 2) =$ | $(3 \times 2) + (3 \times 2)$ |
|---|---|
| ☺ ☺ + ☺ ☺ | ☺ ☺ ☺ ☺ ☺ ☺ + ☺ ☺ ☺ ☺ ☺ ☺ |
| ☺ ☺ + ☺ ☺ | |
| ☺ ☺ + ☺ ☺ | |

| Unit Sequence | Reflection |
|---|---|
| **Closure**<br><br>The teacher generates activities that use concrete materials and rectangular arrays to develop understandings for these properties, and helps students organize the facts they learn. After constructing or completing their own tables, students justify the organization by writing their reason for placement and how they know. | Students who are ready for more challenge can construct problem-solving strategies and explain when and how they use a strategy. Students can use charts, tables, diagrams, models, and journals to illustrate how problems are encountered and solved using specific properties. |

**Figure 4.1** Basic Fact Tables for Addition and Multiplication

| Addition Table | | | | | | | | | | |
|---|---|---|---|---|---|---|---|---|---|---|
| Commutative Property | | | | | | | | | | |
| + | 0 | 1 | 2 | 3 | 4 | 5 | 6 | 7 | 8 | 9 |
| 0 | 0 | 1 | 2 | 3 | 4 | 5 | 6 | 7 | 8 | 9 |
| 1 | 1 | 2 | 3 | 4 | 5 | 6 | 7 | 8 | 9 | 10 |
| 2 | 2 | 3 | 4 | 5 | 6 | 7 | 8 | 9 | 10 | 11 |
| 3 | 3 | 4 | 5 | 6 | 7 | 8 | 9 | 10 | 11 | 12 |

**Figure 4.1** (Continued)

| + | 0 | 1 | 2 | 3 | 4 | 5 | 6 | 7 | 8 | 9 |
|---|---|---|---|---|---|---|---|---|---|---|
| 4 | 4 | 5 | 6 | 7 | 8 | 9 | 10 | 11 | 12 | 13 |
| 5 | 5 | 6 | 7 | 8 | 9 | 10 | 11 | 12 | 13 | 14 |
| 6 | 6 | 7 | 8 | 9 | 10 | 11 | 12 | 13 | 14 | 15 |
| 7 | 7 | 8 | 9 | 10 | 11 | 12 | 13 | 14 | 15 | 16 |
| 8 | 8 | 9 | 10 | 11 | 12 | 13 | 14 | 15 | 16 | 17 |
| 9 | 9 | 10 | 11 | 12 | 13 | 14 | 15 | 16 | 17 | 18 |

Commit to Memory

**Multiplication Table**

Commit to Memory

| × | 0 | 1 | 2 | 3 | 4 | 5 | 6 | 7 | 8 | 9 |
|---|---|---|---|---|---|---|---|---|---|---|
| 0 | 0 | 0 | 0 | 0 | 0 | 0 | 0 | 0 | 0 | 0 |
| 1 | 0 | 1 | 2 | 3 | 4 | 5 | 6 | 7 | 8 | 9 |
| 2 | 0 | 2 | 4 | 6 | 8 | 10 | 12 | 14 | 16 | 18 |
| 3 | 0 | 3 | 6 | 9 | 12 | 15 | 18 | 21 | 24 | 27 |
| 4 | 0 | 4 | 8 | 12 | 16 | 20 | 24 | 28 | 32 | 36 |
| 5 | 0 | 5 | 10 | 15 | 20 | 25 | 30 | 35 | 40 | 45 |
| 6 | 0 | 6 | 12 | 18 | 24 | 30 | 36 | 42 | 48 | 54 |
| 7 | 0 | 7 | 14 | 21 | 28 | 35 | 42 | 49 | 56 | 63 |
| 8 | 0 | 8 | 16 | 24 | 32 | 40 | 48 | 56 | 64 | 72 |
| 9 | 0 | 9 | 18 | 27 | 36 | 45 | 54 | 63 | 72 | 81 |

Commutative Property

## LESSON 4.3: BUILDING CONCEPTUAL UNDERSTANDING OF ALGORITHMS

**Length:** One 60-minute session

| Unit Sequence | Reflection |
|---|---|
| **Concepts**<br><br>• Operations<br>• Relationships<br>• Communication<br>• Computation<br>• Estimation | |

| Unit Sequence | Reflection |
|---|---|
| **Principles**<br><br>• Addition, subtraction, multiplication, and division are mathematical operations that have specific properties.<br>• While there may be alternate ways to obtain a right answer, knowing particular steps to follow, often called *algorithms,* when using specific mathematical operations increases the chances of obtaining a correct result.<br>• Numbers can be represented in different ways. | The activities for this lesson provide experiences that develop conceptual understanding of the specific steps used to obtain accurate results when adding, subtracting, multiplying, and dividing. |
| **Skills**<br><br>Compute fluently. | The intent is to provide opportunities for students to understand each step of the algorithm rather than simply memorizing a heuristic that can often become confusing.<br><br>As students learn these algorithms, they can use paper and pencil, mental calculations, calculators, or computers. Although students will be more successful when they know the basic facts, the idea is to focus on the steps and sequence and not necessarily the immediate recall of basic facts. Tools may assist students with recall so they may focus on the algorithms. |
| **Standards**<br><br>SD 1, SD 3, SD 5, SD 6 | |
| **Guiding Questions**<br><br>• What is an algorithm?<br>• When is an estimate considered reasonable? | |
| **Introduction**<br><br>The teacher begins by asking students to recall when they have followed a recipe to cook something, or followed numbered directions to put something together. They then speculate on what happens if a step is skipped or if the steps are out of order. The teacher leads students to articulate that following the steps in the correct order is essential to properly prepared food or assembled items. It is important to review basic facts and the order words *first, next,* and so on. | The lessons are created so that addition and subtraction, and then multiplication and division, are explored simultaneously. The properties for the operations are discussed when these operations are explored. |
| **Teaching Strategies and Learning Experiences**<br><br>Small groups of students work with cubes as the algorithm is demonstrated. Situations that do not require regrouping precede situations that do.<br><br>$$\begin{array}{ccc} 10 & 18 & 19 \\ \underline{+4} & \underline{+1} & \underline{+4} \\ 14 & 19 & 23 \end{array}$$ | Resource 4.4 provides additional explanations of the practice. |

(Continued)

| Unit Sequence | Reflection |
|---|---|
| Students construct rectangles, write the numeral to represent each addend, and then count to determine how many cubes.<br><br>☺ ☺ ☺ ☺ ☺ ☺ ☺ ☺ ☺ ☺   = 10<br>☺ ☺ ☺ ☺   =  4<br>               14 | |
| Represent numbers by tens and ones. | This is important when students begin to work with numbers that require regrouping. |
| ☺ ☺ ☺ ☺ ☺ ☺ ☺ ☺ ☺ ☺   = 10<br>☺ ☺ ☺ ☺ ☺ ☺ ☺ ☺   =  8<br>☺   = +1<br>               19<br><br>The teacher explains that when students add these, the first step is to add the numbers in the ones column. Students combine the cubes that represent ones, count them, and record them in the appropriate column before moving to the tens column. | |
| The next example requires regrouping. Students show how to represent nineteen with tens and ones ($10 + 9 = 19$) before proceeding. | Students need many opportunities to represent numbers using expanded notation before grasping the concept of regrouping. |
| First, students add all the ones and record the answer. They then add the nine and four to get thirteen (one ten and three ones). The teacher prompts them to record thirteen in the ones column, and asks for justification of all responses. | It is important to use the appropriate terms. The students are actually *regrouping* and not *carrying*. |
| Students record the three in the ones column and then add the one ten and one ten to get and record two tens in the tens column for an answer of twenty-three. | It is also important during this process to refer to numbers in expanded notation, that is, one ten and three ones rather than thirteen. They must understand that they are adding tens, and saying "one ten plus one ten" and not "ten plus one" to avoid misunderstandings.<br><br>It is essential to follow the same process and questioning procedures for the other operations. |
| A simple multiplication problem, such as $2 \times 3 = [\ ]$, provides a model for students to build a rectangular array with base-ten blocks. For example,<br><br>☺ ☺ ☺<br>☺ ☺ ☺<br>☺ ☺ ☺ | When students construct rectangular arrays for multiplication, it is important that they represent the first factor vertically, and the second factor horizontally. While the commutative property of multiplication makes this a moot point, it facilitates communication during the process. |

| Unit Sequence | Reflection |
|---|---|
| Students count and record the answer of six.<br>Next, a problem such as<br><br>$$\begin{array}{r} 12 \\ \times\ 3 \\ \hline \end{array}$$<br><br>allows students to build a rectangular array using the tens sticks and unit cubes. For example,<br><br>☺ ☺ ☺     $3 \times 10$<br>☺ ☺ ☺<br>☺ ☺ ☺<br>☺ ☺ ☺<br>☺ ☺ ☺<br>☺ ☺ ☺<br>☺ ☺ ☺<br>☺ ☺ ☺<br>☺ ☺ ☺<br>☺ ☺ ☺<br>☺ ☺ ☺     $3 \times 2$<br>☺ ☺ ☺<br><br>$$\begin{array}{r} 12 \\ \times\ 3 \\ \hline 6 = 3 \times 2 \\ +30 = 3 \times 10 \\ \hline 36 \end{array}$$<br><br>Students show and record $3 \times 2$.<br>Students show and record $3 \times 10$.<br>The teacher then helps students discover the relationship between multiplication and division using the rectangular array. | It is also important for students to talk about each step and identify the appropriate blocks that represent each partial product of the algorithm. They first identify the six ones and then identify the three tens. After they have done this, they add the partial products to reach the final product of thirty-six.<br>    Once students construct the rectangular arrays and find the partial products by trading and representing them with numbers, they articulate the algorithm by showing the partial products. |
| In small groups, students use base-ten blocks for division scenarios, such as $36 \div 12 = [\ ]$. The teacher uses the terminology to ask what is thirty-six divided by twelve, and poses a situation such as,<br><br>*You have thirty-six cookies and twelve students. How many cookies does each student get? What operation do we use to answer this question?*<br><br>Students build a rectangular array using all the blocks, with the array twelve blocks *wide*.<br><br>☺ ☺ ☺ ☺ ☺ ☺ ☺ ☺ ☺ ☺ ☺ ☺<br>☺ ☺ ☺ ☺ ☺ ☺ ☺ ☺ ☺ ☺ ☺ ☺<br>☺ ☺ ☺ ☺ ☺ ☺ ☺ ☺ ☺ ☺ ☺ ☺ | This is the *distributive* scenario for division. Knowing *how many in all* (thirty-six) and knowing *how many sets* to make (twelve) determines *how many* will be *in each set*. |

(Continued)

| Unit Sequence | Reflection |
|---|---|
| After asking students how many blocks *long* the array is, the teacher explains that this is the quotient.<br><br>$36 \div 12 = 3$ | |
| **Closure**<br><br>Students build multiplication and division arrays and come to understand the relationship between multiplication and division, and also to see there is a reason for each step of the algorithms and that this leads to reasonable and accurate answers to questions requiring these operations. | Advanced students can be given manipulatives and problems and be challenged to come up with all the ways to solve the problem.<br><br>They write down, in words and symbols, their method for solving the problems. |

## LESSON 4.4: RELATIONSHIPS BETWEEN OPERATIONS

**Length:** One 60-minute session

| Unit Sequence | Reflection |
|---|---|
| **Concepts**<br><br>• Operations<br>• Relationships<br>• Communication<br>• Computation<br>• Estimation | |
| **Principles**<br><br>• Addition, subtraction, multiplication, and division are mathematical operations that have specific properties.<br>• While there may be alternate ways to obtain a right answer, knowing particular steps to follow, often called *algorithms*, when using specific mathematical operations increases the chances of obtaining a correct result.<br>• Mathematical ideas are related and build on one another. | |
| **Skills**<br><br>• Distinguish between situations that require different operations.<br>• Compute fluently. | |
| **Standards**<br><br>SD 2, SD 6, SD 18, SD 19 | |

| Unit Sequence | Reflection |
|---|---|
| **Guiding Question**<br><br>How do you show how different numbers and operations are related? | |
| **Introduction**<br><br>The lesson begins with a review of the *how many* concept and the symbols related to the operations that are the lesson focus. For example, if the lesson is about addition and subtraction, symbols and terms including + *(and);* = *(the same as);* − *(less); addend, sum, subtrahend, minuend,* and *difference* are reviewed.<br><br>    Beginning with a number such as five, students in small groups work with five concrete materials and show different ways to make five, using the materials (i.e., $4 + 1 = 5$, $3 + 2 = 5$, etc.). Students record number sentences for each physical grouping using the + symbol. | The activities for this lesson provide experiences for students that establish a foundation for the relationships of operations, along with an understanding of how this knowledge helps them remember mathematical facts; the activities also facilitate computational fluency.<br><br>    As the class discusses the sentences, it is important to relay the idea that five is the same number as all of these. The property of *transitivity of equality* (conceptually) helps students to understand that these sentences are all (the same as) five.<br><br>    For example, $a = b$ and $b = c$; if $a = 5$ and $b = 4 + 1$ and $c = 3 + 2$, then $a = c$ since $5 = 3 + 2$. |
| **Teaching Strategies<br>and Learning Experiences**<br><br>Students work with ten concrete materials and show different ways to make five using the concept of *less* and write sentences to represent those groupings using the minus (−) symbol ($10 − 5$, $7 − 2$, etc.). | |
| The teacher reviews the basic facts of addition and the strategies used to develop these. Students use manipulative materials to represent a number sentence, such as $3 + 2 = 5$. They next arrange the materials in one group with all five objects and then separate them into groups that look like the addition grouping they just made ($5 − 3 = 2$). Students finally make one more grouping that uses the same numerals ($5 − 2 = 3$). The teacher leads students, through questioning, to see the association and helps them articulate the generalization that for every number appearing on the addition table, there are two related subtraction facts. | The same ideas and scenarios for addition and subtraction may by adapted to illustrate the relationship between multiplication and division.<br><br>    Resource 4.5 provides additional sample activities that may be used for student practice. |
| **Closure**<br><br>Students may need to be told explicitly that for each addition fact, there are two related subtraction facts. Questions calling for subtraction scenarios can be posed as addition ideas are modeled and explored. | Advanced students can put number sentences with sums less than ten into families and write a narrative story about these families and their relationships. |

## LESSON 4.5: CONNECTING PROBLEM SOLVING TO THE REAL WORLD

**Length:** One 60-minute session

| Unit Sequence | Reflection |
|---|---|
| **Concepts**<br><br>• Operations<br>• Relationships<br>• Communication<br>• Computation<br>• Estimation | |
| **Principles**<br><br>• Mathematical ideas are related and build on one another.<br>• Communicating mathematical processes builds new mathematical knowledge.<br>• Real life requires applying and adapting a variety of problem-solving strategies. | |
| **Skills**<br><br>Solve problems in a real context. | |
| **Standards**<br><br>SD 11, SD 12, SD 20 | |
| **Guiding Questions**<br><br>• What is an algorithm?<br>• When is an estimate considered reasonable? | |
| **Introduction**<br><br>Posing a problem related to some subject-matter content (e.g., science or social studies), the teacher uses questioning to demonstrate how the problem relates to the real world. Discussion follows about the topic, allowing students to study and solve the problem. | The activities for this lesson provide many stimulating problem-solving activities and develop problem-solving skills while giving students a sense of accomplishment and confidence.<br><br>A problem-solving approach fosters mathematical reasoning and thinking. The focus becomes the process of problem solving, reasoning, and communicating. The mathematical skills should not be too difficult, nor too easy. Students use calculators, because the focus is on the process and not necessarily the facts or rules of mathematics. |
| **Teaching Strategies and Learning Experiences**<br><br>The teacher presents the following scenario:<br><br>*The third grade is planning a field trip to the local museum. There are five first-grade classrooms with twenty students in each class. The district has two different sized buses. One bus has twenty-two seats and the other has only twelve seats. Each seat holds three students or two adults. Assuming the teacher and two chaperones* | This is used in conjunction with a lesson on school-bus safety. Students learn about rules governing how many students can ride on a bus and how these laws were established. |

| Unit Sequence | Reflection |
|---|---|
| *for each class will go on the field trip, how many buses should the school order for the trip?*<br><br>Resource 4.6 provides a student activity page, along with a scoring rubric to evaluate the steps of the problem-solving process. | |
| Students use manipulative materials such as base-ten blocks or cubes and follow the following steps to solve the problem.<br><br>• Write a sentence that states what the problem is about and what the question is asking.<br>• Develop a plan for solving the problem that includes the identification of all operations involved.<br>• Follow the plan to a solution.<br>• Reflect and evaluate the plan and the solution. Revise the plan and rework the problem if it didn't lead to a correct response. | Students identify the information necessary to solve the problem, as well as any information that is not needed to solve the problem.<br>   Students keep records of their work on the problem, recording all attempts whether they succeed or not. They also record explanations of their thinking and reasoning.<br>   Students devise their own plans. Different approaches are possible, so discussions should be facilitated for different ways to look at a problem. |
| **Closure**<br><br>The teacher concludes by making sure that students used the laws and safety regulations to solve this problem. To connect to social studies, the following assignments may be made:<br><br>• What is the history of bus safety in the United States?<br>• How are laws made?<br>• Are the laws related to school-bus safety state or national laws? How do you know? How would you find out?<br>• What were the incidents in history that led to the establishment of these regulations? | Posing extensions to the problem, the teacher encourages students to consider what would happen if one of the components in a problem were different—that is, if it had a different value. In the problem posed in this situation, they can explore the idea that bus capacity is based on height and weight rather than number of people.<br>   Students write an explanation of how this problem is similar or different from other problem solutions. |

## LESSON 4.6: WHAT IS A MATHEMATICIAN?

**Length:** One 60-minute session

| Unit Sequence | Reflection |
|---|---|
| **Concepts**<br>Communication | |
| **Principles**<br>Real life requires applying and adapting a variety of problem-solving strategies. | |

(Continued)

| Unit Sequence | Reflection |
|---|---|
| **Skills** <br> Solve problems in a real context. | |
| **Standards** <br> SD 13 | |
| **Guiding Question** <br> What is a mathematician? | |
| **Introduction** <br><br> The teacher begins by asking students if they have ever heard of the Pythagorean theorem or the mathematician Pythagoras, allowing anyone to share and accepting all ideas and responses. If students are not familiar with the subject, the teacher simply explains that Pythagoras was a famous mathematician, and provides a few details. United Streaming (http://streaming.discoveryeducation.com) may assist in locating information about his life and contributions. | The activities for this lesson are designed to help students see the practical nature of mathematics and understand that one does not have to have a particular aptitude or talent in order to be a mathematician. |
| Students next illustrate their mental picture of what a mathematician is. They then label all parts of their drawing with specific terms. <br><br>     Students share pictures and explain their drawings; they also share experiences that may have given them these ideas. | Typically, students will have the notion that mathematicians are those with exceptional mathematical skills and abilities. Drawings may be of people with wild hair, glasses, and working with calculators or long strings of formulas written on a chalkboard. |
| **Teaching Strategies and Learning Experiences** <br><br> Students now go to different workstations where there are scenarios written on pieces of paper that require ordinary mathematics, such as the following: <br><br>     It is 7:00 a.m. The bus comes at 7:16. It takes you 20 minutes to eat breakfast and prepare your lunch. Will you be able to complete these tasks before the bus comes? Why? Why not? Please explain and show your work. | The teacher provides appropriate addition and subtraction or multiplication and division problems that people face in daily chores or on the job. Resource 4.7 provides a mathematician survey along with workstation sample activities. |
| **Closure** <br><br> The teacher discusses the different real-life situations in which mathematics helps answer common questions. Students share all the ways they used mathematics since they got out of bed that day. The teacher leads them to understand that mathematicians are those who use mathematics as a tool and not necessarily only those who solve complex equations or develop new theorems. | Students who need a challenge can read about famous mathematicians and write a brief report on their contributions. <br><br>     More advanced students may come up with a conjecture on which they might pose as a new mathematical idea. <br><br>     Those interested may go to www.teachersnetwork.org/readysettech/vargese to learn more about Pythagoras, his life, and to engage in activities created by Vargese that teach about his theorem. |

## LESSON 4.7: THE TOOLS OF A MATHEMATICIAN

**Length:** One 60-minute session

| Unit Sequence | Reflection |
|---|---|
| **Concepts**<br><br>• Communication<br>• Estimation<br>• Computation<br>• Systems<br>• Relationships | |
| **Principles**<br><br>• While there may be alternate ways to obtain a right answer, knowing particular steps to follow, often called *algorithms,* when using specific mathematical operations increases the chances of obtaining a correct result.<br>• Real life requires applying and adapting a variety of problem-solving strategies. | |
| **Skills**<br><br>• Distinguish between situations that require different operations.<br>• Solve problems in a real context. | |
| **Standards**<br><br>SD 3, SD 8, SD 11 | |
| **Guiding Question**<br><br>What are the tools of a mathematician? | |
| **Introduction**<br><br>The first lesson begins with students identifying tools that make work and tasks around the house easier, that is, the dishwasher, mop, broom, microwave, and so on. Students brainstorm and the teacher accepts all responses.<br><br>Through a discussion about why these tools were invented, students speculate about the reasons humans need and develop tools.<br><br>The teacher extends this discussion by explaining how computers and calculators have impacted science, business, industry, society, and individuals in recent years.<br><br>It is helpful to share examples of how some supermarkets put calculators on shopping carts to help customers estimate their shopping totals, how computer | In this parallel, students identify the tools and approaches that mathematicians employ to solve problems and reach reasonable and accurate answers.<br><br>Children need many opportunities to work with the appropriate technology in all mathematics. It should not be reserved for one lesson. These experiences are formal and informal and allow students to check estimates, confirm answers, and importantly, learn how to use the tools appropriately.<br><br>The discussions in this parallel help students consider the relevance of the role mathematics plays in their daily lives. |

(Continued)

| Unit Sequence | Reflection |
|---|---|
| programs and software help individuals figure out what monthly payments will be on cars or homes they purchase, and so forth.<br><br>The teacher builds on the ideas developed in the earlier lesson on what a mathematician is and what a mathematician does. | |
| **Teaching Strategies and Learning Experiences**<br><br>The teacher gives students stimulating problems to solve that involve appropriate numbers and operations. Students may use the website www.aplusmath.com/games/ and practice addition, subtraction, multiplication, or division skills in a game format using the computer.<br><br>Students use calculators as they work on these games. | The ideas behind the suggested learning experiences in this parallel allow students to see the applications of math by using the same tools that mathematicians commonly use in everyday life. Resource 4.8 provides additional student activities. |
| **Closure**<br><br>Students speculate on what life would be without computers or calculators.<br><br>Students select one mathematician from history (e.g., Pythagoras) and identify the tools he used. Students then research which tools might be used in the same branch of mathematics today. | **Homework**<br><br>Students record all the ways mathematics is used in one room of their house. They determine how often mathematics is used (once daily or how many times per day) and what tools are used to facilitate this use. |

## LESSON 4.8: THE ETHICS OF THE USE OF THE TOOLS OF MATHEMATICS

**Length:** One 60-minute session

| Unit Sequence | Reflection |
|---|---|
| **Concepts**<br><br>• Communication<br>• Estimation<br>• Computation | |
| **Principles**<br><br>While there may be alternate ways to obtain a right answer, knowing particular steps to follow, often called *algorithms*, when using specific mathematical operations increases the chances of obtaining a correct result. | |
| **Skills**<br><br>Distinguish between situations that require different operations. | |

| Unit Sequence | Reflection |
|---|---|
| **Standards**<br>SD 8 | |
| **Guiding Question**<br>When is it appropriate to use a calculator and when is it not? | |
| **Introduction**<br>The lesson begins with defining the term *ethics* through examples of ethical dilemmas to which students can relate. For example,<br><br>*If you found a dollar on your desk and knew it was not yours, what would you do? Would you put it in your desk and tell no one about it? Why or why not? Would you give it to the teacher? Why or why not?*<br><br>The discussion continues as the teacher engages students in sharing their thoughts about how and when calculators should be used in the classroom. | The purpose of this lesson is for students to consider the ethics of the use of calculators and computers in the mathematics classroom. |
| **Teaching Strategies and Learning Experiences**<br>A debate is staged where students take arbitrary positions on the use of calculators on daily work and tests in mathematics. They must defend their arguments with logical and rational thinking. | |
| **Closure**<br>Students complete the Calculator Place Value activity (Resource 4.8), either individually or working with a partner. The lesson closes with the teacher asking students if they thought completing the tasks would be easier or harder if they had not been able to use their calculators, and why or why not. | Many more lessons could be added to this unit and to this parallel to extend and expand students' understanding. |

# REFERENCE

Schwartz, D. M. (1985). *How much is a million?* New York: HarperCollins.

## RESOURCE 4.1: PREASSESSMENT

You have been given the task of counting the number of cars that pass by your school playground between 10:00 a.m. and 11:00 a.m. Your job is to count the number of cars during this time slot for a week, and then report to the principal the number of cars as well as summarize the information and come up with a statement of what you believe to be true about the traffic-flow pattern.

In small groups, devise a plan for how you will conduct this investigation. Decide what materials you will need, how to organize the information (think in terms of tables and charts), and what mathematical operations and skills you will need to complete this assignment.

Record your information on the second page of this handout.

Examine the following mathematical sentences. Look for any patterns, relationships, or rules. Explain your observations in writing, using appropriate mathematical terms.

| | | | |
|---|---|---|---|
| $2 + 2 + 2 + 2 + 2 + 2 = 12$ | $6 \times 2 = 12$ | $12 \div 6 = 2$ | $12 \div 2 = 6$ |
| $2 + 3 = 5$ | $3 + 2 = 5$ | $5 - 2 = 3$ | $5 - 3 = 2$ |

Read the following word problem. Identify the mathematical operations needed to solve the problem. Explain your thinking. You do not need to carry out the plan or solve the problem, but must clearly explain your thinking.

A dog takes about 61 days to form before it is born. After it is born, it lives about 4,480 days. A red fox takes about 52 days to form before it is born, but it only lives about 2,560 days. How much longer does the dog live than the fox?

Do appearances matter? Think about what or who a mathematician is. In the box below, draw a picture of your visual image of a mathematician.

## RESOURCE 4.2: LESSON 4.1 SAMPLE ACTIVITIES

This is a model and can be used for developing similar scenarios for each of the other operations. This is important so students can begin to recognize when to use specific operations.

### *Combination* Scenario for Addition

Tom has 2 pencils and Mary has 3. How many pencils do they have in all?
Draw pictures to illustrate your plan for solving this problem.
Write a number sentence and solve it.
Label your answer.

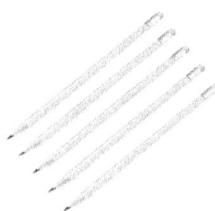

$$2 + 3 = 5$$

There are 5 pencils in all.

### *Static* Scenario for Addition

Dick has 2 pencils in his desk and 4 at home. How many does he have in all?

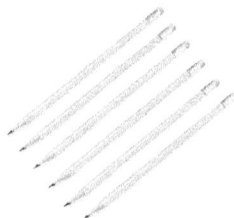

$$2 + 4 = 6$$

There are 6 pencils in all.

*Note:* With static situations, the objects are not actually combined; they are simply counted.

### *Incremental* Scenario for Addition

Tom is 5'4" when he enters fourth grade. At the beginning of the second semester, he has grown 3 inches. How tall is Tom now?

*Note:* With incremental changes there are no objects to count or manipulate.

## RESOURCE 4.3: LESSON 4.2 SAMPLE ACTIVITIES

Show students a sheet of grid paper and draw arrows to show them arrays. Explain that adjacent squares, either vertically or horizontally, form an array. Ask students to look around the room and find examples of arrays (e.g., ceiling tiles, the calendar, etc.).

Point out that the shaded area below represents three rows by four columns. Count the rectangles to see that they represent twelve squares. Explain that this can be represented by $3 \times 4 = 12$. This is easier than counting all rectangles in the array. The number of rows is multiplied by the number of columns to find out how many rectangles this represents.

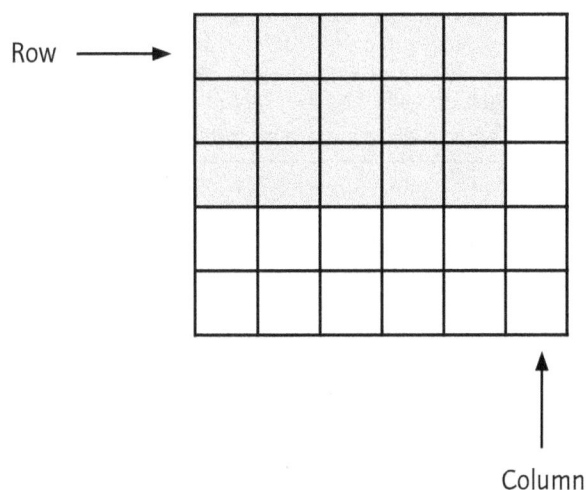

Row $\longrightarrow$

Column

Give students a blank sheet of grid paper. Give multiplication-number sentences that are appropriate for groups or individual students, such as $2 \times 3$ and $3 \times 2$, and have them color in the shapes to represent these sentences that reflect the commutative property of multiplication.

You can make this more challenging by giving students the blank grid paper and asking them to write their own number sentences and then color in the rectangles to represent the commutative property, or another property.

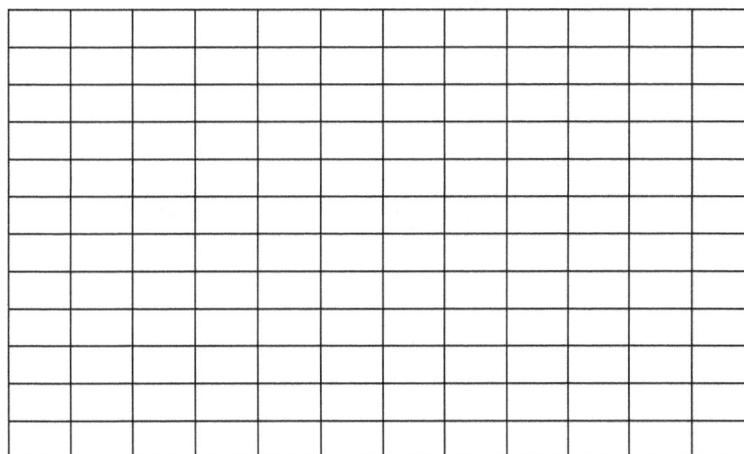

## RESOURCE 4.4: LESSON 4.3 SAMPLE ACTIVITIES

Using the readiness level and skills of individual or groups or students, select the appropriate operation (addition, subtraction, multiplication, and/or division) and the corresponding algorithm, and have them design scenarios and write stories to represent the scenarios.

Use the following interpretations for each operation as the basis for the scenarios.

| Operation | Interpretation | Example Basis for Scenario |
|---|---|---|
| Addition | Combination | Putting together two separate sets of the same thing to determine how many in all |
| | Static | Putting together two sets of the same thing without actually combining them to determine how many in all |
| | Incremental | Determining growth or change where there are no objects to combine |
| Subtraction | Take-away | Removing objects from a given set to determine how many are left |
| | Additive | Determining what is needed when asked to find out what is needed to reach or get a predetermined amount |
| | Comparative | Determining which has more and how much more when comparing two sets of the same type of objects |
| | Partitioning | Determining how many objects are left when separating or partitioning objects into parts with different characteristics |
| | Incremental | Determining decrease or change when there are no objects to combine such as in growth or temperature |
| Multiplication | Repeated addition | Determining how many in all when sets have the same number of objects |
| | Row-by-column | Determining how many in all in a given number of rows with each row having the same number of objects |
| | Combination | Determining the total number of possible pairs when given two sets of objects and one object from the first set is combined with one object from the second set |
| Division | Subtractive | Determining the total number of sets when given the total number of objects and the number of objects in each set |
| | Distributive | Determining the total number of objects in each set when given the total number of objects and the number of sets |

## RESOURCE 4.5: LESSON 4.4 SAMPLE ACTIVITIES

This activity can be very similar to the one for Lesson 4.2, but students write addition sentences and color in rectangles to represent the transitivity of equality property. Students also color in arrays to represent the relationships between operations, using different colors.

For example, ask students to color in rectangles to illustrate that

$$2 + 3 \text{ has a relationship to } 5 - 2 \text{ and } 5 - 3$$

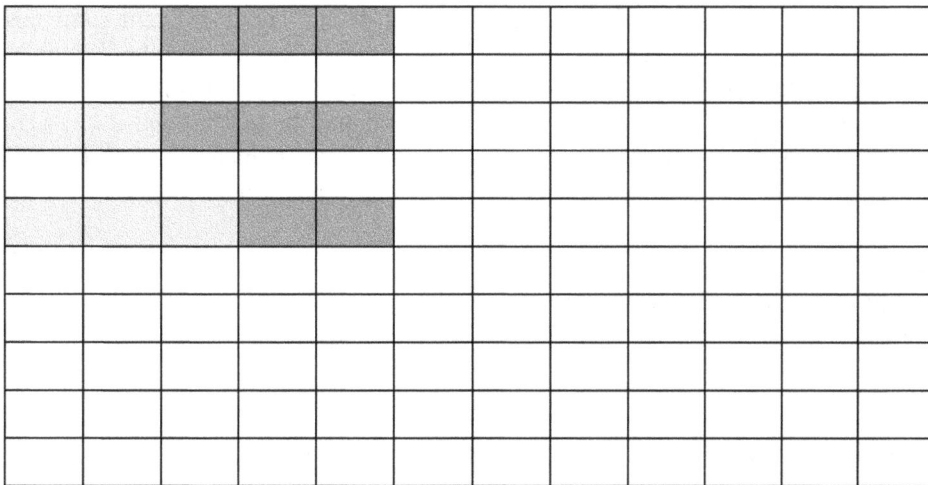

Ask students to complete a graphic organizer to explain the relationship between two operations such as addition and subtraction.

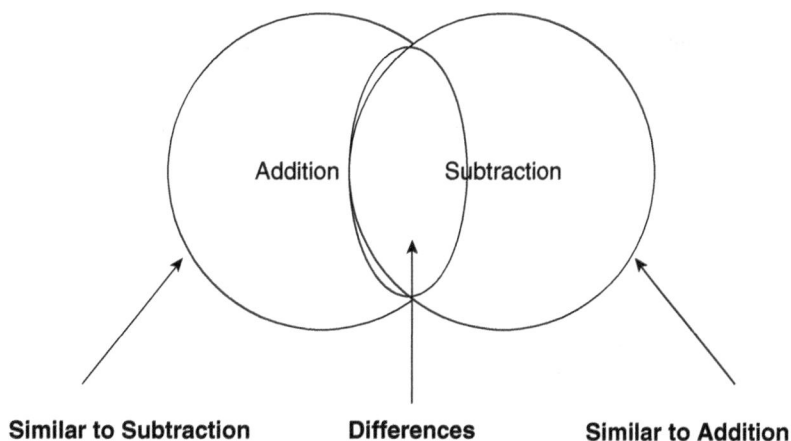

**Similar to Subtraction**          **Differences**          **Similar to Addition**

*Note:* A more challenging activity is for students to illustrate the relationships among all four operations: addition, subtraction, multiplication, and division. Students make their own graphic organizer to illustrate these.

## RESOURCE 4.6: LESSON 4.5 SAMPLE ACTIVITIES

In the spirit of connections, it is important for students to see the connections not only between and among all aspects of mathematics, but to other disciplines and the real world.

> The third grade is planning a field trip to the local museum. There are 5 third-grade classrooms with 20 students in each class.
>
> The district has 2 different sized busses. One bus has 22 seats and the other has only 12 seats. Each seat holds 3 students or 2 adults.
>
> Assuming the teacher and 2 adult chaperones for each class are planning to go on the field trip, how many buses must the school order for the trip?

Write a sentence that states what the problem is about. _____

_____

Summarize your plan for solving the problem that includes the operations. _____

_____

_____

Reflect, evaluate, and if needed, revise the plan and solution. _____

_____

_____

_____

Solve and show your work.

*Rubric for Scoring Problem Solving*

| 3 = Expert: works independently, accurately and quickly<br>2 = Practitioner: works accurately<br>1 = Novice: works with support<br>0 = Not there yet: misses the mark | 3 | 2 | 1 | 0 |
|---|---|---|---|---|
| **Understanding the Problem** | | | | |
| Restated the problem in his/her own words | | | | |
| Identified the unknown | | | | |
| Identified needed and unnecessary information | | | | |
| **Devising a Plan** | | | | |
| Drew a picture | | | | |
| Looked for patterns | | | | |
| Organized the information in the form of a table or chart | | | | |
| Related the problem to a familiar problem | | | | |
| Wrote a number sentence | | | | |
| Worked backwards | | | | |
| Used logical reasoning to eliminate possibilities | | | | |
| Guessed and checked | | | | |
| **Following the Plan** | | | | |
| Carried out the plan | | | | |
| Used logic to decide whether or not the plan was working | | | | |
| **Reflecting** | | | | |
| Decided whether or not the solution was reasonable | | | | |
| Decided whether the solution answered the question | | | | |
| Decided if there were other possible solutions | | | | |

Observations of student thinking:

## RESOURCE 4.7: LESSON 4.6 SAMPLE ACTIVITIES

Conduct a survey to get others' ideas about a mathematician.

**Mathematician Survey**

| Statement | Yes | No |
|---|---|---|
| 1.  A mathematician is a specific *job*. | | |
| 2.  A mathematician is a genius. | | |
| 3.  Mathematicians have special skills and talents. | | |
| 4.  I know a mathematician. | | |
| 5.  Everyone is a mathematician. | | |

Look at the responses. Write a statement that summarizes what you believe the people you interviewed think a mathematician is or is not.

**Friends and Family Survey**

Conduct a survey of family and friends to determine how often they use mathematics.

*Survey Questions*

1. List all the ways you have used mathematics today (e.g., looked at the clock to tell time, balanced the checkbook, figured out how long it would take to drive to school or work).

2. How often do you use a calculator?

3. For what do you use a calculator?

4. What type of calculator do you use?

5. Do you consider yourself a mathematician?

Why or why not?

*Sample Activity for Workstations for Lesson 4.6*

Do you use a digital or analog clock?

Is this clock digital or analog?

How do you know?

**Scenario 1**

It is 7:00 a.m. and the school bus comes to pick you up at 7:16 a.m. It takes you 6 minutes to eat breakfast and 10 minutes to prepare your lunch.

Will you be able to complete these tasks before the bus comes? _____ Yes _____ No

How do you know? Please explain and show your work.

If you can only complete one task, which one would it be? Why?

## RESOURCE 4.8: LESSON 4.7 SAMPLE ACTIVITIES

*1, 2, 3, 4, 5 . . . 10, 20, 30, 40, 50 . . .*

### Counting to 1 Million

Start by asking students to write the numeral representing 1 million. (Adapt this number to fit the skills and needs of particular students or groups of students. It can start with one hundred or even ten.)

Ask students to write the number as many different ways as they can—using expanded notation, and so on.

Program a computer to count to 1 million. Ask students to speculate about how long it will take the computer to complete this task. Write down the time.

Begin the program. After it has run for a few seconds, interrupt the program and allow students to revise their estimates and speculations. The point of this is to demonstrate the magnitude of the number.

Using *How Much Is a Million?* by David M. Schwartz (1985), ask students to use a calculator to figure how long it would take to count to 1 million (or an appropriate number). Ask them to explain their strategy and show their work.

Using a calculator, engage students in the activities to answer the following adaptations of questions Schwartz poses:

- What is the length of 1 million kids standing on each other's shoulders?
- How big would a fish bowl be if it could hold 1 million goldfish?
- How many pages would the book be if it pictured 1 million stars?

### Links to Other Content

Make connections to social studies by talking about the national debt. Define terms such as *surplus* and *deficit*.

Using calculators, have students calculate how long it would take to pay off the national debt using a large number such as $1,000,000,000 per day.

Advanced students take into consideration that debt continues to accumulate. How will they deal with that? Ask them to explain their thinking.

### Calculators to Reinforce Place Value

Instruct students to use only the keys with digits on them.

0   1   2   3   4   5   6   7   8   9

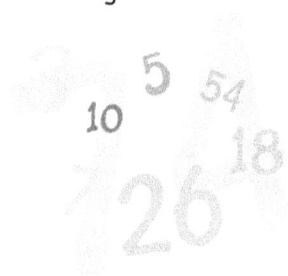

Use one key, one time.

- Make the smallest number possible.                    _____
- Make the largest number possible.                     _____

Use two keys. You can use the same key two times.

- Make the smallest number possible.                    _____
- Make the largest number possible.                     _____
- [Continue for three keys, four keys, etc.]

Use two keys. You cannot use the same key two times.

- Make the smallest number possible.                    _____
- Make the largest number possible.                     _____
- [Continue for three keys, four keys, etc.]

Use any key as many times as you want.

- Make the smallest number possible.                    _____
- Make the largest number possible.                     _____

Adaptation: Add the decimal key to this exercise.

- Which is smaller, 0.1 or 0.01? (etc.)                 _____
- What is the smallest nonzero number possible?         _____
- Find a number other than zero that is smaller than 0.009.   _____

Allow students to make up their own challenges.

# Preserving Our Identity

Learning About the History of Our State (Intermediate)

*Jennifer Beasley*

## INTRODUCTION TO THE UNIT

### Overview of the Unit

In every state social studies curriculum, there exists a unit on state history. For many social studies classrooms, this may incorporate learning the famous names, dates, and state symbols that characterize the state. Often what is missing is the "why" behind this information. Each of us identifies with the place we live. We feel pride in where we live and we want others to know that pride we feel. In the Parallel Curriculum Model (PCM), the four parallels give students a way to identify with and define that pride. They do this by using the concepts and principles that will answer questions as to why they want to study their own state. State history is a way to look at identity in a unique way. Through it students begin to understand what constitutes their own identity.

This unit requires students to delve into the "famous faces and facts" of their state, using the methods and practices of someone who really does work with this information—a public historian. As scholars, students are asked to make connections regarding how they communicate about their state identity and their own identity. Students draw upon these experiences as they see themselves in new ways. Assessments throughout the unit gauge students' understanding of the concepts and principles.

## The Parallels

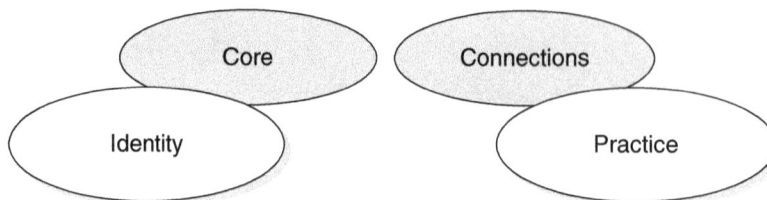

This unit works within all four parallels, but features the parallel of identity and the parallel of practice. In the preceding graphic, the parallels of identity and practice are highlighted to indicate the primary unit focus. Students work within the core parallel to develop the concepts found within this unit. The concepts are essential for understanding how a historian studies and communicates about state history. Students look at the parallel of connections between history and the study of their own identity. There are many parallels between our own characteristics and how we describe our state and it is important to see those connections through this unit.

Identity and practice are highlighted within this unit and are the cornerstones for the lessons. Students begin by looking at their own identity and how they communicate what is important to them. These ideas begin to flow naturally into the identity of their state and how they communicate what is important about their state. As they collect evidence of their identity as well as their state's, they use the tools and methodologies of a disciplinarian who has the responsibility of making history public. Students learn about the job of a public historian and use the methodologies of the public historian as they collect information and work on their final unit project. Students have contact with the authentic tools and documents that public historians use in their jobs.

The questions within this unit are derived from each parallel of the Parallel Curriculum Model. Students work within the discipline-specific field of public history with the concepts of time, change, identity, and culture to organize and make meaning out of their work in each of the parallels. Following are the key curriculum questions that drive the curriculum focus in this unit.

## Guiding Questions for Each Parallel

### Core Curriculum

- What makes me unique?
- How do we authenticate artifacts and sources in history?
- How do we identify and use primary and secondary sources?

### Curriculum of Connections

- How does knowing our own identity help us understand more about our state history?

*Curriculum of Practice*

- Who studies state history?
- What methods and tools does a historian use?
- How does a public historian communicate with an audience about history?

*Curriculum of Identity*

- What makes me unique?
- How do I communicate my identity to someone else?
- What makes my state unique?
- How do I communicate my state's identity to someone else?
- How does the evidence left behind by culture help us understand ourselves as citizens of a state?

## Background Information for the Unit

The following curriculum description and rationale for the unit summarize the unit's key curriculum components and assist teachers in their mental and planning preparation.

| Curriculum Component | Component Descriptions and Rationale |
|---|---|
| Content | Students work within the discipline-specific field of public history with the concepts of time, change, identity, and culture to organize and make meaning out of their work in each of the parallels. |
| | *Curriculum of Identity.* Students discover how their own identity is communicated and perceived through the study of their state history and its identity. |
| | *Curriculum of Practice.* Students assume the role of a public historian to understand how evidence is gathered through the use of multiple sources, how to validate historical artifacts and sources, and how to apply these new skills as they create a museum exhibit to inform others about their state. |
| | *Core Curriculum.* Students focus on the basic structure, organization, and purposes of public history. They also review the foundational knowledge and skills for using state history to reveal and communicate their own identity as well as the identity of a group of individuals. |
| | *Curriculum of Connections.* Students individually and collectively compare the traits and values they identify with themselves as they look at the traits and values that are attributed to their state. Through gathering this evidence about themselves and their state, they begin to see connections between each other as well as the community they live in. |
| Assessments | Conceptual understanding is monitored through varied formats.<br>   The focus is on conceptual understanding rather than learning the specific famous dates and faces of state history. Students choose various ways to demonstrate individual understanding. |

(Continued)

| Curriculum Component | Component Descriptions and Rationale |
|---|---|
| Introductory Activities | Introductory activities engage students by stimulating prior knowledge through tasks and discussions focusing on key concepts.<br><br>*Curriculum of Identity.* The activities ask students to consider how their own identity and how they define and communicate it compare with how a state's identity is defined and communicated.<br><br>*Curriculum of Practice.* The introductory activity engages students in understanding the type of work that a public historian is responsible for when trying to inform others about history.<br><br>*Core Curriculum.* The introductory activity focuses on the importance of identity and how the study of state history reveals the identity of a particular place and people.<br><br>*Curriculum of Connections.* The introductory activities help students to identify traits and values within themselves and connect those with the traits and values that are attributed to their state. |
| Teaching Strategies | In both whole-class and small-group instruction, the teacher emphasizes the unit's key concepts and principles that are identified in each parallel. The teaching strategies are varied to move students from a more foundational look at their own identity to a more transformational look at state identity. |
| Learning Activities | Whole-group, small-group, and individual activities are provided to stimulate active engagement in exploration of the concepts within the unit. The learning activities are all created to emphasize the questions of each parallel and allow students to work together or individually to answer them. In addition, small-group learning activities include a focus on extending research skills.<br><br>*Curriculum of Identity.* Students talk about their own identity through a small investigation at the beginning of the unit. The investigation allows students to define what identity is and then use that definition to guide their investigation into examining what state identity is. They ponder questions such as "How do we dispel or debunk first impressions?" and "How does perspective shape identity?"<br><br>*Curriculum of Practice.* Using the tools and methodologies of a public historian, students locate and analyze historical data about themselves and their state. They research the historical context and identify important factors that shaped the founding of their state. Students then choose the most relevant findings and utilize the information required in the Core Curriculum to help them prepare their museum exhibit using the activities developed within the Curriculum of Practice.<br><br>*Core Curriculum.* Students identify how they and others see themselves through the story of events. They reveal this through the study of history. Students begin to understand themselves in terms of their culture: values, traditions, art, food, and family.<br><br>*Curriculum of Connections.* Students identify how they depart from or fit within their research findings to identify connections between their lives and their state's identity. |

| Curriculum Component | Component Descriptions and Rationale |
|---|---|
| Grouping Strategies | Varied grouping strategies are used in this unit. Whole-group activities stimulate and generate ideas from varied viewpoints. Small-group activities allow students with similar strengths and needs to work collaboratively to support their individual learning. Independent work builds and strengthens understandings through self- and teacher-selected activities that communicate high expectations and worthwhile opportunities for all. |
| Products | Ongoing products and planned student reflections are organized around students demonstrating and providing evidence of understanding the key principles and concepts. |
| Resources | Resources guide the students' focus on the knowledge, understandings, and skills essential to the unit. In addition, they allow students to work at their own level of need to pursue personal avenues of interest. |
| Extension Activities | Opportunities to extend conceptual thinking and explore ideas based on student interest and need are provided throughout the unit. |
| Differentiation Based on Learner Needs, Including Ascending Intellectual Demand (AID) | Students bring different experiences and levels of readiness, interest, and learning profiles to each learning opportunity that may affect their ability to connect with the ideas in this unit. High expectations and worthwhile opportunities are provided based on specific needs through the varied activities and resources designed to support all students.<br><br>AID for advanced students requires them to work at more advanced levels, to provide deeper analyses and richer explanations of historical thinking. |

*Note:* During the first two lessons of the unit, students learn about the definitions of primary and secondary sources that are used throughout this unit. They also look at the methodologies of a public historian—interviewing, preserving artifacts, and communicating information in an articulate manner to the public—as they tell the story of their own lives.

The teacher may choose to provide a specific area of the room in which to collect and display a running vocabulary bank.

### Vocabulary for the Unit

*Artifacts.* Objects that were used by people long ago.

*Community.* Any group living in the same area or having interests, work, and so on in common.

*Culture.* Learned behavior of people that includes belief systems, languages, social relationships, institutions, organizations, and material goods (food, clothing, buildings, tools).

*Folklore.* The traditional beliefs, myths, tales, and practices of a people, passed from person to person orally.

*Identity.* The distinguishing character or personality of an individual.

*Natural resource.* Resources (fields, forests, the sea, and other gifts of nature) used to produce goods and services.

*Primary source.* A firsthand account of an event, person, or place (official document, diary, letter, historical photograph, oral testimony).

*Region.* An area with one or more common characteristics or features that make it different from surrounding areas.

*Secondary source.* An account of an event, person, or place that is not firsthand (textbook information, historically based movies, biographies).

*State.* A politically organized body of people usually occupying a definite territory.

# CONTENT FRAMEWORK

## Organizing Concepts

### Macroconcepts

M1: Adaptation

M2: Community

M3: Systems

### Discipline-Specific Concepts

C1: Time

C2: Identity

C3: Culture

C4: Perspective

## Principles

P1: Culture helps us to understand ourselves as both individuals and members of various groups.

P2: Our identity is shaped by the actions we take, the traits that help define who we are, and the choices that we make.

P3: The study of state history reveals the identity of a particular place and people.

P4: Humans seek to understand their historical roots and to locate themselves in time.

P5: Public historians use a set of tools and methods in their research to profile, chronicle, and communicate about the history of people.

P6: Public history is a way to transform the two-dimensional to the three-dimensional.

P7: The study of history helps people see change over time.

P8: The perspective of the historian impacts the interpretation of history.

## National or State Standards

*National Council for the Social Studies
Standards and Example State Standards*

SD 1: Social studies programs should include experiences that provide for the study of the ways human beings see themselves over time.

SD 2: Students will understand the people, events, problems, and ideas that were significant in creating the history of their state.

SD 3: Students will understand how culture and experience influence people's perceptions of places and regions.

SD 4: Students will explore different experiences, beliefs, motives, and traditions of people living in their neighborhoods, communities, and state.

SD 5: Students will view historic events through the eyes of those who were there, as shown in their art, writings, music, and artifacts.

SD 6: Students will consider different interpretations of key events and/or issues in history and understand the differences in these accounts.

SD 7: Students will demonstrate an understanding of the physical and human geographic features that define places and regions in their state.

SD 8: Students will study how personal identity is shaped by one's culture, by groups, and by institutional influences.

## Skills

S1: Identify the state capital and describe the various regions of students' particular state, including how their characteristics and physical environments (e.g., water, landforms, vegetation, climate) affect human activity.

S2: Identify and communicate about the lives of people who helped build the students' particular state.

S3: Use research skills (e.g., select relevant information, organize and share information in his/her own words, discuss ideas, formulate broad and specific questions at both the knowledge and comprehension level, with help know there are different formats of information, and record information).

S4: Use information to frame important historical questions.

S5: Identify and compare information from primary and secondary sources.

S6: Retell historical stories about the community using a variety of sources: maps, photos, oral histories, newspapers, and letters.

S7: Analyze and discuss issues both orally and in writing.

S8: Determine cause and effect relationships.

S9: Compare and contrast historical events.

S10: Draw conclusions and make generalizations.

S11: Make connections between past and present.

S12: Identify tasks that require a coordinated effort and work with others to complete those tasks.

S13: Plan and make written, oral, or visual presentations for a planned purpose and audience.

## UNIT ASSESSMENTS

### Preassessment

Before starting the unit, the teacher preassesses students' current understandings about the purposes of and experiences with state history. This preassessment provides evidence of the depth of content and conceptual understanding students have previously mastered. It is important to acknowledge what students have already learned about their state as well as their research skills.

The following questions provide a starting point for this assessment:

- What do you think is important about our state?
- What is a primary and a secondary source?

    o What is an example of a primary and a secondary source?
    o What makes these good examples of a primary and a secondary source?

To determine student knowledge and familiarity with the concepts of this unit, the teacher administers the Frayer Diagram for Conceptual Knowledge (Resource 5.1) and students fill in the information pertaining to the concepts of the unit. In order to collect information for the final project, preassessment of interests is also obtained. The following exercise provides a starting point for this:

I like to

- Draw
- Use computers
- Speak in front of others
- Write stories
- Organize and label
- Build things

The Frayer Diagram provides a great tool for uncovering student understanding about topics or concepts. Placing the concept or topic (i.e., state history) in the center and letting students share what they already know is a wonderful resource for making decisions.

For the final project, students work together to prepare a museum exhibit. This interest survey provides a starting place for grouping students according to their comfort level.

### Postassessment

As a part of the final assessment, all students complete a reflection sheet, responding to the following questions:

- What did you learn about the content as you completed this product?
- What did you learn about yourself as a learner by creating this product?

Students use a rubric in planning for and evaluating their presentation skills from basic to advanced performance (Resource 5.6).

Students complete a group evaluation on their final product (Resource 5.14).

# UNIT SEQUENCE AND TEACHER REFLECTION

## LESSON 5.1: INTRODUCING THE HISTORICAL METHOD

**Length:** One 30–40-minute session

| Unit Sequence | Reflection |
|---|---|
| **Concepts**<br><br>• Identity<br>• Culture | |
| **Principles**<br><br>• The actions we take, the traits that help define who we are, and the choices that we make all shape our identity.<br>• The study of state history reveals the identity of a particular place and people.<br>• Humans seek to understand their historical roots and to locate themselves in time.<br>• Public history is a way to transform the two-dimensional to the three-dimensional. | |
| **Skills**<br><br>• Use research skills.<br>• Use information to frame important historical questions.<br>• Draw conclusions and make generalizations.<br>• Make connections between past and present. | |
| **Standards**<br><br>SD 1, SD 8 | |
| **Guiding Questions**<br><br>• What is a historian?<br>• What does a historian do?<br>• What do historians mean by *evidence?*<br>• How might evidence be important in the work of historians? | |

(Continued)

| Unit Sequence | Reflection |
|---|---|
| **Introduction**<br><br>The lesson opens with a letter to the class.<br><br>*Who is this letter from? How can we find out who sent us the letter?*<br><br>The class brainstorms all the ways they can discover the identity of the letter writer. Some suggestions students may come up with are<br><br>• The handwriting<br>• The paper that was used<br>• The content of the letter<br>• The place it was found<br><br>The class concludes that there are certain characteristics that help define identity, that is, the identity of who wrote the note. Students make guesses about the identity of the writer, and the teacher probes further, asking what they are basing their guesses on. | It is important to provide a hook to introduce the unit as the class explores the significance of a historian. Starting with a mystery that needs to be solved can translate to the real practice of a historian. Students look at historical evidence and use tools to understand the unknown. This activity gets at the deeper understanding behind learning about state history, that *all humans seek to understand their historical roots and to locate themselves in time.* |
| **Teaching Strategies and Learning Experiences**<br><br>At this point, a discussion ensues about the goals of the upcoming unit on state history. In order to study state history, the teacher shares with the students that they will use the tools and methodologies of historians.<br>The teacher may use the following definition of a public historian:<br><br>*History is the events involving or affecting large numbers of human beings, and a public historian makes those events known to the public. Public historians are working "behind the scenes" any time you visit a museum, a historical reenactment, or even a historical theme park!*<br><br>The teacher posts and discusses vocabulary needed for the unit. The Pathway to Discovery Chart (Resource 5.2) guides discussion about how a historian talks about historical evidence.<br><br>*Did we use some of these same questions and methods when we examined our letter?* | This discussion is most effective in a whole-class setting. It is important to articulate where the class is going with this unit and give students an idea of the path the class is following. Posting the principles of the unit for the students may also be valuable at this time. The evidence files example (Resource 5.3) is one way to post the unit principles in the classroom. |
| **Closure**<br><br>Giving each student an index card, the teacher asks students to think of a question that a historian might want to ask about their state.<br>Students write that question on the card. On the other side, they answer the following question:<br><br>*How might these questions help us as we learn about our own state history?* | This exit card provides an idea of how students processed the idea of thinking like a historian. It also allows these questions to be included within the unit itself. Many of these questions might be ones that students are really interested in and including them in future lessons keeps students engaged and motivated. |

## LESSON 5.2: UNDERSTANDING THE TOOLS OF A PUBLIC HISTORIAN: LEARNING ABOUT OUR OWN LIVES

**Length:** Two 45–60-minute sessions

| Unit Sequence | Reflection |
|---|---|
| **Concepts**<br><br>• Identity<br>• Culture<br>• Change | |
| **Principles**<br><br>• Culture helps us to understand ourselves as both individuals and members of various groups.<br>• The actions we take, the traits that help define who we are, and the choices that we make shape our identity.<br>• Humans seek to understand their historical roots and to locate themselves in time.<br>• Public historians use a set of tools and methods in their research to profile, chronicle, and communicate about the history of people.<br>• The study of history helps people see change over time. | |
| **Skills**<br><br>• Use research skills.<br>• Use information to frame important historical questions.<br>• Analyze and discuss issues both orally and in writing.<br>• Make connections between past and present.<br>• Identify tasks that require a coordinated effort and work with others to complete those tasks.<br>• Plan and make a written, oral, or visual presentation for a planned purpose and audience. | |
| **Standards**<br><br>SD 1, SD 3, SD 4, SD 5, SD 6 | |
| **Guiding Questions**<br><br>• What do you think about when you hear the word *culture?*<br>• In what ways might your (state's) culture differ from (another state's) culture? | |

*(Continued)*

(Continued)

| Unit Sequence | Reflection |
|---|---|
| **Introduction**<br><br>In the first session, the teacher brings in a baby book or some other information to tell his or her own story as a baby. After presenting the information, the teacher leads the class in a discussion about what they learned.<br><br>*How did I find out information about myself?*<br><br>*What helped you learn about my history?*<br><br>*What do you know about my culture?* (Culture is learned behavior of people that includes belief systems, languages, social relationships, institutions, organizations, and material goods [food, clothing, buildings, tools].)<br><br>*Can you tell what is important to me from listening to me talk about my history?* | Before the lesson, the teacher sends home a letter to parents or guardians about the upcoming project. (The Example Parent Letter, Resource 5.5, provides an example of content.) It is important to let parents know about the On the Day I Was Born project. Some families may not have access to information documenting their child's birth and some children may be in adoptive or foster care situations. Therefore, letting parents or guardians know ahead of time the type of information needed for the project gives them an idea of what to begin collecting. In the letter, there is a section that each child will return, stating the type of evidence they will collect for this project. The examples are intended to be easy for most families to find. |
| **Teaching Strategies and Learning Experiences**<br><br>The teacher reads the story *On the Day You Were Born* by Debra Frasier (1991).<br><br>*What is the author saying? How is this different from my own story?*<br><br>*As a historian, where do we begin if we want to answer the question: What happened on the day I was born?* (This is step 1 in the pathway to discovery.)<br><br>Students refer to the Pathway to Discovery Chart (Resource 5.2) as they begin to go through the steps in the process.<br><br>The students meet with a partner to talk about what they might bring in and how they might use their evidence in a presentation about the day they were born (step 2 in the pathway to discovery).<br><br>*Homework*<br><br>Students collect their items for the project and bring them in for the second session. | On the day of this lesson, it is helpful to have the note back from the parents indicating what evidence they will be able to find at home.<br><br>The book, *On the Day You Were Born* is particularly focused on the surrounding world (gravity, moon, ocean, trees, etc.). Some students may understand that the author writes this way so the book can appeal to a wider audience.<br><br>*Author's note:* I wanted students to meet with a partner who collected similar information so they could help each other think about how they would present that type of evidence. |

| Unit Sequence | Reflection |
|---|---|
| *Second Session* <br><br> This activity extends to a second session when the students bring in evidence they have collected. Students meet with their original partners to look over their collections. <br><br> Using a copy of the Graphic Organizer for Step 3 (Resource 5.4), each student chooses one piece of evidence they brought and answers the questions. <br><br> After meeting with their partners to go over the evidence they brought, students prepare a way to present their information to an audience (step 4 in the pathway to discovery). | |
| Multiple product options (poster, oral presentation, model, story, report, poem, or book) assist students in thinking about how to communicate their information, along with the assessment criteria (Resource 5.6). | The Curriculum Project (2010), located at www .curriculumproject.com, provides product guides with criteria for many products. The product ideas are organized by learning profiles (visual, kinesthetic, oral, and written). These profiles provide a resource for teachers and students alike and will help when thinking about assessment. |
| **Closure** <br><br> Students share their presentations about the day they were born. As students share, it may enhance the following lessons to pinpoint each student's place of birth on a map. This is a concrete way to introduce the relationship between place and identity. <br><br> The book *On the Day You Were Born* is illustrated on the paper collage medium, which lends itself to an art lesson on the techniques of collage. If the class has access to an art teacher, partnering provides a great opportunity to work with the students on collage. Students may want to create a cover for a book about the day they were born. This activity gives students an opportunity to further connect with the style found in the book they read. | **AID or Modifications for Learner Need** <br><br> The basic and advanced presentation illustrates how an assessment can be modified for advanced learners. The criteria for the advanced learners are written in an open way to allow for the possibility of moving beyond the basic criteria. The basic presentation criteria are written in the form of questions to prompt students who may need guidance as they plan their presentations. Both rubrics measure the same elements for the presentation; yet they allow students to work in a more open or structured way. <br><br> **Optional Extension Activity** <br><br> The book *On the Day You Were Born* provides a wonderful source for extension activities. Some students may want to write their own stories for the classroom library. Students may want to use templates that follow the pattern within the story. Each page begins with one extreme (high above) and follows up with a page at the other extreme (far below). Students think of directional opposites as well as other opposites (e.g., soft, hard) to compose a book using their own information. |

## LESSON 5.3: UNDERSTANDING THE TOOLS OF A HISTORIAN: LEARNING ABOUT OUR STATE HISTORY

**Length:** Two 45–60-minute sessions

| Unit Sequence | Reflection |
| --- | --- |
| **Concepts**<br><br>• Identity<br>• Culture<br>• Change | |
| **Principles**<br><br>• Culture helps us to understand ourselves as both individuals and members of various groups.<br>• The study of state history reveals the identity of a particular place and people.<br>• Public historians use a set of tools and methods in their research to profile, chronicle, and communicate about the history of people.<br>• The perspective of the historian impacts the interpretation of history. | |
| **Skills**<br><br>• Identify and communicate about the lives of people who helped build the students' particular state.<br>• Use research skills.<br>• Use information to frame important historical questions.<br>• Analyze and discuss issues both orally and in writing.<br>• Determine cause and effect relationships.<br>• Compare and contrast historical events.<br>• Draw conclusions and make generalizations.<br>• Make connections between past and present.<br>• Identify tasks that require a coordinated effort and work with others to complete those tasks.<br>• Plan and make a written, oral, or visual presentation for a planned purpose and audience. | |
| **Standards**<br><br>SD 1, SD 2, SD 3, SD 5, SD 6, SD 8 | |
| **Guiding Questions**<br><br>• How do we see our descriptions of a place similar or dissimilar to descriptions about a person?<br>• What would a historian want to know?<br>• What questions would a historian ask?<br>• What helps us understand the identity of a place?<br>• What is so special about our state? | |

| Unit Sequence | Reflection |
|---|---|
| **Introduction**<br><br>During this part of the unit, students apply the skills they were introduced to in the day they were born project to their own state. They will also explore the idea that perspective has a direct impact on how state history and state identity are viewed.<br><br>The teacher begins by asking the class to identify the people, places, and events that are typically associated with the region known as "the West."<br><br>Students begin to brainstorm how they would characterize the West. The teacher then prompts them to consider how descriptions of a place are similar or dissimilar to descriptions about a person.<br><br>The class views the first part of an old western (such as *The Lone Ranger*) and speculates how someone watching that clip might describe the West.<br><br>Students might raise the following points:<br><br>• The show describes the West as a lawless place, a wild place.<br>• The show depicts Native Americans as unable to communicate and dependent on the "white man."<br>• The show describes people in one-dimensional ways: half-breed, villain, and hero.<br><br>The teacher asks,<br><br>*What would a historian want to know? What questions would a historian ask?* | As students begin to transition to learning about the identity of their state, it is important to begin to look at ways they originally spoke of their own identity and see similarities and differences when describing a place. Starting with a place that is known and often misunderstood (the "Wild West") provides the hook for students to discover that oftentimes people have misconceptions about places that color their views. In the case of the West, people have often romanticized or generalized to such an extreme, some of so-called history is now known to be folklore. This introduction leads into an activity where students look at the methods a historian uses to validate artifacts and events. |
| **Teaching Strategies and Learning Experiences**<br><br>*(Sessions 1 and 2)*<br><br>Public historians believe that history and historical-cultural memory matter in the way people go about their day-to-day lives.<br><br>Showing the beginning of the film *The West* (only until the title caption) by Ken Burns (1996) allows students to understand how landscape, interviews, photographs, myths, folklore, music, and events tell the history of the region.<br><br>Looking at the two "pictures" of the West told from the two sources, the teacher asks what students understand about the identity of this region, and how they would find out the true identity of the region.<br><br>The teacher leads the whole class in a discussion about how the study of state history helps with | **AID or Modifications for Learner Need**<br><br>Students may extend this research about how state stereotypes are perpetuated or dispelled. Still other students may need more practice finding materials on their state or understanding perspective's role in history.<br><br>*Author's note:* To help extend or reinforce learning, I created a learning center in the room that I kept in place for two weeks. The following is a description of the center:<br><br>*Spot the Stereotype Center*<br><br>Cards that contain quotes or phrases referring to different states are mounted on the wall. These quotes or phrases can come from found materials or from impressions students themselves have about the states. California may be known as the Sunshine State, or students may think about |

(Continued)

| Unit Sequence | Reflection |
|---|---|
| understanding the identity of a place, and then asks what helps with understanding the identity of a place. This leads into the evidence list for the pathway to discovery (Resource 5.2, step 2).<br><br>The class looks at evidence that was consciously left by their state—their state license plate. A great resource is www.worldlicenseplates.com/world/NA_USAX.html.<br><br>This investigation can be set up as a computer activity with students working in teams to explore their state license plate. Resources can also be printed out and made accessible to individual students or partners.<br><br>It is important to make clear to students through this activity that the perspective of the historian impacts the interpretation of history. In this activity, they look at their state license plates and dig into the facts that surround the plate and its symbols. As historians, students interpret what they think the message is. Students use the graphic organizer to help identify facts that surround a state's license identity and their own interpretations.<br><br>As students work alone or with a partner, they fill out a Right There, or History and Me observation sheet (Resource 5.10). | surfing or Disneyland when they think of California. These may be stereotypes that we have developed over time.<br><br>*Are they based at all in reality? Whether it is or isn't, where might we find sources to prove or disprove this stereotype?*<br><br>For this center, three tasks (Resource 5.9) are modified to reinforce or extend the concepts featured in this lesson. |
| **Closure**<br><br>Under pictures of the state license plate, students post their Right There, or History and Me activity. Students walk around the room and look at other responses. The sessions end by bringing the class back to the "big ideas" of the lesson:<br><br>*The study of state history reveals the identity of a particular place and people, and the perspective of the historian impacts the interpretation of history.* | An example of how students may use the Right There, or History and Me (Resource 5.10) activity follows:<br><br>On Hawaii's license plate, there is a picture of King Kamehameha the Great who unified all eight Hawaiian Islands under his rule, creating a united royal Hawaiian Kingdom in 1810. This fact is posted under the Right There side of the graphic organizer. It is a fact that few debate. After reading about why Hawaii is called the Aloha State, students may end up putting their response in the History and Me section. (There are quite a few stories about why Hawaii is called this.) Students may also put their reasons why there is a palm tree on the license plate in the History and Me section because this is up to interpretation. Students' own stereotypes may even influence their responses.<br><br>Right There, or History and Me can be used to assess where students are in terms of understanding perspective as well as use of resources. This activity can guide modification for learner needs leading into using primary and secondary sources. |

## LESSON 5.4: USING PRIMARY SOURCES

**Length:** One 45–60-minute session

| Unit Sequence | Reflection |
|---|---|
| **Concept** <br><br> • Identity <br> • Culture <br> • Perspective | |
| **Principles** <br><br> • Culture helps us to understand ourselves as both individuals and members of various groups. <br> • The actions we take, the traits that help define who we are, and the choices that we make all shape our identity. <br> • The study of state history reveals the identity of a particular place and people. <br> • Public historians use a set of tools and methods in their research to profile, chronicle, and communicate about the history of people. <br> • The study of history helps people see change over time. <br> • The perspective of the historian impacts the interpretation of history. | |
| **Skills** <br><br> • Identify and communicate about the lives of people who helped build the students' particular state. <br> • Use research skills. <br> • Use information to frame important historical questions. <br> • Identify and compare information from primary and secondary sources. <br> • Retell historical stories about the community using a variety of sources: maps, photos, oral histories, newspapers, and letters. <br> • Analyze and discuss issues both orally and in writing. <br> • Draw conclusions and make generalizations. <br> • Make connections between past and present. <br> • Identify tasks that require a coordinated effort and work with others to complete those tasks. <br> • Plan and make a written, oral, or visual presentation for a planned purpose and audience. | |

*(Continued)*

(Continued)

| Unit Sequence | Reflection |
|---|---|
| **Standards**<br><br>SD 1, SD 2, SD 3, SD 4, SD 5, SD 6, SD 8 | |
| **Guiding Questions**<br><br>• How does the evidence a culture leaves behind help us understand ourselves as citizens of a state?<br>• Do you think it is important for historians to collaborate with other historians? Why? | |
| **Introduction**<br><br>The teacher begins by introducing the definition of primary and secondary sources.<br><br>• *Primary source.* A firsthand account of an event, person, or place (official document, diary, letter, historical photograph, or oral testimony).<br>• *Secondary source.* An account of an event, person, or place that is not firsthand (textbook information, historically based movies, or biographies).<br><br>Creating Internet links through Ribit (http://ribit.tielab.org/index.php) or Filamentality (http://www.kn.pacbell.com/wired/fil/) can help organize the resources for this lesson. This newly created website can be a storehouse for websites that collect primary as well as secondary sources on state history (and they are both free).<br><br>The resources are displayed for the class or students visit the computer lab where they can pull up the new website and explore the links. Students look at the gathered resources to promote curiosity and interest.<br><br>If the class does not have access to computers, the teacher can create a central area in the classroom where all the state resources are kept. | It is important to teach the skills and methodologies that underlie primary and secondary sources. As a result of this lesson, students begin to question resources as well as define primary and secondary sources. To group students by readiness, the teacher can use the preassessment from the beginning of the unit as well as the previous lesson. Some students will likely be familiar with primary and secondary sources and be able to identify examples of each. Other students may leave the answer blank on the preassessment, or not be able to fully define the terms. |
| **Teaching Strategies and Learning Experiences**<br><br>The activity on identifying primary sources centers the exploration on the following question:<br><br>*How does the evidence a culture leaves behind help us understand ourselves as citizens of a state?*<br><br>It is helpful to review or introduce that culture is the learned behavior of people, which includes belief systems, languages, social relationships, institutions, organizations, and material goods (food, clothing, buildings, tools). | The aim is to build upon the information collected during this activity to use for the final activity of the unit—the creation of the museum exhibit. |

| Unit Sequence | Reflection |
|---|---|
| *We can find out about a particular culture through the evidence they leave behind. This evidence can be examined through primary and secondary sources. As historians have access to more and more sources, they need to interpret more and more sources.*<br><br>*This expanded source work can lead to more error. Historians sometimes joke that it is easier to write about the ancient Mediterranean world than it is about the present world—due to the fact that the ancient Mediterranean world left very little evidence behind!* | |
| The students then examine primary and secondary sources through a jigsaw activity. The teacher uses the following descriptions to explain the directions:<br><br>*Home Group*<br><br>*Today your team's task is to learn about the variety of primary sources available for our state. Decide which member of your group will explore each type of artifact and begin your expert group activity.*<br><br>*Expert Groups*<br><br>Primary/Secondary Task Cards<br><br>For each object the team explores, a Graphic Organizer for Step 3 (Resource 5.4) is filled out. The students will be familiar with this organizer from a previous lesson. Specific instructions for primary sources follow (these should not be read aloud to the class, but written on task cards at the station): | Jigsaw is a cooperative learning strategy in which all students become experts on a small piece of a topic and then teach each other. Students start in the home group to touch base, receive introductory information, and choose tasks. They then move into expert groups to become experts on one "piece" of the puzzle. After spending time becoming an expert on their assigned piece, they return to their home group to present their piece of the puzzle to the other group members. The home group works together to complete a project or outcome that ties all the pieces of information together. Jigsaw ends with a whole-class discussion, as well as a check for individual understanding. |
| Task 1: Photos<br><br>*Directions:* Physical remains are defined by the fact that they offer no language. Historians sometimes refer to them as *mute evidence.* Photos are an example of a physical remain that recent historians use to uncover the identity of a culture. We can tell a lot about our state identity from the photographs that are left behind. Take a look at one or more photographs at your station. Fill out the artifact label for your photo (Graphic Organizer for Step 3, Resource 5.4) and then complete the green or blue task that you have been assigned.<br><br>*Green task.* Students who are not as familiar with primary sources. | In selecting sources for this activity, the following questions are helpful:<br><br>• What kinds of sources are of particular interest to my students?<br>• How difficult is the reading level of the primary source compared to my students' readiness?<br>• Do I need to provide a glossary of terms?<br>• How long is the source?<br>• Do I need to excerpt a portion?<br>• Are various points of views represented?<br>• Is there a balance among competing points of view?<br>• Where can I find the sources we need? (school or public library, a local historical society, etc.) |

*(Continued)*

(Continued)

| Unit Sequence | Reflection |
|---|---|
| *Blue task.* Students who are more familiar with primary and secondary sources. <br><br> (Task descriptions are provided in Resource 5.11.) <br><br> Task 2: Oral and Written History <br><br> *Directions:* Oral and written history provide historians with information from cultures that were able to document their history in written form as well as cultures that communicated through retelling. Historians use interview and folktales as well as documents to interpret history. Many of these objects need to be examined for bias and stereotype. Take a look at one or more artifacts at your station. Fill out the artifact label for your object (Graphic Organizer for Step 3, Resource 5.4) and then complete the green or blue task that you have been assigned. <br><br> *Green task.* Students who are not as familiar with primary sources. <br><br> *Blue task.* Students who are more familiar with primary and secondary sources. <br><br> (Task descriptions are provided in Resource 5.11.) <br><br> Task 3: Artwork <br><br> *Directions:* Artwork can be a physical remain or an oral or written history. Physical remains are defined by the fact that they offer no language. Historians sometimes refer to them as *mute evidence*. Oral and written history includes plays, folktales, poetry, and so forth. Many of these objects need to be examined for bias, values, and stereotypes. We can tell a lot about our state identity from the art that is left behind. Take a look at one or more artworks at your station. Fill out the artifact label for your object (Graphic Organizer for Step 3, Resource 5.4) and then complete the green or blue task that you have been assigned. <br><br> *Green task.* Students who are not as familiar with primary sources. <br><br> *Blue task.* Students who are more familiar with primary and secondary sources. <br><br> (Task descriptions are provided in Resource 5.11.) | **AID** <br><br> During this activity (task 2), the questions as well as the primary source can be modified to allow students to work with varying degrees of complexity. Some primary source data is harder to analyze than other, more straightforward sources. In each state, there may be sources in which many historians have conflicting evidence. Students may enjoy trying to throw their own hat in the ring in regards to the controversy. Students may want to collaborate with media specialists or historians in the area as they explore the sources for their state. |

| Unit Sequence | Reflection |
|---|---|
| **Task 4: Physical Artifacts**<br><br>*Directions:* Physical remains are defined by the fact that they offer no language. Historians sometimes refer to them as *mute evidence.* We can tell a lot about our state identity from the physical artifacts that are left behind. Take a look at one or more artifacts at your station. Fill out the artifact label for your object (Graphic Organizer for Step 3, Resource 5.4) and then complete the green or blue task that you have been assigned.<br><br>*Green task.* Students who are not as familiar with primary sources.<br><br>*Blue task.* Students who are more familiar with primary and secondary sources.<br><br>(Task descriptions are provided in Resource 5.11.)<br><br>*Home Group*<br><br>*Now that you are back with your home group, take time for each person in your group to share the artifacts they explored in their expert group. Each expert needs to conclude their presentation by talking to the group about the challenges and benefits of their particular source. Are there any hints you want to pass along to your home group?*<br><br>*As a home group, answer the question that was posed at the beginning of the activity: How does the evidence left behind by a culture help us understand ourselves as citizens of a state?*<br><br>*Be prepared as a group to present your ideas to the whole class.* | |
| **Closure**<br><br>As a whole class, each home group shares what they have prepared. The following links can be used for students to explore for primary and secondary sources.<br><br>www.50states.com//song/. This source contains many of the facts and fun trivia about all fifty states.<br><br>http://hlab.org/links/index.php?catid=2. The History Lab has put together an extensive list of primary sources related to U. S. history.<br><br>www.lib.washington.edu/subject/History/tm/state.html. The University of Washington has organized links to many artifacts on all states.<br><br>http://memory.loc.gov/ammen/index.html. The Library of Congress has collected its primary sources in the American Memory website. Specifically, in the culture/folklore section, there are examples of all four types of primary sources. | **Optional Extension Activity**<br><br>The Library of Congress (LOC) is a resource for exploring primary sources. Students who want to learn more about primary sources can visit the American Memory website and play games with the vast resources found at the LOC, at http://memory.loc.gov/learn/features/index.html. |

## LESSON 5.5: IF YOU'RE NOT FROM . . . , YOU DON'T KNOW . . .

**Length:** Two 30–45-minute sessions

| Unit Sequence | Reflection |
|---|---|
| **Concepts**<br><br>• Identity<br>• Culture<br>• Perspective | |
| **Principles**<br><br>• Culture helps us to understand ourselves as both individuals and members of various groups.<br>• The actions we take, the traits that help define who we are, and the choices that we make all shape our identity.<br>• The study of state history reveals the identity of a particular place and people.<br>• The perspective of the historian impacts the interpretation of history. | |
| **Skills**<br><br>• Identify the state capital and describe the various regions of the students' particular state, including how their characteristics and physical environments (e.g., water, landforms, vegetation, and climate) affect human activity.<br>• Identify and communicate about the lives of people who helped build the students' particular state.<br>• Use research skills.<br>• Identify and compare information from primary and secondary sources.<br>• Retell historical stories about the community using a variety of sources: maps, photos, oral histories, newspapers, and letters.<br>• Analyze and discuss issues both orally and in writing.<br>• Draw conclusions and make generalizations.<br>• Make connections between past and present.<br>• Plan and make a written, oral, or visual presentation for a planned purpose and audience. | |
| **Standards**<br><br>SD 1, SD 2, SD 4, SD 5, SD 6, SD 7 | |
| **Guiding Questions**<br><br>• Why is it important to collect information from both primary and secondary resources?<br>• What are the differences between the two resources? | |

| Unit Sequence | Reflection |
|---|---|
| **Introduction**<br><br>The teacher reads aloud *If You're Not From the Prairie . . .* by David Bouchard (1995), and asks the class:<br><br>*What is this author saying about where he lives? Do you think he has a definite view of what is important about where he lives?* | Students have spent time identifying primary sources on their state. In many states, the curriculum asks that students be familiar with dates, events, geography, and the remarkable people of their state. At this point, students collect information about their state from secondary resources as well. The information collected from the secondary resources assists students in preparing for their final museum exhibit project.<br><br>The website www.lib.washington.edu/subject/History/tm/state.html contains a wealth of information about state history. |
| **Teaching Strategies and Learning Experiences**<br><br>The teacher explains that students will learn about the dates, events, geography, and remarkable people of their state that contribute to the state's identity.<br><br>Materials about the dates, events, geography, and remarkable people of the state are provided to the students, and can include the state symbols. Students look through the information and record on their If You're Not From . . . Example Brainstorming sheet (Resource 5.7) all the information they find that is unique about their state.<br><br>After students fill out some important facts or information about their state on the brainstorming sheet, the teacher meets with students individually to talk about which area of interest intrigues them. The students put a star next to these areas and this is information they work on during the second session of this lesson. | |
| *Second Session*<br><br>During the second session, students continue their work on their state, and have chosen a specific interest area to research in more depth. Some students may concentrate on geographical identity; others may look at famous or extraordinary individuals of their state. Students may want to use some of the resources from their primary source discovery work to contribute to their product outcome. | **Modification for Learner Need**<br><br>Some students may benefit from using the brainstorming sheet and templates provided in this lesson. It provides a structured way to record their information. |
| Students use the information they collect to create a page for a book titled, *If You're Not From (state name). . . .* Using the same structure as the book read in class, students complete a template using the information they collected.<br><br>Some students may want to use the If You're Not From . . . Template (Resource 5.8) as a guide. It provides a final template to use as students put together a class-made book about their state. | *Author's note:* To make this class book, I used a student publishing company called Student Treasures (www.studenttreasures.com), which provides all the materials to publish an illustrated hardback copy of a classroom book. Students loved it because it looks like a real book. |

*(Continued)*

(Continued)

| Unit Sequence | Reflection |
|---|---|
| **Closure**<br><br>As part of the wrap-up of this lesson, another class can be invited in to hear the students share from their classroom book.<br><br>    It is now appropriate to assess how students are progressing in terms of learning about their state. The teacher can administer a traditional test concerning the facts about their state, or follow up the original preassessment:<br><br>• What do you think is important about our state?<br>• What are primary and secondary sources?<br>• What are examples of a primary and a secondary source?<br>• What makes these good examples of a primary and secondary source?<br><br>The Frayer Diagram for Conceptual Knowledge (Resource 5.1) determines student knowledge and familiarity with the concepts of the unit. Students fill in the information pertaining to the concepts of the unit. | At this point, the larger concepts of this unit are integrated and students have wrestled with the concepts the unit is built upon. Before moving into the culminating project, students need certain skills and tools. This assessment determines which students still need work to reinforce the skills associated in this unit. |

## LESSON 5.6: MAKING OUR STATE PUBLIC: CULMINATING PROJECT

**Length:** Two to four 45-minute sessions

| Unit Sequence | Reflection |
|---|---|
| **Concepts**<br><br>• Identity<br>• Culture<br>• Perspective<br>• Time | |
| **Principles**<br><br>• Culture helps us to understand ourselves as both individuals and members of various groups.<br>• The actions we take, the traits that help define who we are, and the choices that we make all shape our identity.<br>• The study of history helps people see change over time.<br>• The perspective of the historian impacts the interpretation of history. | |

| Unit Sequence | Reflection |
|---|---|
| **Skills**<br><br>• Retell historical stories about the community using a variety of sources: maps, photos, oral histories, newspapers, and letters.<br>• Identify tasks that require a coordinated effort and work with others to complete those tasks.<br>• Plan and make a written, oral, or visual presentation for a planned purpose and audience. | |
| **Standards**<br><br>SD 2, SD 3, SD 6 | |
| **Guiding Questions**<br><br>• What did you learn about the content as you completed the unit product?<br>• What did you learn about yourself as a learner by creating the unit product? | |
| **Introduction**<br><br>For the final project, students create an exhibit that communicates to others information about their state.<br><br>If the class is not able to get a museum curator in to talk about being a curator and how an exhibit is created, the teacher can begin by introducing students to museums through pictures and examples. Bringing a collection of brochures, maps, and pictures from a variety of museums in the area allows students to begin to think about what is involved in creating a museum exhibit. | It is beneficial to bring in an expert such as a museum curator to talk about the job of curatorship. Museum curatorship is concerned with all aspects of the development, study, preservation, and interpretation of a museum's collections. The curatorial role's in exhibitions is focused on interpretation.<br><br>*The Manual of Museum Exhibitions*, edited by Barry Lord and Gail Dexter Lord (2001), is an excellent resource for providing information about museum exhibits and roles. |
| **Teaching Strategies and Learning Experiences**<br><br>The class returns to the Pathway to Discovery Chart (Resource 5.2) and discusses the role of the public historian. The public historian helps transform the two-dimensional to the three-dimensional. For this project, the class creates a museum exhibit that communicates to others the identity of their state.<br><br>The teacher discusses project goals with the students and gives them choices of museum roles based upon the interests they indicated on the unit preassessment.<br><br>Students receive the following information and directions (Resource 5.12) to set up the final project: | |

*(Continued)*

(Continued)

| Unit Sequence | Reflection |
|---|---|
| *We have spent this unit understanding how the study of state history reveals the identity of a particular place and people. We now want to make that identity known to a real audience.*<br><br>*We are going to create a state museum containing exhibits that convey our state identity. I am going to post the job descriptions for the exhibit roles, as well as general exhibit topics. Each of you will have a chance to apply for three positions. I will try to give you one of your choices so that all the jobs will be filled.*<br><br>*Now is the time to bring all of what we have collected, catalogued, and learned about our state to an audience! We will each be a part of an exhibit team that will contribute to our state history museum. The following jobs are open for your application: museum curator, public historian, exhibit designer, and museum docent.* | |
| *Curator*<br><br>Your role focuses on how the exhibit is interpreted. You are responsible for<br><br>• Formulating the exhibit concept<br>• Researching the interpretation of the historical evidence<br>• Evaluating, selecting, and developing collection<br>• Documenting<br>• Preparing the exhibition brief (the short paragraph about the exhibit)<br><br>*Public Historian*<br><br>Your role focuses on how the information for the exhibit is collected and displayed. You are responsible for<br><br>• Collecting and tagging historical evidence<br>• Working with the curator to determine the exhibit concept<br><br>*Exhibit Designer*<br><br>Your role focuses on designing and executing the museum space. You are responsible for<br><br>• Designing the space and visual elements that enhance the information you are sharing | Students may simply turn in statements for their positions. They can also fill out an application for this process. In order to assure that the class has a well-rounded museum, exhibits should represent all aspects of their state. Some examples of this might be: famous places, famous faces, key events, and defining traditions.<br><br>*Optional Extension*<br><br>The Smithsonian sponsors a website that allows students to look at historical objects and create their own virtual museum (http://objectofhistory .org). Some students may be interested in exploring this website to get ideas for their own exhibit.<br><br>*Modifications for Learner Need*<br><br>Some students may feel more comfortable working with partners for a particular job. It is important to make sure that each job has carefully delineated roles to allow all students to feel successful in making each exhibit. Students may also use specific dates and checklists.<br><br>*AID*<br><br>Students can accurately reference the resources for their exhibit using a free online tool called BibMe. Students type in their resource and it is printed in the appropriate reference style (www.bibme.org). |

| Unit Sequence | Reflection |
|---|---|
| • Working with the public historian and curator to make their "big idea" come to life<br>• Working with the writer to place the artifact signs in the appropriate places<br><br>*Museum Docent*<br><br>Your role focuses on conducting tours and encouraging visitors to explore the exhibit. You are responsible for<br><br>• Preparing a script to lead audiences through the museum exhibit<br>• Working with all members of your group to make sure that the "big idea" of the exhibit is clear to all audiences<br>• Being cheerful and willing to work with visitors to the museum exhibit | |
| **Closure**<br><br>Students have an opportunity to answer questions, look at their original preassessment choices, and apply for a job.<br><br>*Following Sessions*<br><br>After students are employed in their respective jobs for their assigned exhibit, each group follows an Action-Planning Guide (Resource 5.13) as they prepare their exhibits.<br>    As a part of the final assessment (Resource 5.14), all students complete a reflection sheet, responding to the following questions:<br><br>• What did you learn about the content as you completed this product?<br>• What did you learn about yourself as a learner by creating this product? | As a culminating event, the class can invite parents and classrooms to visit the museum exhibits. The museum docents act as guides for each exhibit. Some hold index cards to follow as each group visits their exhibit.<br><br>*Author's note:* In my class, one inventive group made an audio tour of their exhibit. They simply prerecorded the tour on a tape recorder and visitors listened to it while they looked at their display.<br><br>    The project can take a lot of managing on the teacher's part, but students begin demonstrating their creative ability to pull together all they have been learning throughout the unit. As a facilitator, the teacher needs to continue keeping students focused on the big idea behind their exhibit. It is easy to get wrapped up in the creative process and lose sight of the message the exhibit tries to convey. This is a great conversation to have with students. Many museums wrestle with this idea all the time. |

# REFERENCES

Bouchard, D. (1995). *If you're not from the prairie. . . .* New York: Simon & Schuster.

Burns, K. (1996). *The west* (Part 1) [Video series episode]. Arlington, VA: PBS.

Frasier, D. (1991). *On the day you were born.* New York: Harcourt.

Lord, B., & Lord, G. D. (Eds.). (2001). *The manual of museum exhibitions.* Walnut Creek, CA: Altimara Press.

The Curriculum Project (2010). *Product guides: Level 2 (Grades 3–5).* Retrieved from www.curriculumproject.com.

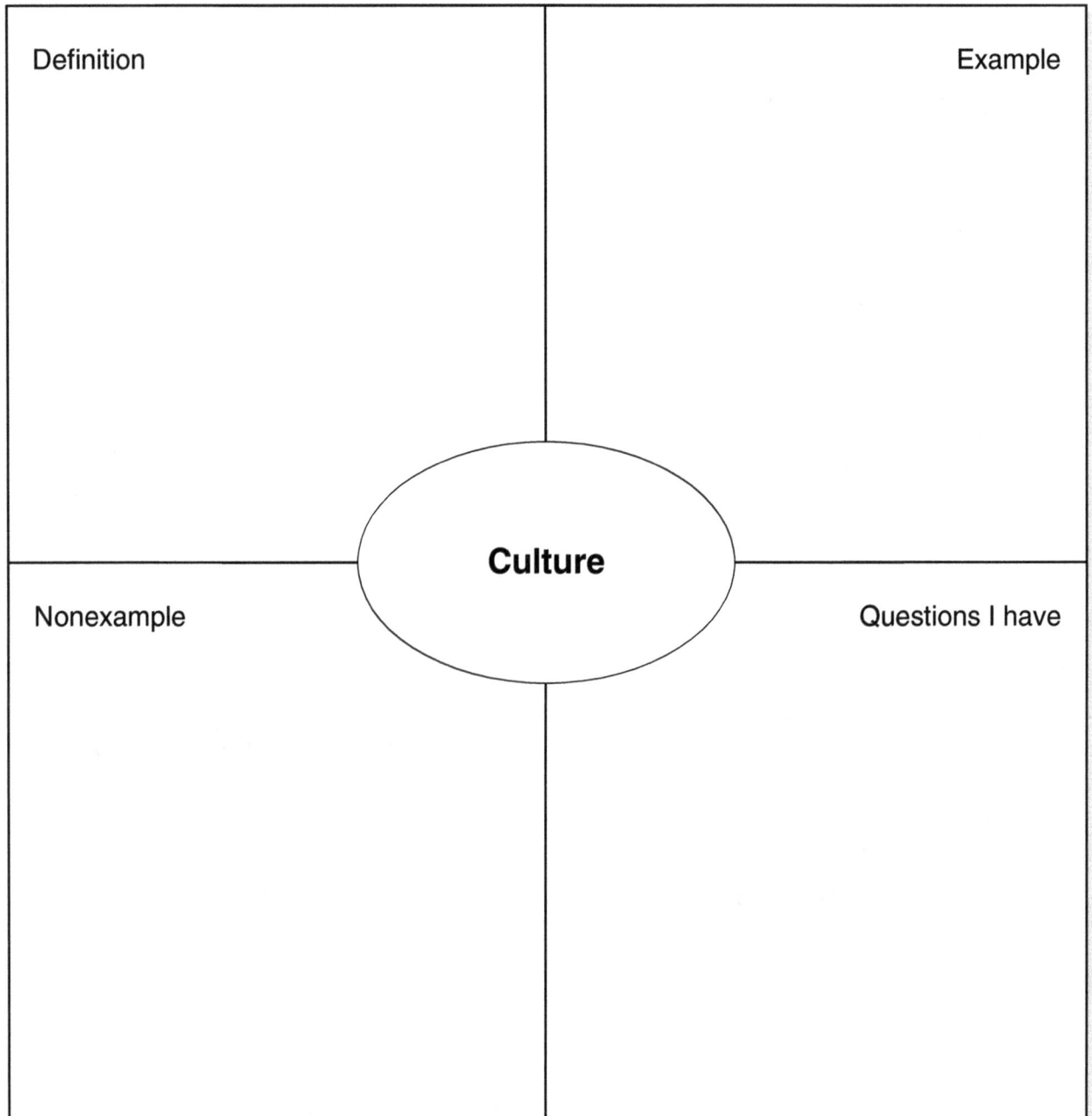

## RESOURCE 5.1: FRAYER DIAGRAM FOR CONCEPTUAL KNOWLEDGE

Example

| Definition | Example |
|---|---|
| | |

**Culture**

| Nonexample | Questions I have |
|---|---|
| | |

## RESOURCE 5.2: PATHWAY TO DISCOVERY CHART

*The Pathway of Discovery: Using the Tools of a Public Historian*

**1. Decide upon a topic or question.**

**2. Choose what evidence needs to be collected.**

Historical evidence can be *consciously* transmitted:

- Written (chronicles, inscriptions, diaries, memoirs, or genealogies)
- Oral (traditional: ballads, tales, or sagas; contemporary: interviews)
- Artwork (paintings, mosaics, portraits, scenic sculpture, coins medals, or films)

Historical evidence can be *unconsciously* transmitted:

- Human remains
- Written ("mere" records such as those from business, military, or government)
- Oral (wiretapped conversations)
- Language
- Customs and institutions
- Artifacts (artistic works or tools)

**3. Collect and examine evidence, using the following questions:**

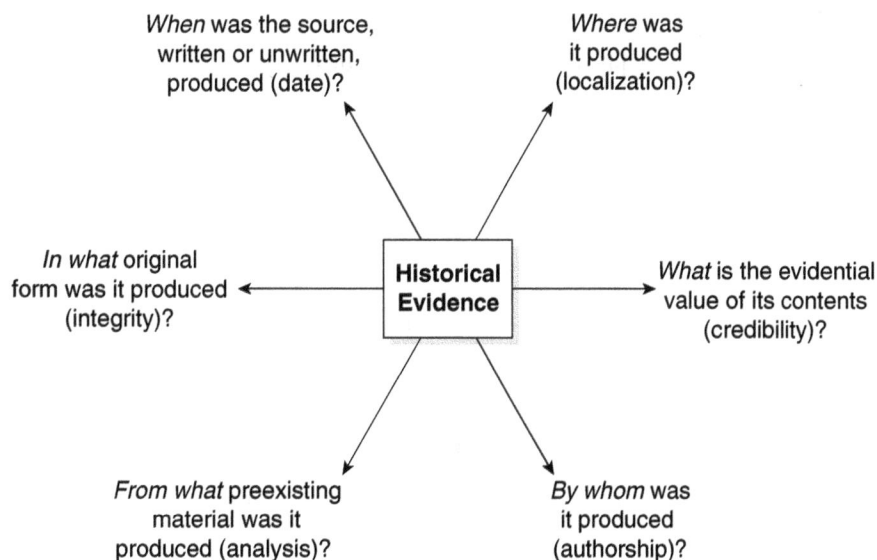

*When* was the source, written or unwritten, produced (date)?

*Where* was it produced (localization)?

*In what* original form was it produced (integrity)?

**Historical Evidence**

*What* is the evidential value of its contents (credibility)?

*From what* preexisting material was it produced (analysis)?

*By whom* was it produced (authorship)?

## RESOURCE 5.3: PRESENT YOUR FINDINGS

*Our Evidence Files: An Example of One Way to*
*Explicitly Post Principles (Our Big Ideas) for the Unit*

As the unit progresses, students often need assistance organizing the information that they have learned in a way that helps them remember the "big ideas" of the unit. One idea is to post the principles in the room under the title "Our Evidence Files." This may fit in with the idea of collecting and examining evidence as historians and following this through with collecting and examining evidence of their learning.

G3    G4    G5

G3: The study of state history reveals the *identity* of a particular place and people.

G4: Humans seek to understand their historical roots and to locate themselves in *time*.

G5: Public historians use a set of tools and methods in their research to profile, chronicle, and communicate about the history of people.

In this example, manila folders can be laminated for posting in the room. Using a transparency marker, write the principle on the folder. Under each folder, write the activities and assignments students will work on that day that tie into the principle. For Lesson 5.1 in this unit, post the Pathway to Discovery chart under the folder labeled G5. During this unit, students may even begin thinking of what to put into each folder as evidence for uncovering a principle of the unit.

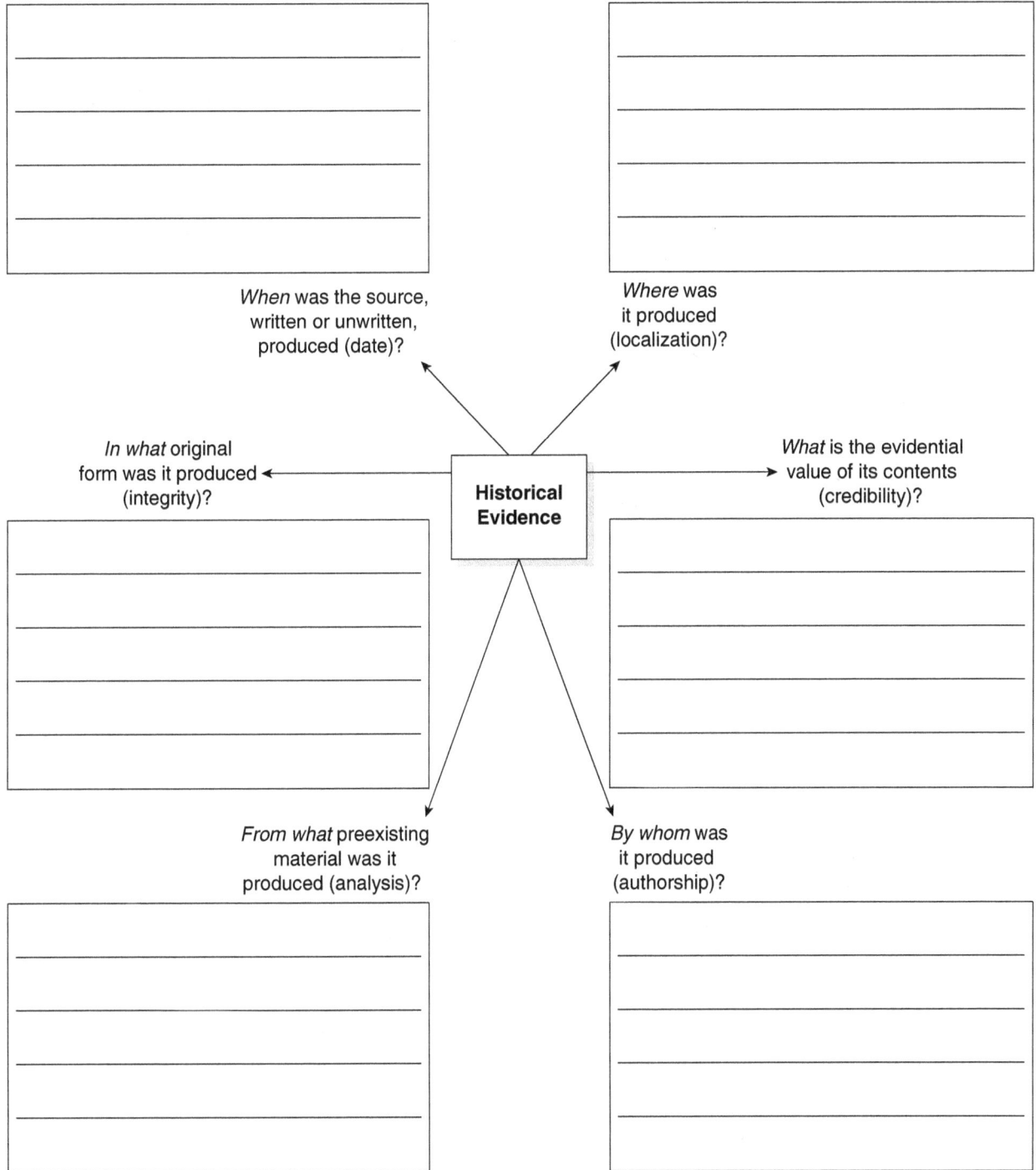

## RESOURCE 5.4: GRAPHIC ORGANIZER
## FOR STEP 3 IN THE PATHWAY TO DISCOVERY

Evidence _____

*When* was the source,
written or unwritten,
produced (date)?

*Where* was
it produced
(localization)?

*In what* original
form was it produced
(integrity)?

*What* is the evidential
value of its contents
(credibility)?

**Historical Evidence**

*From what* preexisting
material was it
produced (analysis)?

*By whom* was
it produced
(authorship)?

## RESOURCE 5.5: PARENT LETTER

Dear parents,

We are starting a new unit on our state history. As a part of this unit, students will learn that the study of state history reveals the *identity* of a particular place and people, that people seek to understand their historical roots, and that people seek to locate themselves in *time*. In order for students to understand their state identity, they will begin by learning how we communicate our own history.

We will read the book *On the Day You Were Born* by Debra Frazier. Each student will then start a mini-research project and will be asked to bring in historical evidence to communicate with others what happened on the day he or she was born. Please take a look at our list (below) of possible items you can help your child find for this project. Please mark items you and your child can collect and return this list to me by _____.

Your child will then collect items you've marked on the list and bring them to class on _____.

Thank you for your help with this project!

*(Teacher)*

------------------------------------------------------------------------------------------------

For the On the Day I Was Born project, _____ will bring

- ☐  Baby photo
- ☐  Congratulation card or shower invitation
- ☐  Birth certificate
- ☐  Baby footprint, handprint, or baby clothes
- ☐  Newspaper article or news from the day of birth
- ☐  Audio or written interview with family member talking about that day
- ☐  Baby blanket or toy
- ☐  Other _____

## RESOURCE 5.6: RUBRICS

### Basic Presentation (Rubric for Student Self-Assessment)

| Content | Is the content correct and complete? | 1 | 2 | 3 | 4 | 5 | 6 |
|---|---|---|---|---|---|---|---|
| | Is the content put together in such a way that people understand it? | 1 | 2 | 3 | 4 | 5 | 6 |
| Presentation | Did your presentation begin with an opening statement? | 1 | 2 | 3 | 4 | 5 | 6 |
| | Did the main body of your presentation give the audience a clear understanding of the topic? | 1 | 2 | 3 | 4 | 5 | 6 |
| | Were your gestures and eye contact purposeful? | 1 | 2 | 3 | 4 | 5 | 6 |
| | Was your voice clear and loud? | 1 | 2 | 3 | 4 | 5 | 6 |
| | Did the objects used in your presentation help to make the points in the presentation clearer? | 1 | 2 | 3 | 4 | 5 | 6 |
| Creativity | Is the content presented in a new way? | 1 | 2 | 3 | 4 | 5 | 6 |
| | Is your presentation done in a new way? | 1 | 2 | 3 | 4 | 5 | 6 |
| Reflection | What did you learn about the content as you completed this product? | 1 | 2 | 3 | 4 | 5 | 6 |
| | What did you learn about yourself as a learner by creating this product? | 1 | 2 | 3 | 4 | 5 | 6 |

### Advanced Presentation (Rubric for Student Self-Assessment)

| Content | Is your information accurate? | 1 | 2 | 3 | 4 | 5 | 6 |
|---|---|---|---|---|---|---|---|
| | Is your information well organized? | 1 | 2 | 3 | 4 | 5 | 6 |
| Presentation | Did you use a strong opening statement? | 1 | 2 | 3 | 4 | 5 | 6 |
| | Are the main points of your presentation supported with evidence? | 1 | 2 | 3 | 4 | 5 | 6 |
| | Did you use eye contact and gestures to enhance your presentation? | 1 | 2 | 3 | 4 | 5 | 6 |
| | Did you use a clear speaking voice? | 1 | 2 | 3 | 4 | 5 | 6 |
| | Did you use visual aids to support your main points? | 1 | 2 | 3 | 4 | 5 | 6 |
| Creativity | Did you show insight in how you related your ideas to the content? | 1 | 2 | 3 | 4 | 5 | 6 |
| | Did your enthusiasm and passion shine through in your presentation? | 1 | 2 | 3 | 4 | 5 | 6 |
| Reflection | Did you reflect on your learning from developing this product? | 1 | 2 | 3 | 4 | 5 | 6 |
| | Did you reflect on what you learned about yourself as a learner from completing this product? | 1 | 2 | 3 | 4 | 5 | 6 |

*Source:* Adapted from Roberts, J. L., & Inman, T. F. (2007). *Strategies for differentiating instruction: Best practices for the classroom.* Waco, TX: Prufrock.

Name _____

## My Brainstorming Sheet

I love Kansas!

## RESOURCE 5.8: IF YOU'RE NOT FROM . . . TEMPLATE

My choice _____

If you are not from Kansas,

You don't know _____

You can't know _____

_____

_____

_____

If you are not from Kansas,

You don't know _____

By _____

## RESOURCE 5.9: SPOT THE STEREOTYPE

*Center Task Cards*

### Task A

*(For students needing practice locating and recording resources)*

1. Pick a state that is displayed at the center. Read the quote or phrase that people have associated with that state. Add one of your own if you have one.

2. Sometimes states are given stereotypes that may be grounded in fact but don't tell the whole story of the state. Using the resources at this center, where might we locate information to help us determine the stereotype from reality? Please list all resources you found.

### Task B

*(For students needing practice determining the difference between Right There and History and Me)*

1. Pick a state that is displayed at the center. Read the quote or phrase that people have associated with that state. Add one of your own, if you have one.
2. Sometimes states are given stereotypes that may be grounded in fact but don't tell the whole story of the state. Use the resources at this center to determine the difference between fact and fiction. Fill out a Right There, or History and Me graphic organizer for the state you chose.

### Task C

*(For students who want more challenge)*

1. Pick one or more states that are displayed at the center. Read the quote or phrase that people have associated with that state. Add one of your own, if you have one—or add a display for another state not listed at this center.
2. Sometimes states are given stereotypes that may be grounded in fact but don't tell the whole story of the state. Use the resources at this center to determine the difference between fact and fiction. Fill out the Right There, or History and Me graphic organizer for the state you chose. For each "right there," please write the resource you used to find this information.

## RESOURCE 5.10: RIGHT THERE, OR HISTORY AND ME

When you look at state history or any history, there are many facts that are not debatable. Many dates and names are found "right there" in the historical evidence. There are also many facts that are debatable; they demand historians to make a decision on their own.

State _____

| Right There! | Artifact and Me |
|---|---|
|  |  |

**Resources Used**

| Title | Page Numbers or Web Address |
|---|---|
|  |  |
|  |  |
|  |  |

## RESOURCE 5.11: PRIMARY SOURCE LESSON-TASK DIRECTIONS

**Green Task**

| Observation | Knowledge | Interpretation |
|---|---|---|
| Describe what you see or have read. | What do you know about this time period, person, or event? | Describe your personal feelings and judgments about the source. Always anchor your subjective response in something that is seen. For example, "I see . . . , and it makes me think of. . . ." What can you conclude about our state? |

**Blue Task**

| Observation | Knowledge | Interpretation |
|---|---|---|
| Describe what you see or have read. Describe the "who, what, when, and where" that you can find. | What do you know about this time period, person, or event? | Describe your personal feelings and judgments about the source. Always anchor your subjective response in something that is seen. For example, "I see . . . , and it makes me think of. . . ." What can you conclude about our state? |
| Further research: What questions have this artifact raised? What is missing? What other sources might you need to answer your questions? | | |

## RESOURCE 5.12: MUSEUM EXHIBIT ROLES

### Curator

Your role focuses on how the exhibit is interpreted. You are responsible for

- Formulating the exhibit concept
- Researching the interpretation of the historical evidence
- Evaluating, selecting, and developing collection
- Documenting
- Preparing the exhibition brief (the short paragraph about the exhibit)

### Public Historian

Your role focuses on how the information for the exhibit is collected and displayed. You are responsible for

- Collecting and tagging historical evidence
- Working with the curator to determine the exhibit concept

### Exhibit Designer

Your role focuses on designing and executing the museum space. You are responsible for

- Designing the space and visual elements that enhance the information you are sharing
- Working with the public historian and curator to make their "big idea" come to life
- Working with the writer to place the artifact signs in the appropriate places

Resources you can look at to help you include http://photo2.si.edu/infoage/infoage.html and http://digitalhistory .uwo.ca/ma0607/index.php/Image:Exhibitlayout.jpg

### Museum Docent

Your role focuses on conducting tours and encouraging visitors to explore the exhibit. You are responsible for

- Preparing a script to lead audiences through the museum exhibit
- Working with all members of your group to make sure that the "big idea" of the exhibit is clear to all audiences
- Being cheerful and willing to work with visitors to the museum exhibit

## RESOURCE 5.13: ACTION-PLANNING GUIDE

An action plan is an outline or description of a project that serves as a step-by-step guide to making your team's project a success. Complete the steps below as you organize your project.

| Exhibit Topic or Theme | Team Members |
|---|---|
|  |  |

### Step 1: Define the "Big Idea" for Your Exhibit

Determining the "big idea" for your exhibit provides the focus your team needs to make things happen. Here is where you want to talk about how you want your state to be identified. What kinds of resources will you need to make this happen? List your ideas and resources.

_____

_____

_____

_____

### Step 2: Ask Questions

Finding out the important questions related to your exhibit topic ensures that you will have a set of guidelines for taking action in accomplishing your mission.

_____

_____

_____

_____

### Step 3: Design Activities, Create Timelines, and Assign Roles

Describe the actions that will help the team answer the questions developed in the previous step. Put together a step-by-step outline or plan for each task associated with each activity. This plan should include which team members will participate, when the activity will take place, and where it will happen.

| Action | Who | When | Where |
|---|---|---|---|
|  |  |  |  |
|  |  |  |  |

### Step 4: List Materials

List the materials and resources your team members need to complete the project.

| Human Resources | Materials | Equipment | References |
|---|---|---|---|
|  |  |  |  |
|  |  |  |  |

### Step 5: Implement Your Plan

Begin your team's plan by implementing the activities that you listed in Step 3. Keep track of your team progress by recording findings in a notebook.

_____

_____

_____

_____

### Step 6: Develop the Product

Determine the type of exhibit that is best for the type of project that you selected. In certain cases, some of you will create a virtual exhibit or audio tour as products, while others may create a traditional artifact-centered exhibit. Describe the type of exhibit you will create.

_____

_____

_____

_____

### Step 7: Reflect

Don't wait until the last minute to evaluate your team project. Take time to reflect along the way. This way, you can revise your plans and make the necessary adjustments to ensure success.

_____

_____

_____

_____

_Source:_ Adapted from Leppien, J.H., & Bobbit, C. (2006). Using biography and autobiography to understand challenge, choice and chance. In C. A. Tomlinson, S. N. Kaplan, J. H. Purcell, J. H. Leppien, D. E. Burns, and C.A. Strickland (Eds.), _The parallel curriculum in the classroom, book 2: Units for application across the content areas, K–12_ (pages 293–362). Thousand Oaks, CA: Corwin.

## RESOURCE 5.14: MUSEUM EXHIBIT GROUP RUBRIC

| Content | Is the content correct and complete? | 1 | 2 | 3 | 4 | 5 | 6 |
|---|---|---|---|---|---|---|---|
| | Is the content put together in such a way that people understand it? | 1 | 2 | 3 | 4 | 5 | 6 |
| Exhibit | Did the exhibit remain true to its "big idea"? | 1 | 2 | 3 | 4 | 5 | 6 |
| | Did all artifacts in the exhibit give the audience a clear understanding of the topic? | 1 | 2 | 3 | 4 | 5 | 6 |
| | Did the labels and signs help to make the points clear? | 1 | 2 | 3 | 4 | 5 | 6 |
| | Was the information accurate? | 1 | 2 | 3 | 4 | 5 | 6 |
| | Did the team members each work together to fulfill their roles? | 1 | 2 | 3 | 4 | 5 | 6 |
| Creativity | Is the content seen in a new way? | 1 | 2 | 3 | 4 | 5 | 6 |
| | Is the presentation done in a new way? | 1 | 2 | 3 | 4 | 5 | 6 |
| Reflection | What did you learn about the content as you completed this product? | 1 | 2 | 3 | 4 | 5 | 6 |
| | What did you learn about yourself as a learner by creating this product? | 1 | 2 | 3 | 4 | 5 | 6 |

# 6

# Conundrums in Criminalistics

Clues, Culprits, and Conclusions (Grades 4–5)

*Lisa DaVia Rubenstein*

## INTRODUCTION TO THE UNIT

### Overview of the Unit

This unit is designed for fourth-, fifth-, and sixth-grade enrichment classes to occur in a once-a-week pull-out class, lasting 90 minutes per session for ten weeks. There are a total of nine lessons. However, a teacher can easily adapt the unit to teach daily over a period of three to four weeks.

The purpose of Conundrums in Criminalistics is to teach the knowledge of the field of forensics, the methods of the practicing forensic scientist, the connections between forensic science and other disciplines, and the relationship between the student and the field. The foundation of the unit is the Core Curriculum because it is built on key facts, concepts, principles, and skills that are essential to the forensic science discipline. The unit, however, branches into the Curriculum of Connections within the opening lesson and the Curriculum of Practice throughout the body of the unit. The Curriculum of Identity also plays an important role as the students debrief at the end of the unit and reflect on the impact it had on them.

The unit begins by examining all types of knowledge and seeing where criminalistics fits within the scope of all knowledge, using the Curriculum of Connections. This lesson connects what the students will learn within the unit to other disciplines to find similarities between them and to see the varying perspectives of the disciplines. The unit progresses into examining how practicing professionals approach problems in the field, which brings in the Curriculum of Practice. The unit then examines specific subfields and techniques within the field. Finally, the unit allows students to talk to a practicing professional and use their knowledge to solve a simulated crime.

## Guiding Questions for Each Parallel

The questions within this unit were derived from each parallel of the Parallel Curriculum Model (PCM).

### Core Curriculum

- What constitutes a valid conclusion, and how can we verify it?
- Does science produce truth?
- How much evidence is enough to draw a conclusion?

### Curriculum of Connections

- How do our perceptions affect the way we view the world?
- How do our questions lead and guide our search for knowledge?
- What are the different types of knowledge? Where does forensic science fit within the scope of all knowledge?

### Curriculum of Practice

- What is the purpose of forensic science? What are the specialties within the field?
- How is forensic science studied? What kind of questions do forensic scientists ask and answer?
- Which processes and skills are essential in analyzing evidence?
- How is evidence collected? What are the procedures and experiments that forensic scientists use to analyze a crime?
- How is evidence used to solve crimes? What is the relationship between evidence and truth?

### Curriculum of Identity

- What part of the field is most personally appealing?

The unit fits best within a science curriculum, but it is an interdisciplinary unit that requires the students to write, read, reason, create, and think logically. It fits well at the beginning of the year when science teachers tend to go over the scientific method. This unit surely captures the students' imaginations and introduces them to a specific scientific discipline that most may not even classify as science. It weaves in many different types of science as it looks at bugs (entomology), motion (physics), chromatography (chemistry), and DNA (microbiology).

## Background Information for the Unit

This unit assumes that the students know very little about forensic science. The most challenging lesson conceptually is the DNA section of Lesson 6.6. Students may need more support in coming to understand DNA. Teachers are encouraged to consult a fingerprint expert in advance to confirm or enhance their own understanding.

The unit is often a favorite for students because they enjoy the experiments, the simulations, and the technology component. The questions are very challenging and may push students to think at higher levels than they may have in the past.

*Author's note:* Conundrums in Criminalistics was truly my students' idea. They desperately wanted to take a course in forensic science at a nearby museum, but the course was already full. Hearing the disappointment in their voices, I thought that I should be able to design a similar yet unique experience for them.

As is the case with any unit of study, there are specific materials that are recommended to successfully implement this unit. The following list is noted by individual lesson.

### Lesson 6.1

- Bulletin board area with the title "The Universe of Knowledge"
- Galaxies, stars, planets, and moon pictures to hang in appropriate places as the class constructs the universe
- Stapler, tape, or Velcro
- Bags for small groups including everyday items: toilet paper, a few pieces of candy, a picture of a dog, and a necklace

### Lesson 6.2

- Detective story DVD (Any detective story can work, but some of the current *CSI* stories can be quite gruesome. *The Adventures of Sherlock Holmes* works well (boxed DVD set collection, but the box set also is not necessary, only one episode that fits the class.)
- DVD player
- *Crime Files: Four-Minute Forensic Mysteries,* by Jeremy Brown (2006) (Other forensic mysteries can substitute for this book.)
- Blank class poster

### Lesson 6.3

- Computers with Internet connectivity

### Lesson 6.4

- Possible video download: http://www.videojug.com/interview/documenting-a-crime-scene-2
- Yellow streamers or police tape
- Poster paper
- Crime scene re-creation: masking tape to mark the location of the body, telephone, one large earring, cigarette butt, tube of lipstick, note ("Meet me at 9:00 tonight at Buck's Place. Love, Sam"), a turned over chair (the teacher can re-create the scene as appropriate)
- Evidence bags (either ziplock bags with a sticker that has room to write the date, time, who handled the evidence, description, and location; or official police evidence bags)
- Gloves
- Tape measures for students

- Rulers
- Sample maps
- Calculators
- Digital or Polaroid camera

### Lesson 6.5

- Check Mystery: magnifying glass, documents in question, black pens, prep work (explanation follows), ruler, protractor, and paper clips
- Chromatography Mystery (in each basket): beaker (or a clear glass cup), wire, hole puncher, water, three paper clips, ruler, pencil, filter paper with samples, and paper towels
- Poster paper

### Lesson 6.6

- Four shoe prints, a pan of dirt with one of the four prints in it, casting boards, plaster of paris, water, bowl, and one physical shoe
- Paper, scissors, tape, and computers (A poster of the genome works well.)

### Lesson 6.7

- Serology: ketchup in cups, spoons, newspapers, cardboard, plastic coverings, protractors, and tape measures
- Fingerprinting: pencils, tape, and fingerprinting chart
- Online resources and books for students' individual evidence projects

### Lesson 6.8

- Forensic scientist and tools (and a prescheduled guest from the local police)

### Lesson 6.9

- An integrated crime scene case (The story in Resource 6.9 from *Court TV*'s website [www.courttv.com/forensics_curriculum/about.html] is adjusted for this unit, but Great Explorations in Math and Science [GEMS] from the University of California, Berkeley produces an excellent case for the students to solve.)
- At the crime scene: ransom note, fingerprints, footprints, a puddle, dog hair, and human hair
- Three different types of pens
- Three different shoe prints
- Rubbing alcohol and water for use in chromatography
- Filter paper
- Yellow streamers or police tape
- Camera (if possible)
- Evidence bags
- Sketch paper
- A dropper
- Tape measure

# CONTENT FRAMEWORK

## Organizing Concepts

### Macroconcepts

M1: Systems

M2: Relationships

M3: Perspective

### Discipline-Specific Concepts

C1: Organization

C2: Models

C3: Cause and effect

C4: Association (linking evidence to suspect or conclusion)

## Principles

P1: A relationship exists between evidence and conclusions, and in order to establish that relationship, the evidence must be scientifically analyzed through proper identification, collection, and experimentation.

P2: Astute observations are essential in order to arrive at an accurate conclusion.

P3: We must ask the right questions in order to get the right answer.

P4: Our perspective affects how we process new information. Two different individuals may assert different conclusions when given the same situation.

P5: There is no standard procedure that works all the time in every situation. Thinking is allowed.

P6: In every discipline, there is a structure with general principles and specific modes of study.

## National or State Standards

### Pennsylvania State Standards

Science and Technology

3.2.4 Inquiry and Design

   A. Identify and use the nature of scientific and technological knowledge.

      o Distinguish between a scientific fact and a belief.

      o Provide clear explanations that account for observations and results.

      o Relate how new information can change existing perceptions.

B. Describe objects in the world using the five senses.

  o Recognize observational descriptors from each of the five senses (e.g., see-blue, feel-rough).
  o Use observations to develop a descriptive vocabulary.

C. Recognize and use the elements of scientific inquiry to solve problems.

  o Generate questions about objects, organisms and/or events that can be answered through scientific investigations.
  o Design an investigation.
  o Conduct an experiment.
  o State a conclusion that is consistent with the information.

### National Science Standards

NS.5–8.1 Science as Inquiry

As a result of activities in Grades 5–8, all students should develop

  o Abilities necessary to do scientific inquiry
  o Understandings about scientific inquiry

NS.5–8.7 History and Nature of Science

As a result of activities in Grades 5–8, all students should develop understanding of

  o Science as a human endeavor
  o Nature of science
  o History of science

## Skills

S1: Design

S2: Analyze

S3: Infer

S4: Present

S5: Question

S6: Conclude

S7: Compare and contrast

# UNIT ASSESSMENTS

| Preassessment | Preassessment graphic organizer |
| --- | --- |
| Formative Assessment | Journal entries, contributions to discussions, mini-projects |
| Summative Assessment | Final crime scene analysis |

## Preassessment

The preassessment addresses the main components of the discipline in a very open manner in order to allow the students to demonstrate as much as they know. It can be used to guide or change the content of the lessons within the unit.

## Formative Assessments

The formative assessments occur on a daily basis and vary from lesson to lesson. Most lessons have a journal prompt or a discussion to help evaluate the key principles and concepts addressed that day. There are also mini-projects throughout the unit that give the students choices on the content, process, and product. These also contain individual challenges for students who grasp the content quickly or want to delve deeper into the field to work on throughout the unit.

## Summative Assessment

The final assessment is most like an authentic assessment within the field of forensic science. The students ask their own questions, design experiments, and come to a conclusion based on the results. It is evaluated based on the thought processes carried out by the students, including the types of questions, the experiments proposed, and the support for the conclusion. Whether or not they actually solve the mystery correctly is not as important.

A generic rubric is provided at the end of the unit to evaluate the content, process, and product that an individual demonstrates or produces. For each individual assignment, the teacher should put in the expected principles for the content and the skills for the process to evaluate the product (Resource 6.10).

# UNIT SEQUENCE AND TEACHER REFLECTION

## LESSON 6.1: THE UNIVERSE OF KNOWLEDGE

**Length:** One 90-minute session

| Unit Sequence | Reflection |
|---|---|
| **Concepts**<br><br>• Systems<br>• Relationships<br>• Perspective | |
| **Principles**<br><br>• All aspects of our world can be explored through the five types of knowledge.<br>• Our perspective affects how we process new information.<br>• We must ask the right questions to get the right answers. | This lesson draws on the Curriculum of Connections. It looks at all disciplines and what they have in common: they all ask questions. The questions are quite different, but all knowledge starts with a question. |

(Continued)

| Unit Sequence | Reflection |
|---|---|
| **Skills**<br><br>• Develop relevant questions.<br>• Seek relationships.<br>• Brainstorm. | |
| **Standards**<br><br>*PA*<br><br>3.2.4 A, 3.2.4 C<br><br>*National*<br><br>NS. 5–8.1, NS.5–8.7 | |
| **Guiding Questions**<br><br>• How do our perspectives affect the way we view the world?<br>• How do our questions lead and guide our search for knowledge?<br>• What are the different types of knowledge?<br>• Where does forensic science fit within the scope of all knowledge? | |
| **Lesson Structure**<br><br>1. Examine types of knowledge.<br><br>2. Construct the universe of knowledge.<br><br>3. Examine the bag of items and review question cards.<br><br>4. Complete preassessment.<br><br>5. Introduce forensic science and its location within the universe. | This lesson is designed to help students to see the big picture. There is a systematic way in which knowledge is organized. The unit contains knowledge that has its own place within the system. It is helpful for students to glimpse the whole system before looking at its pieces. |
| **Introduction**<br><br>The teacher begins the lesson by telling students to close their eyes.<br><br>*Everyone close your eyes for a moment. Imagine all of the information you have learned this summer, last year, and throughout your entire life.* (Pause) *Open your eyes. What pictures did you see? What learning experiences have you had?*<br><br>The teacher records students' answers on the board. If discussion slows, the teacher can ask about the students' favorite projects, book topics, and interests. | This introduction is designed to help the students see how much information is available and to pique their interest in the information they will study by tying it to information they already have. |
| **Teaching Strategies and Learning Experiences**<br><br>After the discussion winds down, the teacher looks at the board and remarks that it is "sort of messy." | It is important for students to relate to the concept of organization and relationships within a system. They need to hook that idea onto something to which they |

| Unit Sequence | Reflection |
|---|---|
| *Think of your room at home. Some of you are very neat and some of you are a little messy. Although we may hate to admit it, when our rooms our messy, it is sometimes hard to find what we need. This happens to me frequently when I look for my keys. If I simply had a specific place for them, it would make my life so much easier.*<br><br>*It is very similar with this board. If I need to find a certain piece of knowledge, I can search each row and column, or I can organize the knowledge logically. Now, I would like to give you the opportunity to clean up this knowledge.*<br><br>Then the teacher organizes the class into partners with the task to design an organizing structure for all of this knowledge. The students will have about 10 minutes to create their own organizational structure, and then there will be about 15 minutes for them to share their ideas. As the students share, the teacher continues to ask the students to explain why they grouped their ideas the way they did.<br><br>The teacher then hangs each of the students' organizational structures on the board and picks pieces from the students' ideas that fit with the universe of knowledge construct. Once the basic organizational structure (logic and mathematics, philosophy, science, and history or humanities) and any of the subcategories the students named are defined and placed on the permanent bulletin board, the teacher distributes the official names for the remaining subjects. The students then have an opportunity to place the names where they think the names belong. They also add their own. | already can relate, such as organizing their rooms.<br><br>As they work, the teacher circulates, asking the groups questions to make sure they have a structure that they are following. Some students may decide their structure is alphabetical order or number of letters, and they may need a little scaffolding to think about connecting fields of study.<br><br>*Author's note:* The universe is my organizational structure in which the universe represents all of knowledge and the galaxies are the overarching categories: logic and mathematics, philosophy, science, and history or humanities. Within the galaxies, there are stars that get more specific. Logic and mathematics may have stars labeled number operations, geometry, measurement, proofs, algebra, and data analysis. Then there are planets around those stars, so number operations include addition, subtraction, multiplication, and division. If needed, there are moons around the planets.<br><br>It is important for students to construct their own structure and that the teacher really tries to blend ideas from everyone to create the bulletin board. |
| The teacher explains that there are many possibilities within this universe (flexibility). For example, art can be placed under the humanities because it is something humans have constructed, but it can also be placed under anthropology if looking at how art describes a culture. The teacher then asks students for several other examples. Some topics require a trip to a few different areas in the universe (interdependence). For example, an architect not only needs to know physics, engineering, and math, but also needs to understand the culture in which the building is created. The teacher again asks for several examples.<br><br>Each discipline has its own purpose and asks its own questions to reach that purpose (individuality). The teacher asks the students to group themselves according to interest in each basic knowledge type (logic and mathematics, philosophy, science, and history or humanities). The teacher gives each group a bag of items and question cards, explaining that each discipline will look at the world differently and ask different questions. The teacher gives an example. | This section asks the students to take on the disciplines' perspectives. This will be challenging at first as they struggle with looking at everyday items from a different perspective. It connects the principle of asking questions to multiple disciplines. |

*(Continued)*

(Continued)

| Unit Sequence | Reflection |
|---|---|
| *Questions are the most important part of any field. I recently read about a little girl who came home from school every day to her mother, who asked her if she had asked any good questions in school that day. Her mother believed more than anything else that it was important for her daughter to ask good questions.*<br><br>*First, I will ask you, "Have you asked any important questions in school today?" Why do you think questions are so important? Here is a lightbulb. A chemist may ask how the atoms move when the light bulb is plugged in. A dancer may wonder how to use the lightbulb in motion as a prop. A mathematician may ask how much space the light bulb takes up. These are all very different questions about the same object. Why do you think that happens?*<br><br>*Now you are going to examine several objects and ask questions about them from your chosen discipline's perspective. Brainstorm many varied and numerous questions. Then we will share them and hang them up.*<br><br>The students then open their bags and formulate questions that their discipline would ask about the object. They will have about 10 minutes to think and write questions and 10 minutes to share. After their discussion, the teacher explains that throughout this unit they are expected to always be thinking of appropriate questions.<br><br>*Travel Plan*<br><br>*As we begin this new unit of study, we need to create a travel plan to help us direct our study through the universe of knowledge. First, we need to define criminalistics. Criminalistics is the study of the evaluation of evidence in the commission of crimes and dealing with the detections of crime and the apprehension of criminals. Now we need to decide where this fits within the universe of knowledge. Remember, there could be several locations.*<br><br>The students then formulate a travel plan for where they need to go to truly understand criminalistics. | This plan illustrates flexibility and interdependence. Criminalistics uses mathematics, different pieces of science (chemistry, physics, and others), and even psychology.<br><br>After completing the small group task, the teacher distributes the forensic science preassessment (Resource 6.1) and asks students to complete all that they can. An analysis of students' responses reveals what students already know or do not know, and what areas of interest they want to pursue. The data also suggests pairings or groupings that will be advantageous during the course of the unit. |
| **Closure**<br><br>The students record information throughout the unit in their "conundrum journals," which can be simple notebooks. Each lesson ends with at least 10 minutes of reflective writing and sharing. This lesson's questions include the following:<br><br>• What is the purpose of the universe of knowledge? Why is it important, and how is it organized?<br>• Which type of knowledge interests you the most? Why?<br>• Why are questions important?<br>• What are some questions in any field that you are curious about?<br>• What questions do you have within the criminalistics field? | Throughout the closure discussion, it is important to keep the students thinking about the system of knowledge, the relationships between types of knowledge, and the perspectives of that field. |

| Unit Sequence | Reflection |
|---|---|
| **Homework and Individual Challenges**<br><br>Students record one good question about any subject every day that week.<br><br>   If time, students can begin a web quest and be responsible for each part as an individual or within a group situation. The following link from San Diego City Schools can assist: http://projects.edtech.sandi.net/kearny/forensic/. | The teacher can give the students file cards or mini-notebooks to record their various questions throughout the week. This likely helps them avoid interrupting the class every time they have a question. After the class, the teacher can sit down with the particular student and discuss questions. |

## LESSON 6.2: THOUGHTS AND TOOLS OF THE TRADE

**Length:** One 90-minute session

| Unit Sequence | Reflection |
|---|---|
| **Concepts**<br><br>• Systems<br>• Relationships<br>• Perspective | |
| **Principles**<br><br>• A relationship exists between evidence and conclusions. In order to establish that relationship, the evidence must be scientifically analyzed through proper identification, collection, and experimentation.<br>• Astute observations are essential in order to arrive at an accurate conclusion.<br>• Our perspective affects how we process new information.<br>• There is no standard procedure that works all the time in every situation. Thinking is allowed. | |
| **Skills**<br><br>• Compare and contrast.<br>• Seek relationships.<br>• Apply inductive thinking.<br>• Analyze data. | |
| **Standards**<br><br>*PA*<br><br>3.2.4 A, 3.2.4 B, 3.2.4 C<br><br>*National*<br><br>NS.5–8.1, NS.5–8.7 | |

*(Continued)*

(Continued)

| Unit Sequence | Reflection |
|---|---|
| **Guiding Questions**<br><br>• What constitutes a valid conclusion, and how can we verify it?<br>• How do our questions lead and guide our search for knowledge?<br>• How do our perspectives affect the way we view the world?<br>• How much evidence is enough to draw a conclusion?<br>• What is the purpose of forensic science?<br>• How is forensic science studied? What kinds of questions do forensic scientists ask and answer?<br>• What processes and skills are essential in analyzing evidence?<br>• How is evidence collected? What are the procedures and experiments that forensic scientists use to analyze a crime?<br>• How is evidence used to solve crimes? What is the relationship between evidence and truth? | |
| **Lesson Structure**<br><br>1. Examine the discipline's methodology by reading and discussing fictional cases.<br><br>2. Watch detective story and analyze the detective's processes.<br><br>3. Apply knowledge to create new fictional detectives. | Through this lesson students identify the tools, language, and processes that people in the field use. It is important for students to identify these themselves, rather than the teacher dictating the discipline's characteristics. |
| **Introduction**<br><br>The teacher begins the lesson by asking the students to recall the universe of knowledge.<br><br>*Let's rewind our thinking back to the universe of knowledge. What is the purpose of the universe of knowledge? How is each discipline similar or different from one another? What types of questions did you write down this week in your conundrum journal? How did your questions change what you learned this week?* (Discussion)<br><br>*For this entire unit of study, we are all going to become forensic scientists. That means we have to learn the discipline of forensic science. How do you think we can learn to think like forensic scientists?* (Answers recorded on board)<br><br>*Today we are going to look at several cases that exhibit forensic scientists and how they operate.* | The introduction reviews the ideas of system and relationships, and then helps the students focus on the discipline at hand. |
| **Teaching Strategies and Learning Experiences**<br><br>The teacher reviews the analysis sheet with the students before they begin examining specific cases, prompting the students to think about why those categories are on the analysis sheet. | The analysis sheet is a great tool to look at any discipline. It guides the study of how practicing professionals operate in the field. Resource 6.2 provides a sample analysis sheet. |

| Unit Sequence | Reflection |
|---|---|
| *Crime Cases*<br><br>The teacher makes a few copies of several of the cases in the book *Crime Files, Four-Minute Forensic Mysteries* by Jeremy Brown (2006). Then the students group themselves according to which case they would like to read. The students read the cases aloud or independently. The students then work within their groups to fill out the analysis sheet for their specific case. It is important to remind students that their writing doesn't have to be complete sentences. After all groups finish, they share their findings with the entire class. The teacher records what each group found on a class poster. | This experience allows students to choose which type of case they are most interested in and the choices also enhance interest. In addition, it allows for greater group analysis by covering more mysteries than if the whole class only read one. |
| The teacher then shows the students one episode from a detective story. The teacher tells the students that they will return for further discussion, but there is now a very famous forensic scientist for them to see in action. (The teacher can choose an episode based on appropriate content.) While the episode plays, students fill in another analysis sheet for the story. | *The Adventures of Sherlock Holmes* works well, because Sherlock Holmes does not always point out the clues that he gathers until the end. The teacher may ask students to take notes of clues they think are important, or questions they think he asks, even if he doesn't verbalize those ideas. |
| **Closure**<br><br>After adding the students' thoughts from the film to the class poster, the class compares and contrasts different methodological strategies and tools that forensic scientists use, seeking relationships between the cases to come up with the overarching principles of forensic science and the specific studies within the general discipline. A few guiding questions help the students with the challenge of thinking about their experiences.<br><br>*Teacher Guiding Questions*<br><br>*Let's compare, find the similarities between, and contrast, find the differences between, the different cases we have read and viewed. What words did the different forensic scientists use? What kind of questions did they ask? Did they all follow a certain format for solving the crime? What kind of evidence did they examine?*<br><br>Here the teacher can discuss how the different types of evidence all have their own special field within forensic science. For example, a dactylographer studies fingerprints.<br><br>*Can you imagine how these scientists are thinking? Did any of them approach a case similarly? How did they draw conclusions based on the evidence? Do you think the evidence was strong enough to warrant that conclusion? Could the evidence be interpreted in another way? Would any additional evidence make another conclusion possible?* | This closure activity specifically introduces several new thinking skills as ways for students to further process the content they learned through the body of the lesson. The students compare and contrast, use inductive thinking, and infer based on evidence. Depending on the ability level, the group may look at these skills in more depth with more examples, or the group may split into small groups and discuss these ideas in more independent settings than a whole-class discussion. |

*(Continued)*

(Continued)

| Unit Sequence | Reflection |
|---|---|
| The teacher then explains that the students just used an inductive thinking skill. This is a skill that many forensic scientists must use often to be successful in their jobs. This skill applies specific observations from one example to the general study of forensic knowledge.<br><br>*How did the individual forensic scientists use this skill?* | |
| **Homework/Individual Challenges**<br><br>*For homework, use your new knowledge in forensic science to create your own fictional detective with a crime to solve. Use your analysis page to review how forensic scientists think and make sure your detective shares some characteristics with the forensic scientists we observed today. Also, consider how your detective is different from these detectives.*<br><br>The teacher may also use the following prompts to assist students in creating their stories.<br><br>1. *Fictional forensic scientist.* Your forensic scientist is at the scene of one of the same crimes that you have witnessed today, but finds a new piece of evidence. Record how this new piece of evidence changes the investigation. Make sure to record your forensic scientist's thinking throughout the story.<br>2. *Fictional forensic scientist.* Your forensic scientist is in a completely new crime location. What is the crime? What kind of evidence is involved? Are there any witnesses? What kind of thought process does your forensic scientist follow? Are there any misleading clues? | The fictional story challenge relates back to the key concepts of the field. The students use the language, tools, and thinking skills or processes that the practicing professionals use in order to create their own fictional story. It also allows students who enjoy using their creativity a way to demonstrate their understanding. |

## LESSON 6.3: WHO'S WHO IN FORENSIC SCIENCE?

**Length:** One 90-minute session

| Unit Sequence | Reflection |
|---|---|
| **Concepts**<br><br>• Systems<br>• Relationships<br>• Perspective | |
| **Principles**<br><br>• We must ask the right questions in order to get the right answer.<br>• In every discipline, there is a structure with general principles and specific modes of study. | |

| Unit Sequence | Reflection |
|---|---|
| • A relationship exists between evidence and conclusions, and in order to establish that relationship, the evidence must be scientifically analyzed through proper identification, collection, and experimentation. | |
| **Skills**<br><br>• Develop relevant questions.<br>• Gather data and evidence.<br>• Record, organize, and compile data from specific tests.<br>• Seek relationships.<br>• Use inductive thinking.<br>• Analyze data.<br>• Predict next steps and draw conclusions. | |
| **Standards**<br><br>*PA*<br><br>3.2.4 A, 3.2.4 B, 3.2.4 C<br><br>*National*<br><br>NS.5–8.1, NS.5–8.7 | |
| **Guiding Questions**<br><br>• What constitutes a valid conclusion, and how can we verify it?<br>• How do our questions lead and guide our search for knowledge?<br>• What are the specialties within the forensic science field?<br>• How is forensic science studied? What kind of questions do forensic scientists ask and answer?<br>• How is evidence collected? What are the procedures and experiments that forensic scientists use to analyze crime? | |
| **Lesson Structure**<br><br>1. Look at the different specialties within the field.<br>2. Assume roles of one of these specialists in order to solve a crime.<br>3. Work together, combining knowledge in order to come to a conclusion. | |
| **Introduction**<br><br>*Personal Story*<br><br>Teachers may use the following anecdote as a model.<br><br>*When I was little, I remember that I didn't want help with anything. I was quite capable of putting on my own socks and making my own lunch, but "thanks anyway Mom." This independent streak has carried over into my adult life. I still want to work by myself on group projects. Do you think this is a good characteristic or not?* (Discussion) | Within any field, there are subfields or specialties that work together to further the field. This is a key concept needed to understand the structure of all disciplines. For example, the medical field has genetic researchers, drug researchers, scientific equipment researchers, pharmacists, doctors, and administrators who work together to further their field or to help a patient. |

*(Continued)*

(Continued)

| Unit Sequence | Reflection |
|---|---|
| *Now, let's think about our universe of knowledge. Do you think someone could know everything about even one specific galaxy? Take a few minutes and think about this question, then pair up and discuss, and finally we will share as an entire class. In your pairs, also ask the following questions:*<br><br>*What if you are responsible for knowing everything about a specific field such as forensic science? What would be the consequences of this idea?* | Students easily relate to this introduction and it provides them with an interactive opportunity to participate. |
| **Teaching Strategies and Learning Experiences**<br><br>*Each one of you will be placed within a team of five students. Each student will be given a role card and take on the role of the specialist within the forensic science field.*<br><br>*A crime has been committed. I am going to give you a picture of the scene of the crime, but you need to look at it through your specialist's eyes. You will research your assigned role, ask me questions regarding the current crime, collect evidence, make conclusions, and finally work with the other students to solve the crime.*<br><br>The Interactive Crime Simulation is found in Resource 6.3 along with the roles and websites that students research to find out about the specialist.<br><br>The teacher divides students into groups of five, and distributes a role card to each student, explaining that all of the sites to explore are listed on one website, Filamentality, www.kn.pacbell.com/wired/fil/ (AT&T, 2010).<br><br>On this site, the teacher can create hotlists to eliminate students' wasted time on the web looking for appropriate sites. They complete their research, record their answers in their notebooks, and formulate appropriate questions. When they ask the appropriate question for their field, the teacher can hand them a clue or simply verbally tell them the clues. They then formulate some predictions while the other fields are also getting their clues. Then the group meets and puts all the clues together. Last, they develop their group conclusion report. | This experience allows students to become practicing professionals. They do not obtain any information unless they ask appropriate questions. They analyze a scene of a crime just like their assigned specialist would, from the specialist's perspective. They then work with other specialists to form a conclusion.<br><br>The Filamentality website is a suggestion to make visiting the other websites easier for students. The students can also type in their given sites. The teacher may also add sites to the suggested ones. The sites introduce students to the tools the specialists use and the types of questions they ask. |
| **Closure**<br><br>Once all groups are finished, the teacher leads a small discussion on their findings. Several questions can be asked in a discussion format and several can be for students to write about in their journals. Debriefing questions include the following:<br><br>• What constitutes a valid conclusion, and how can we verify it? How do our questions lead and guide our search for knowledge?<br>• What are the specialties within the forensic science field? | The closing discussion summarizes what the students learned during their inquiry- and inductive-based learning activity. |

| Unit Sequence | Reflection |
|---|---|
| • How is forensic science studied?<br>• What kind of questions do forensic scientists ask and answer?<br>• How is evidence collected?<br>• What are the procedures and experiments that forensic scientists use to analyze crime?<br>• How is evidence used to solve crime?<br>• What is the relationship between evidence and truth?<br>• Why is it important to have specialties within a field? | |
| **Homework/Individual Challenge**<br><br>Students complete a RAFT assignment (Resource 6.4) in order to assess or demonstrate their understanding of the role that specialists contribute in solving crimes. | This challenge is interesting for students because they choose which role to play and complete that strip for that role. It reinforces a specialty field within forensic science. |

## LESSON 6.4: SCENE ANALYSIS AND EVIDENCE DOCUMENTATION

**Length:** One 90-minute session

| Unit Sequence | Reflection |
|---|---|
| **Concepts**<br><br>• Systems<br>• Relationships<br>• Perspective | |
| **Principles**<br><br>• A relationship exists between evidence and conclusions, and in order to establish that relationship, the evidence must be scientifically analyzed through proper identification, collection, and experimentation.<br>• Astute observations are essential in order to arrive at accurate conclusions.<br>• We must ask the right questions in order to get the right answers. | |
| **Skills**<br><br>• Develop relevant questions.<br>• Gather evidence.<br>• Record, organize, and compile evidence.<br>• Draw conclusions.<br>• Use observation techniques.<br>• Seek relationships.<br>• Apply inductive thinking. | |

*(Continued)*

(Continued)

| Unit Sequence | Reflection |
|---|---|
| **Standards**<br><br>*PA*<br>3.2.4 A, 3.2.4 B, 3.2.4 C<br><br>*National*<br>NS.5–8.1, NS.5–8.7 | |
| **Guiding Questions**<br><br>• How do our questions lead and guide our search for knowledge?<br>• How much evidence is enough to draw a conclusion?<br>• How is forensic science studied? What kinds of questions do forensic scientists ask and answer?<br>• Which processes and skills are essential in analyzing evidence?<br>• How is evidence collected? What are the procedures and experiments that forensic scientists use to analyze a crime? | |
| **Lesson Structure**<br><br>1. Watch and analyze an expert describing how to investigate a crime.<br>2. Create a procedural plan.<br>3. Execute the plan on a simulated scene. | This lesson allows the students a chance to develop their own procedure with guidance from an expert. |
| **Introduction**<br><br>*Would you agree or disagree with the statement, "The scene of the crime is the most important piece in solving a crime." Think-pair-share.*<br><br>*Before we analyze the scene within our own room, we will watch a short clip of a real forensic scientist discussing how to properly analyze a scene of a crime. While you are watching, record the procedure for analyzing a crime scene and think about how you will use this information to analyze our crime scene that is set up in the back of the room.*<br><br>The teacher shows a clip from Videojug (2007), located at www.videojug.com/interview/documenting-a-crime-scene-2. | Think-pair-share is a technique that allows students to think about a topic on their own, discuss it with a partner, and then share with the whole class. It gives students a chance to be actively involved rather than relying on the fastest responder.<br><br>*Troubleshooting:* If the suggested video is no longer available, clicking "videos" on www.google.com allows a search for crime scene techniques or forensic science education. |
| **Teaching Strategies and Learning Experiences**<br><br>The teacher first discusses the strategies mentioned in the video, and then asks the students what methods were introduced (e.g., securing the crime scene, taking photographs, sketching details, combing the scene for evidence: grid, a weave, or a spiral pattern). | Viewing a video allows students to acquire information they can use to create their own methodologies and procedures for carrying out the crime scene investigation.<br><br>Teachers may change the crime to meet the needs of their students. With younger students, a scene where something was vandalized or stolen can |

| Unit Sequence | Reflection |
|---|---|
| *What methods do you find most important? Which may be the hardest to remember? Let's design a plan for the crime scene that we have in the back of the room. Here is the background information:*<br><br>*Last night a crime was committed. The victim was identified as a twenty-five-year-old single female. At 9:00 p.m., she was discovered by her neighbor. The victim had been stabbed in the chest and was face down when she was found. Before she was removed from the scene of the crime, the position of her body was outlined with tape. None of the other items were disturbed.* | work well, being careful to leave different types of evidence. For this case, there is no specific right answer. |
| *What should we do first? What kind of questions would an investigator ask? Remember, in order to get the right answer, we must first ask the right questions.* | This brings the focus back to asking the right questions. |
| Recording student questions first, the teacher then asks them to answer them, and later transfers their answers to a poster to display in the room. (Throughout the methodological studies of this unit, the teacher keeps posters displayed of procedures that the students develop.)<br><br>The students develop the procedure as much as possible themselves, but the following outline helps the teacher guide properly guide students.<br><br>1. *Secure the crime scene and hold onto witnesses.* In this scene, there are no witnesses.<br><br>2. *Take pictures.* Document everything!<br><br>3. *Comb the crime scene for evidence.* Use grids, weaves, or spirals. Can you think of cases when each would be appropriate?<br><br>4. *Create detailed sketches.* Note the important locations of the evidence, the length and width of the room, and the direction of the room; measure the distance from two fixed points to each piece of evidence marked on the map by using dashed lines; and note the windows and the doors. Try to make your drawings to scale.<br><br>5. *Collect the evidence.* What type of procedure should be followed to collect the evidence?<br><br>Once the students have developed a procedure, they explain why it is important to take their time on these sketches and scene evaluation. They are now ready to follow the procedure they created. | By recording their questions, the teacher shows the students that their thoughts are worth holding onto. The students develop their knowledge, while the teacher facilitates and records.<br><br>Depending on the class, the students may need more scaffolding, so these steps allow the teacher to help the students develop the procedure themselves. The teacher can ask about what happens when they first arrive on the scene, what kinds of evidence are important to preserve, and how they will find and preserve the evidence.<br><br>To assist with step 4, the teacher may teach a mini-lesson on how to draw the scene to scale. The teacher may also show maps and what the scale factor is on the map. The students can record the distances of evidence from each other or from the door or the body.<br><br>In step 5, it is important for students to identify these main points: (1) Material evidence must be collected with gloves and placed in correctly labeled bags. Sometimes the investigators will use two sets of gloves so when they change gloves to pick up a new piece of evidence, they will not contaminate the scene. (2) Blood evidence must be photographed. The best option for blood is to submit the entire piece that it is on, but if that is not possible, a Q-tip may be used to swab the area. Then the Q-tip is placed in a bag and then in a refrigerated area. (3) Fingerprints are the last item to be collected. Black powder can be applied to the scene and if any prints show up, photographed. (There is much more to fingerprint finding, but this is the basic idea.) |

*(Continued)*

(Continued)

| Unit Sequence | Reflection |
|---|---|
| **Closure**<br><br>When students finish analyzing the crime scene, they write in their journals a story about what could have happened, or an analysis about what they found and where they would go next with this case. Students each then have a few minutes to discuss their sketches and their journal entries as a conclusion. | This closure asks students to extend the lesson to the next stage in solving a crime.<br>   Students can turn in their journals, if time is short and time to share in class is not available. |
| **Homework/Individual Challenges**<br><br>Students respond to this statement with examples from forensic science as well as from other fields: astute observations are essential in order to arrive at accurate conclusions. | This prompt may need a graphic organizer so the students give examples and connect it to other fields. |

## LESSON 6.5: DOCUMENT ANALYSIS

**Length:** One 90-minute session

| Unit Sequence | Reflection |
|---|---|
| **Concepts**<br><br>• Systems<br>• Relationships | |
| **Principles**<br><br>• We must ask the right questions in order to get the right answers.<br>• Astute observations are essential in order to arrive at an accurate conclusion.<br>• A relationship exists between evidence and conclusions, and in order to establish that relationship, the evidence must be scientifically analyzed through proper identification, collection, and experimentation. | |
| **Skills**<br><br>• Develop relevant questions.<br>• Gather evidence.<br>• Perform scientific tests on the evidence.<br>• Compare and contrast.<br>• Record, organize, and compile data from the tests.<br>• Draw conclusions.<br>• Use observation techniques.<br>• Apply inductive thinking. | |

| Unit Sequence | Reflection |
|---|---|
| **Standards** <br><br> *PA* <br><br> 3.2.4 A, 3.2.4 B, 3.2.4 C <br><br> *National* <br><br> NS.5–8.1, NS.5–8.7 | |
| **Guiding Questions** <br><br> • What constitutes a valid conclusion, and how can we verify it? <br> • How do our questions lead and guide our search for knowledge? <br> • How much evidence is enough to draw a conclusion? <br> • What is the purpose of forensic science? What are the specialties within the field? <br> • How is forensic science studied? What kind of questions do forensic scientists ask and answer? <br> • What processes and skills are essential in analyzing evidence? <br> • How is evidence used to solve crimes? What is the relationship between evidence and truth? | |
| **Lesson Structure** <br><br> 1. Analyze personal handwriting samples to develop the characteristics that can be used to identify and connect unique samples. <br><br> 2. Apply that knowledge to a specific case. <br><br> 3. Use the process of chromatography to identify the composition of specific inks. <br><br> *Preparation for Lessons* <br><br> The teacher completes the following steps to prepare for the handwriting lesson: <br><br> 1. Enlist six friends to sign "Mrs. Alicia Zoey Davis" on a piece of paper. <br><br> 2. Ask the friends to make up names of whom they represent, and designate one friend the true culprit who also signs the back of the check. <br><br> 3. Make enough copies of the check in question and all the suspect handwriting samples for all students. <br><br> For the chromatography lesson, the teacher completes the following steps: | This lesson allows students to come up with the distinct features of different people's handwriting. Rather than telling them to look for the swirls or letter slant, the students come up with it on their own. <br><br> The chromatography lesson is a more teacher-directed session, because the students are not likely to have heard of chromatography before. |

(Continued)

| Unit Sequence | Reflection |
|---|---|
| 1. Gather several black or blue pens.<br><br>2. Obtain a sample of the evidence (have someone use one of the pens to write a note—the students' job is to figure out which pen they used).<br><br>3. Cut several coffee filters into 1/2″ strips.<br><br>4. Set up the chromatography apparatus. Place a skewer or other long object across two supports. Place a pan underneath the skewer and fill it about 1/2″ deep with the solvent (water or alcohol). | |
| **Introduction**<br><br>*Let's take a moment and think back to some of our past experiences with forensic science. First, what are some of the things we have learned so far in this unit? How did your homework assignment go? What questions are still looming large in your head about forensic science?*<br><br>The teacher can either connect these questions to the planned lessons or plan additional lessons that will address them, letting students know that they may not all be answered that day, but hopefully many will be answered before the end of the unit. | The beginning of the introduction is an informal assessment gauging where the students are and where else they want to go. It is important to be flexible so that if the students have an interesting question, the unit can address it. |
| *Have you ever used any aspect of forensic science in your life without even realizing it? Well, as a teacher, there is one specialty that I always use. I am going to give you a clue: all teachers warn you, most try to remind you, and many will get very angry with you if you don't do this.*<br>    *Any guesses about what experience most teachers have with forensic science on a daily basis? (Discussion) That is right; we all have to have an ability to analyze the handwriting of our students to conclude who forgot to put their names on their papers.* | This section helps students connect individually with the information, as well as engages them with a personal story connecting teaching to forensic science. |
| **Teaching Strategies and Learning Experiences**<br><br>*Today we are going to be looking at some specific skills that forensic scientists use in the document analysis department. Any guesses as to where document analysis might be used? (money forgery, document or art forgery, handwriting analysis, typewriter or paper analysis, code breaking, etc.)* | These experiences all focus on mastering the methods that a practicing professional uses. |

| Unit Sequence | Reflection |
|---|---|
| *We have two mysteries to solve today dealing with document analysis. Please get into groups of four, and copy down this statement, "My favorite class is forensic science, and I love to write in my journal." Now, compare and contrast your handwriting to the other students in your group. Make a list of the traits that are different. Start a class list on a poster paper. Why would handwriting analysis be useful in forensic science?* | This section provides a way for students to create their own criteria for analyzing handwriting. Allowing them to create their own criteria gives them more opportunities to develop inductive thinking skills. |
| *Our first mystery, today, is dealing with a forged check. Here is the background information. Butler Area School District mails checks to the teachers for their work. Mrs. Davis was supposed to be paid October 10, 2010, but she claims that she hasn't received a check in the mail. Under further investigation, the canceled check was in Butler's bank statement. Mrs. Davis and Butler Area School District decided to contact the bureau of investigation, and you have been placed on the case. Mrs. Davis feels as if one of the mail workers picked it up before it even got to her mailbox, because her mail slides into a locked box awaiting her arrival.* | Here again the students ask the questions that lead to the experiment. The teacher does not tell them what experiment should be performed next, but rather, guides the students to discover for themselves. |
| The teacher gives the students copies of the forged check (Resource 6.5). Then the teacher asks what they would do first. If they ask about fingerprints, they are informed that no fingerprints were found on the check. The criminal must have been wearing gloves or it passed through so many hands that the prints wore off. If students suggest analyzing handwriting, the teacher asks how they can do that.<br><br>Eventually, students come to the conclusion that they need samples from all the postal workers who worked that week. When they ask, the teacher distributes samples of all the employees' names and forged signatures of Mrs. Alicia Zoey Davis. They examine these, make a list of how they analyzed them, identify whom they believe took the check, name two checks that are close matches, and identify what helped them to rule them out. After the students finish their examination, the teacher leads a discussion that develops the criteria for analyzing handwriting. All their information is recorded on chart paper and displayed in the room for future additions and reference. | This experiment requires careful preparation. A master key may be used, with labels of whose sample signature belongs with whom in real life.<br><br>*Author's note:* I somehow lost this list once and had a hard time deciding which sample really did forge the check. If this does happen, it brings up a good point that in real investigations, more evidence than just the handwriting may be necessary. The teacher can even ask the students why this might be the case. |

*(Continued)*

(Continued)

| Unit Sequence | Reflection |
|---|---|
| *We are going to move on to our next mystery in document analysis. Look back at the specialties that you brainstormed. We are now going to examine the different types of ink used. Why would this be helpful?* (Discussion) <br><br> *Now I am going to tell you the mystery, and you need to tell me what we can do about it.* <br><br> *Pete owns a computer business and he has become quite successful in the last several years. To save money, Pete refuses to hire an accountant to help him file his taxes. A month ago, Pete received a letter from the IRS informing him that he is being audited. Pete panicked and began collecting everything he could find. The IRS suspects that he wrote an incriminating note to a friend describing his changing the numbers on the receipts. Here is the note they found.* <br><br> The note is written in print without enough variation to use a handwriting sample. The teacher explains that pens were found in Pete's house, and asks, "Could one of these pens have written the note?" The class then splits into teams of three, and each team receives a basket of materials. <br><br> *Procedure* <br><br> The teacher guides students with the following steps: <br><br> 1. Use a long 1/2" wide strip of your evidence and hang it from the skewer so that the end just touches the solvent. Don't let the ink get wet. <br><br> 2. Use each of your suspect pens to place a dark spot of ink about 1/4" to 1/2" from the end of each coffee filter strip. <br><br> 3. Hang these strips from the skewer so that the tips of the strips just touch the solvent. <br><br> 4. Allow the inks to separate for about 15 minutes. <br><br> 5. Examine the banding patterns and determine which of your known suspect pens is the pen used to write the note. | |

| Unit Sequence | Reflection |
|---|---|
| The teacher explains that if the pattern of the ink is the same on the note as one of the test pens, then Pete wrote the letter. Students make observations and answer the following questions:<br><br>• Did Pete write the note?<br>• How do you know?<br>• Could there be another explanation?<br>• What would you do next? | |
| The teacher explains the proper terms for what the students experienced. Black ink is a mixture of a variety of colors. The black ink separates into colors when placed in water. This is an example of ink chromatography. *Chromatography* is the method of separating parts of a mixture. *Chromatograms* are the samples of the mixture after a liquid is run through it.<br><br>When the coffee filter is dipped in water, some of the water sticks to the coffee filter and gets it wet. There is a force between the water molecules and the molecules in the coffee filter. This is called *adhesion*. The water also sticks to itself. This is called *cohesion*.<br><br>Both of these sticky forces—adhesion and cohesion—cause the water to travel up the coffee filter, moving against gravity. When the water reaches the ink, it dissolves some of the dyes in the ink, and the dyes travel up the coffee filter with the water. This is how all the different colors that make up the ink appear. The teacher then asks the students if there could be any other uses for chromatography. | It is important to remind students that this is the kind of vocabulary that practicing forensic scientists use when they work. Knowing the correct vocabulary is a part of skills and processes for students to learn in the Curriculum of Practice. |
| **Closure**<br><br>For their final activity, the students examine the journal prompt, write a response, and share with their classmates.<br><br>*Journal Prompt*<br><br>Professor Y. N. Howe was very excited because he had just prepared a great exam to give his students. He arrived at work today and found a note taped to the classroom door. It read, "Class is cancelled." What are some techniques the professor can use to identify who was trying to get out of the exam? How could he design his experiment? Think of as many experiments as possible. | This closure activity is ideal for helping students apply their knowledge to a novel situation. The teacher may discuss how multiple experiments that yield the same information make it easier to make a justifiable conclusion. |

*(Continued)*

(Continued)

| Unit Sequence | Reflection |
|---|---|
| **Homework/Individual Challenges**<br><br>This is another lesson to introduce codes and ciphers to students. On the site www.nrich.maths.org, the "packages" link leads to "enigma," and then on to "preview." The codes and ciphers can all be printed out for students to ponder. The teacher can pose an additional individual challenge with the following questions:<br><br>• What role does document analysis play in solving crime?<br>• What other fields use document analysis or the methods used in document analysis?<br><br>Students then research a real life example of a crime solved through document analysis and present their findings through a product of their choice. | Some students enjoy this opportunity and may then develop their own codes and ciphers. Some may try to solve the monthly problems on the nrich website long after they complete the code section.<br><br>*Author's note:* Some of my students even got their solutions published when the answers came out during the following month. |

## LESSON 6.6: DNA AND IMPRINTS

**Length:** One 90-minute session

| Unit Sequence | Reflection |
|---|---|
| **Concepts**<br><br>• Relationships<br>• Systems | |
| **Principles**<br><br>• We must ask the right questions in order to get the right answers.<br>• Astute observations are essential in order to arrive at an accurate conclusion.<br>• A relationship exists between evidence and conclusions, and in order to establish that relationship, the evidence must be scientifically analyzed through proper identification, collection, and experimentation. | |
| **Skills**<br><br>• Develop relevant questions.<br>• Gather evidence.<br>• Perform scientific tests on the evidence.<br>• Compare and contrast.<br>• Record, organize, and compile data from the tests. | |

| Unit Sequence | Reflection |
|---|---|
| • Draw conclusions.<br>• Use observation techniques.<br>• Seek relationships.<br>• Apply inductive thinking. | |
| **Standards**<br><br>*PA*<br><br>3.2.4 A, 3.2.4 B, 3.2.4 C<br><br>*National*<br><br>NS.5–8.1, NS.5–8.7 | |
| **Guiding Questions**<br><br>• What constitutes a valid conclusion, and how can we verify it?<br>• How do our questions lead and guide our search for knowledge?<br>• How much evidence is enough to draw a conclusion?<br>• What is the purpose of forensic science? What are the specialties within the field?<br>• How is forensic science studied? What kinds of questions do forensic scientists ask and answer?<br>• What processes and skills are essential in analyzing evidence?<br>• How is evidence collected? What are the procedures and experiments that forensic scientists use to analyze a crime?<br>• How is evidence used to solve crimes? What is the relationship between evidence and truth? | |
| **Lesson Structure**<br><br>1. Learn how to make shoe imprints and discuss why they are useful.<br>2. Work through a DNA fingerprint case online while doing hands-on activities in the classroom. | This lesson introduces the students to two more methods that forensic scientists use to solve crimes. |
| **Introduction**<br><br>*When I was studying forensic science in order to develop this unit, I ran into an interesting quote. Around 1920, a French forensic scientist named Edmond Locard said, "Every contact leaves a trace" (Locard, n.d.). Our entire study today is going to examine those traces left behind. Right now, I want you to take a few moments and really digest this quote. "Every contact leaves a trace." Is this true for your life? Let's talk about it. What are some examples? Is this true in forensic science studies?* | The students again try to connect forensic science with their own lives and other fields. The teacher asks about what other studies look at contacts, and the traces they leave behind. In history, a meeting with an advisor may have led to a presidential campaign. Specific people may leave a trace in their field. |
| **Teaching Strategies and Learning Experiences**<br><br>*Part 1: Shoe Print Impressions*<br><br>This takes 25 minutes, with a 30-minute wait time, so in the middle of the next section, students can take a break and spend 5 minutes to extract and label the cast. | |

*(Continued)*

(Continued)

| Unit Sequence | Reflection |
|---|---|
| *A new crime has been reported. Brandon's Burger Bonanza was robbed late last night several hours after closing. When the police arrived, they parked a few yards away from the restaurant. Then they surrounded the area with yellow crime scene tape to preserve the evidence.* <br><br> *Since onlookers were kept at bay, some valuable evidence was found near the restaurant. A light rain had fallen at closing time, causing the surrounding dirt to be very soft. Detectives, what are some things you may look for?* | This offers students a simulation experience that mimics one a professional would encounter. <br><br> The students use the skill of brainstorming and creative thinking. They once again guide the instruction. |
| Students brainstorm, and then focus on the shoe print idea. The teacher asks them how they can preserve this evidence, and then tell them that they will examine one way to preserve the evidence, using a cast. The students split into four groups, and each group has a bucket of dirt with shoe prints in it. Each student group also receives four pieces of wood. <br><br> The students gently press the planks into the soil without distorting the frame, pressing the pieces as deep as the imprint. They place enough water in a bowl to fill the cast and then add plaster to reach the consistency of pancake batter. They next pour the liquid gently into the cast, and allow the cast to dry about 30 minutes. <br><br> In 30 minutes, they return to these casts, remove them, and mark names and dates on the cast. They then let them dry, and analyze at a later time. (The teacher can show the students the shoes that were picked up from the suspect's house and see if the students can determine if any of the shoes were indeed used to make the print.) <br><br> *Part 2: DNA Analysis* <br><br> This takes 60 minutes. Depending on the students' familiarity with the content, they may progress through the online activity independently. The material, however, is quite complex and some instruction may be needed. <br><br> *Today we are going to examine what DNA is and how it is created in each of us. Then we will discuss how DNA has been used to solve crimes. First, what do you already know about DNA?* <br><br> The teacher gauges the introduction based on students' current knowledge. | This section tends to be the most challenging for teachers in the whole unit, but the students usually pick it up easily if the teacher takes a few minutes to explicitly teach. |
| *Introduction* <br><br> The teacher shows the cell picture (Resource 6.6). <br><br> *Everyone is made up of cells. Each part within the cell has a different job, and each cell has a different job within the body. Just like in forensic science, there are toxicologists who study chemicals and poisons, psychologists who study the mental state of the victim and suspect, and entomologists who study bugs found at the scene.* | Here the discussion connects back to the system and relationship concepts. The students should at this point name many systems and relationships within the systems. |

| Unit Sequence | Reflection |
|---|---|
| *What other systems can be broken down into different jobs?* (basketball teams, computers, fans, businesses, etc.) <br><br> *Some cells in our body make up our bones, some make up our heart, and some our brain. The interesting thing is that all these cells have the same instruction manual. Each cell just references a different section of the manual. The instruction manual is DNA.* <br><br> *DNA is most often found within the nucleus. DNA tells the cells what to do and gives an outsider an idea of the entire person. You have very unique DNA because you got half of your mom's DNA and half from your dad. It is random which half you got within their cells. There are over 8 million different possible combinations just from one of your parents!* <br><br> *The only people who have exactly the same DNA are identical twins. This is why examining DNA at a crime scene is especially helpful. How do you think scientists find DNA at a crime scene?* (hair, skin cells, saliva, etc.) | |
| *Website* <br><br> The teacher directs everyone to www.pbs.org/wgbh/nova/ sheppard/analyze.html and reads through the article with the students (Groleau, 2000). After asking if they have any questions, the teacher progresses to the next section. <br><br> *Restriction Enzymes* <br><br> Students pour the restriction enzymes into the DNA, but the teacher initiates a pause for the explanation. Giving each student a strip of DNA, the students take their scissors and cut after the two Gs and before the A. It is important for the teacher to reiterate that restriction enzymes cut the DNA at specific places. <br><br> *Share with your neighbor. Do the sizes of your DNA pieces look similar?* <br><br> The teacher reviews that because all DNA is different and because restriction enzymes only cut at specific points, there will be different sizes of DNA. The teacher then asks the students what will happen with more codes. <br><br> *If we did it with codes that were 10,000 letters long instead of just around 50, would there be more matches between individuals or fewer?* <br><br> *Agarose Gel* <br><br> After pouring the gel into the tray, each student receives a blank piece of paper that is to represent the agarose. <br><br> *Electrophoresis* <br><br> *DNA has an overall negative charge, and the gel has a positive charge on the one end. The DNA is attracted to the positive charge* | This experience alternates between a computer lab activity and a classroom physical activity. After each step is taken on the computer, the students replicate the step in a way that helps them understand what they just did. If the students don't do both at the same time with guidance, they tend to rush through the simulation and not understand what they just did. <br><br> The scissors cutting the paper DNA is like the restriction enzymes students added to their sample. |

(Continued)

| Unit Sequence | Reflection |
|---|---|
| *and tries to move closer. What does this remind you of? (magnet) Why do the smaller pieces move the farthest?* <br><br> The teacher can set up a human gel, where students have to hold out their arms, bend their elbows, or do nothing as they try to move through a sea of other students to the other side of the room. A discussion follows about why the one not holding out his or her arms made it there the fastest. The smallest pieces slip through the pores in the gel faster. <br> On the computer, students begin their electrophoresis. <br><br> *Now with your DNA slices, I want you to label the top of your paper, positive (+) and the bottom negative (–) and arrange your slices from smallest to largest. Then tape down your pieces.* <br><br> *Probes* <br><br> *Now I want you to take a highlighter and highlight your individual strands. Label the highlighting "probes." Probes stick to the various slices of DNA and help the slices show up in the X-ray process. You may finish this developing activity on your own, but wait for the rest of the class once you have your fingerprint.* <br><br> *Matching* <br><br> *Now all you have to do is match your DNA fingerprint with the fingerprint from one of the suspects. Who do you think is guilty?* | |
| **Closure** <br><br> *In your journal, record the method that scientists use to create DNA fingerprints and what questions a DNA fingerprint can be used to answer.* <br><br> After the cast has dried, the students also respond to these questions: <br><br> *Describe the criteria you would use to choose the print that best matches your cast. What is your final answer regarding the culprit? What is the purpose in casting frames? What other impressions might be helpful in solving a crime? What other questions would you ask within this case to build a solid conclusion to present to the jury?* | Students look back at the methods of a practicing professional and the thought process the professional uses. |
| **Homework/Individual Challenges** <br><br> The teacher may offer the following prompt: <br><br> *Prepare a persuasive argument about which evidence you would prefer to find at the scene of the crime. You can use any type of evidence that you know about, such as scene analysis, documents, shoe imprints, or DNA. Describe how you could process it to solve the mystery.* | |

## LESSON 6.7: FINGERPRINTING, BLOOD, QUESTIONS, AND EVIDENCE

**Length:** One 90-minute session

| Unit Sequence | Reflection |
|---|---|
| **Concepts**<br><br>• Systems<br>• Relationships | |
| **Principles**<br><br>• We must ask the right questions in order to get the right answers.<br>• Astute observations are essential in order to arrive at an accurate conclusion.<br>• A relationship exists between evidence and conclusions, and in order to establish that relationship, the evidence must be scientifically analyzed through proper identification, collection, and experimentation.<br>• There is no standard procedure that works all the time in every situation. Thinking is allowed. | |
| **Skills**<br><br>• Develop relevant questions.<br>• Gather evidence.<br>• Perform scientific tests on the evidence.<br>• Compare and contrast.<br>• Record, organize, and compile data from the tests.<br>• Draw conclusions.<br>• Use observation techniques.<br>• Seek relationships.<br>• Apply inductive thinking. | |
| **Standards**<br><br>*PA*<br><br>3.2.4 A, 3.2.4 B, 3.2.4 C<br><br>*National*<br><br>NS.5–8.1, NS.5–8.7 | |
| **Guiding Questions**<br><br>• What constitutes a valid conclusion, and how can we verify it?<br>• How do our questions lead and guide our search for knowledge?<br>• How much evidence is enough to draw a conclusion?<br>• What is the purpose of forensic science? What are the specialties within the field? | |

*(Continued)*

(Continued)

| Unit Sequence | Reflection |
|---|---|
| • How is forensic science studied? What kinds of questions do forensic scientists ask and answer?<br>• What processes and skills are essential in analyzing evidence?<br>• How is evidence collected? What are the procedures and experiments that forensic scientists use to analyze a crime?<br>• How is evidence used to solve crimes? What is the relationship between evidence and truth? | |
| **Lesson Structure**<br><br>1. Investigate blood splashes and draw a conclusion about the events surrounding a blood splash.<br><br>2. Analyze fingerprints to design a system of classification.<br><br>3. Write informed questions for the visiting professional. | |
| **Introduction**<br><br>The teacher prints two words on the board: *serologists* and *dactylographer*. The students then write a few statements about the conversation that would occur if these two people went out to dinner together. It is up to the teacher whether to wait until after they have written their conversation to inform them that a serologist studies blood and a dactylographer studies fingerprints. After students share for a few minutes, they learn that they are going to become serologists and dactylographers. | This seems to spark excitement because the students seem to love big words. They likely see themselves impressing their family and friends with their extensive vocabulary. It is also a creative thinking exercise that reminds the students of the specialties within the field. |
| **Teaching Strategies and Learning Experiences**<br><br>*Part 1: Blood Analysis: Serology (30 minutes)*<br><br>*Blood is often found at the scene of the crime. What kind of questions do serologists ask? What kind of information do you think forensic scientists can gain from finding blood spots?*<br><br>*A crime was committed and this blood spot was found on the scene. Your job for the next 20 minutes is to discover how this spot was created. What kinds of variables are there in creating a blood spot?*<br><br>If the students struggle, introducing these concepts can help: different amounts of "blood," different heights, different angles, and even the velocity of the blood. Then each group receives a container of "blood," a spoon, newspaper, sheet of plastic, and cardboard. (They can use their books to work on the angle of the surface.)<br><br>After they have performed the experiments, the groups discuss how the spot was created and what that can tell them about the crime. | This first part of the lesson allows the students to practice making astute observations in order to arrive at an accurate conclusion. They test their own hypotheses to re-create how the spot was made. They have to make observations and then adjust their next experiment accordingly. It is important that the original blood spot is carefully constructed with detail to amount, distance, and angles, so that the teacher can inform students of their accuracy. |

| Unit Sequence | Reflection |
|---|---|
| *Part 2: Fingerprinting: Dactylography (30 minutes)*<br><br>*What do you already know about fingerprinting?* (Discussion about the uniqueness of everyone's fingerprints) *What kinds of questions do dactylographers ask? Can we invent a way to classify fingerprints?*<br><br>The students then attempt to design an experiment to help them classify. If they need scaffolding, an appropriate plan is for them to work groups and compare their own fingerprints. First, they must take their own prints. To do this, they rub a pencil on a piece of paper. Then they each rub their finger over top of their pencil mark, and place a piece of tape over top of their finger. The piece of tape is next placed on a white piece of paper and labeled with which finger of which hand.<br>    The students next compare their own fingerprints to their friends' fingerprints. They write the criteria and the differences they notice and identify if there are any specific patterns. Once they describe their findings, proper terms are introduced, and they identify their fingerprints as *whorls*, *arches*, or *loops*. Examples are found in Resource 6.7. | This is another example of students organizing information, and determining how the pieces fit into the system. |
| *Student Questions*<br><br>The teacher explains that a forensic scientist will come to the next class. It is very important that they prepare meaningful questions for the guest to answer. Each student must think back through everything that has been discussed in class and what they have seen on television. Then they formulate serious questions about forensic science. If students struggle, the teacher can suggest topics such as evidence, controversies, villains, schooling, life stories, helpful tips, and techniques for solving crimes. | It is important to remind students of the principle: we must ask the right questions in order to get the right answers. Their goals are to find out (1) all they need to know about forensic science to solve their final mystery and (2) how to make a contribution to the field. |
| **Closure**<br><br>*Blood Analysis Journal Questions*<br><br>• What can blood analysis tell forensic scientists?<br>• What questions do serologists ask when they find a spot of blood?<br>• What did you find out about the sample blood spot found at the scene of the crime through your own investigation?<br><br>*Fingerprint Analysis Journal Questions*<br><br>• What questions do you think dactylographers ask?<br>• How did you originally organize the fingerprints?<br>• What are some different characteristics that you notice between the fingerprints?<br><br>    At the end of the lesson, the students share their journal entries and discuss questions they plan to ask the expert. | This closure addresses the key questions the students have learned how to answer throughout the experience. The students can present their information in a less typical way, such as (1) making a commercial to recruit people for either field, (2) creating a television drama that uses one of these specialists, or (3) designing a forensic science blog that houses information about what they have come to learn from the unit. It is quite simple to create a blog at www .blogger.com. |

*(Continued)*

(Continued)

| Unit Sequence | Reflection |
|---|---|
| **Homework/Individual Challenges**<br><br>The Student Choice Project (Resource 6.8) allows students to choose either the creative, analytical, or practical assignment based on their intelligence preference. This challenge is particularly interesting and the students will share it with the incoming expert. If this unit is taught on more of a daily basis, the students may take a few days to work through this challenge. | This assignment uses Robert Sternberg's intelligences and allows each student to pick a topic and product that is most interesting. The possibility of sharing it with an expert is also quite thrilling. |

## LESSON 6.8: MEET A FORENSIC SCIENTIST

**Length:** One 90-minute session

| Unit Sequence | Reflection |
|---|---|
| **Concepts**<br><br>• Systems<br>• Relationships<br>• Perspective | |
| **Principles**<br><br>• We must ask the right questions in order to get the right answers.<br>• Astute observations are essential in order to arrive at an accurate conclusion.<br>• A relationship exists between evidence and conclusions, and in order to establish that relationship, the evidence must be scientifically analyzed through proper identification, collection, and experimentation.<br>• There is a responsibility to humanity to properly analyze evidence and substantiate the conclusion made from that evidence.<br>• Our perspective affects how we process new information.<br>• Scientific experimentation leads to theories but not steadfast truths. | |
| **Skills**<br><br>• Develop relevant questions.<br>• Draw conclusions.<br>• Use observation techniques.<br>• Seek relationships.<br>• Apply inductive thinking.<br>• Determine the strength of an argument. | |

| Unit Sequence | Reflection |
|---|---|
| **Standards**<br><br>*PA*<br><br>3.2.4 A, 3.2.4 B, 3.2.4 C<br><br>*National*<br><br>NS.5–8.1, NS.5–8.7 | |
| **Guiding Questions**<br><br>• What constitutes a valid conclusion, and how can we verify it?<br>• How do our questions lead and guide our search for knowledge?<br>• How much evidence is enough to draw a conclusion?<br>• Does science produce truth?<br>• What is the purpose of forensic science? What are the specialties within the field?<br>• How is forensic science studied? What kinds of questions do forensic scientists ask and answer?<br>• What processes and skills are essential in analyzing evidence?<br>• How is evidence collected? What are the procedures and experiments that forensic scientists use to analyze a crime?<br>• How is evidence used to solve crimes? What is the relationship between evidence and truth? | |
| **Lesson Structure**<br><br>1. Meet forensic scientist.<br>2. Ask questions and display evidence projects.<br>3. Read and discuss the fingerprint controversy. | This lesson allows the students to become immersed in the field by interacting with a practicing forensic scientist. |
| **Introduction**<br><br>The teacher introduces the speaker, providing background and explaining the details of the visit. | The content expert further ignites students' excitement and interest in the topic. |
| **Teaching Strategies and Learning Experiences**<br><br>The teacher advises the forensic scientist beforehand to bring some equipment to share with the students. The forensic scientist talks about the job and students ask their prepared questions. If the discussion lags, the teacher can ask about the step-by-step process of analyzing a crime, interrogating a witness, television's effect on forensic science, and controversies.<br><br>　If time, students share their evidence projects with the forensic scientist. The forensic scientist can point out how realistic some aspects of their projects are, or inquire as to where they found such good information. | The forensic scientist is most likely not accustomed to speaking with nine-year-olds, so the teacher prepares the scientist for the class. The forensic scientist should be aware that the visit's purpose is to give the students tools they would need to become practicing professionals, such as the appropriate language, tools, and thinking strategies. |

(Continued)

| Unit Sequence | Reflection |
|---|---|
| If there is more time, the class can also discuss controversies, using "Crime Lab Crimes" article from http://whyfiles .org/133crime_lab/3.html (Why Files, n.d.).<br><br>The students read the article and respond to the following prompts in their journals.<br><br>• Why is fingerprinting under suspicion?<br>• Do you think fingerprinting is valid for use as evidence?<br>• How conclusive do you think the evidence has to be for the jury to convict a criminal? What criteria do you use to judge the certainty of evidence?<br>• Would another type of evidence be needed to make a responsible conviction? Why or why not?<br>• How much of a responsibility do forensic scientists have to the accused criminal? How sure do they have to be? Do you think they are ever 100% sure?<br>• Now respond to this statement: "Our perspective affects how we process new information." Is it true? Give fictional examples from forensic science and other fields. | The expert may examine how much evidence is enough and what controversies are currently happening within the local branch. Focus can also be directed on the principles within the lesson, discussing how they apply to the job. |
| **Closure**<br><br>At the end of this lesson, after the expert leaves, the students discuss what surprised them, what they learned, and if they think they might enjoy this field as a career path. These responses can be collected and used as an exit card for the lesson. | After such an intense day, this closure allows an informal gauge of students' progress and learning experiences. |
| **Homework/Individual Challenges**<br><br>Mature and perhaps older students may want to look into The Justice Project, a nonprofit organization that works to increase fairness and accuracy in the criminal justice system (www.aacj .org/justice-project.php). The students research and find out how common this problem is, and what they can do to help. Frequently, the overturned sentences are for rape because the DNA technology confirms or refutes past sentences, but this type of crime is not suitable for most students to research. | |

## LESSON 6.9: SOLVE A SIMULATED CRIME

**Length:** One to two 90-minute sessions

| Unit Sequence | Reflection |
|---|---|
| **Concepts**<br><br>• Systems<br>• Relationships<br>• Perspective | |

| Unit Sequence | Reflection |
|---|---|
| **Principles**<br><br>• We must ask the right questions in order to get the right answers.<br>• Astute observations are essential in order to arrive at an accurate conclusion.<br>• A relationship exists between evidence and conclusions, and in order to establish that relationship, the evidence must be scientifically analyzed through proper identification, collection, and experimentation.<br>• There is a responsibility to humanity to properly analyze evidence and substantiate the conclusion made from that evidence.<br>• Our perspective affects how we process new information.<br>• Scientific experimentation leads to theories but not steadfast truths.<br>• There is no standard process that works all of the time. Thinking is allowed. | |
| **Skills**<br><br>• Develop relevant questions.<br>• Draw conclusions.<br>• Use observation techniques.<br>• Seek relationships.<br>• Apply inductive thinking.<br>• Determine the strength of an argument. | |
| **Standards**<br><br>*PA*<br><br>3.2.4 A, 3.2.4 B, 3.2.4 C<br><br>*National*<br><br>NS.5–8.1, NS.5–8.7 | |
| **Guiding Questions**<br><br>• What constitutes a valid conclusion, and how can we verify it?<br>• How do our questions lead and guide our search for knowledge?<br>• How much evidence is enough to draw a conclusion?<br>• Does science produce truth?<br>• What is the purpose of forensic science? What are the specialties within the field?<br>• How is forensic science studied? What kinds of questions do forensic scientists ask and answer? | |

*(Continued)*

(Continued)

| Unit Sequence | Reflection |
|---|---|
| • What processes and skills are essential in analyzing evidence?<br>• How is evidence collected? What are the procedures and experiments that forensic scientists use to analyze a crime?<br>• How is evidence used to solve crimes? What is the relationship between evidence and truth? | |
| **Lesson Structure**<br><br>1. Implement the final lesson as a performance task and culminating activity.<br>2. Debrief the unit. | |
| **Teacher Preparation**<br><br>This simulation requires considerable preparation. Three different footprints are created, and one of the shoes creates a print at the scene from mud. The note is created, as well as samples of handwriting from each of the suspects. The teacher can also choose who committed the crime. The three suspects to use are Otis Nixon; Melinda Johnson; or Hal's friend, Gerald Hanso. They all have motives, and the teacher can choose the level of difficulty. All the evidence can point to one person, or a footprint from Otis can add complexity, as he was overzealous about his detective skills and broke into the crime scene before the police arrived, even though Gerald was actually the one who stole Magic. | This experience is set up so the students apply what they have come to understand and plan how they will analyze the scene. Most units provide the teacher with step-by-step instructions on how the students should analyze the scene, but this unit is set up to empower the students to determine the tools needed, the tests needed, and the evidence collected. The students learned the necessary methodological skills in the previous lessons to complete the investigation on their own. If, however, they run into problems, there is a list of procedures that can assist the teacher. The teacher's goal is to only give information when the students ask the right questions. Also, if this unit doesn't fill all the steps desired, the teacher can add different pieces of evidence. |
| **Introduction**<br><br>The teacher shows students the crime scene and explains that this is their chance to do the work of a forensic scientist. The detective first on the scene took notes, but he was going on vacation, so he left the case to the class. The teacher says, "Here are his notes," and gives students the scenario (Resource 6.9). | |
| **Teaching Strategies and Learning Experiences**<br><br>Students work in small self-selected groups, with a few groups at a time investigating the scene. The teacher also tells the students that the Jeffersons need to get back to their real life, so the crime scene will only be set up for one week. The investigation can go on to the next week, but they need to be very thorough at the crime scene. | Once again, the idea is for the students to direct this activity, so the grouping is self-selection and coincides with the open nature of this project. The students need to feel comfortable within the group so they can offer ideas for experiments or techniques. |

| Unit Sequence | Reflection |
|---|---|
| The outline of steps is only necessary if the students need help. The teacher provides the equipment or information as needed. | This allows the students to apply the tools of practicing professionals in this field. |
| *Outline of Steps* | |
| 1. Secure the crime scene. | |
| 2. Sketch the crime scene to scale. | |
| 3. Secure all the evidence in bags or with the camera. | |
| 4. Create a plan of how to test the evidence. | |
| 5. Create a suspect list to compare with the evidence. | |
| 6. Carry out the tests on the evidence (and refer to previous lessons if necessary).<br>   a. Paper chromatography: test what kind of pen was used on the note.<br>   b. Handwriting samples: collect and see which handwriting sample matches.<br>   c. Fingerprint and footprint analysis.<br>   d. DNA analysis from the hair found at the scene. | The students' written request contains the detailed description of the experiments and evidence that they believe justifies their recommendation. This is close to an authentic product for this field. Unfortunately or fortunately, the students can't go to an actual crime scene to practice their skills. Their analysis here is the authentic postassessment. |
| 7. Re-create the crime and determine the motive. | |
| 8. Write a request to the police force to arrest the guilty suspect, with evidence to support the recommendation. | |
|    If the students ask to do something that hasn't been thought of yet, they can research a method, and then the teacher can design the information to coordinate with the crime scene. | |
| **Closure**<br><br>The teacher asks the students the following questions and offers final remarks.<br><br>   *Are there any other questions you still have? What impact did this unit have on you? Where do you fit it within this field? Are you passionate about finding evidence or creating arguments?*<br>   *Not everyone will become a forensic scientist as a result of this unit, but you all can take away skills that will help you work in a field that most interests you.*<br><br>During this session, the teacher connects the unit to other fields, discussing how observation plays a role in forensic science as well as other fields.<br><br>   *How does evidence collection and analysis lead to conclusions in forensic science as well as other fields?* | This is a time to for the teacher go back and make sure that the students learned everything they wanted to learn. This is also a time to discuss further opportunities in this field, such as independent research projects as well as mentor opportunities. |

*(Continued)*

(Continued)

| Unit Sequence | Reflection |
|---|---|
| **Homework/Individual Challenges**<br><br>Students research how forensic anthropology has answered many questions regarding the "disappeared" people in Argentina, or the teacher helps them find a mentor in the field of forensic science. | |

# REFERENCES

AT&T Knowledge Network (2010). *Filamentality.* Retrieved from http://www.kn.pacbell.com/wired/fil/

Brown, J. (2006). *Crime files: four-minute forensic mysteries.* New York: Scholastic.

Groleau, R. (2000). Create a DNA fingerprint. *NOVA online.* Retrieved from www.pbs.org/wgbh/nova/sheppard/analyze.html

Locard, E. (n.d.). In *Wikipedia.* Retrieved from http://en.wikipedia.org/wiki/Edmond_Locard.

Videojug. (2007). Documenting a crime scene. Retrieved from www.videojug.com/interview/documenting-a-crime-scene-2

The Why Files. (n.d.). *Crime lab crimes?* Retrieved from http://whyfiles.org/133crime_lab/3.html

## RESOURCE 6.1: PREASSESSMENT GRAPHIC ORGANIZER

*All About Forensic Science*

Name _____ Date _____

| What kinds of tools do forensic scientists use? What kinds of experiments might they do? | What do forensic scientists do? Why are they useful? |
|---|---|

**Forensic Science**
(uses science to solve crimes)

| What else do you know about forensic science? | What would you like to know about forensic science? |
|---|---|

## RESOURCE 6.2: THINKING LIKE A FORENSIC SCIENTIST

| | |
|---|---|
| Language of the discipline: Are there words that forensic scientists use that are unique? | |
| Questions asked by the forensic scientist | |
| Evidence presented | |
| Thinking skills, attitudes, and methods used in the field | |

| | |
|---|---|
| Resources used in forensic science (tools or equipment) | |
| Conclusion based from that evidence and testing | |
| Could the evidence be interpreted in another way? Would any additional evidence make another conclusion possible? | |

## RESOURCE 6.3: INTERACTIVE CRIME SIMULATION

*Who's Who in Forensic Science?*

Each student is placed within a team of five students. Each student is given a role card and takes on the role of the specialist within the forensic science field. The student researches the role, asks questions regarding the current crime, collects evidence, makes conclusions, and finally works with the other students to solve the crime. The research sites may be placed on the Filamentality site (AT&T, 2010) for easy access. When students meet together, they may realize that they still need more information, so they may have to ask questions as general practicing professionals in the field.

*The Scene of the Crime: Mason, Idaho*

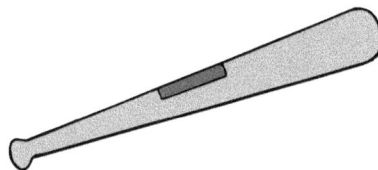

☆   **The Mason Star**   ☆

---

July 7, 2010                    Life, Liberty, and the Pursuit of Happiness                    $1.00

On July 6, 2010 at 7:30 p.m., two armed robbers walked away from the Bricks Building, at 165 Prince Street in Mason, with $1,218,211.19 in cash and more than $1.5 million in checks, money orders, and other securities.

It was a textbook robbery. There were two robbers—both were wearing navy peacoats, gloves, caps, and Halloween masks. The robbers said little and knew exactly what they were doing. They came through a series of locked doors to reach the second floor, where Bricks's employees were counting and storing money.

The only evidence was a chauffeur's cap one of the robbers left behind, but using this one small piece of evidence, police have two suspects: Robert Greene and Jerry Limesta.

It was billed as the "crime of the century," as so many stunning, jaw-dropping crimes are. Bricks offered a $100,000 reward for information leading to the arrest and conviction of the robbers.

*Student Project Cards*

**Pathologist**

Your job is to locate a practicing professional in this field and find out what the professional does. Get to it, sleuth!

*Resources*

- www.discoverychannel.co.uk/crime/forensic_scientists/index.shtml (Click on pathologists.)
- www.pathguy.com/autopsy.htm (This site shows the steps of an autopsy.)
- http://thename.org/index.php?option=com_content&task=category&sectionid=3&id=7&Itemid=42 (This site answers many general questions about forensic pathologists.)
- http://faculty.ncwc.edu/toconnor/425/425lect12.htm http://www.aafs.org/default.asp?section_id=resources&page_id=choosing_a_career#Path/Bio
- www.virtualmuseum.ca/Exhibitions/Myst/en/rcmp/index.html

*Directions*

1. Name and biographical information of a pathologist:
2. What does a pathologist study in the field?
3. What kinds of questions would a pathologist ask?
4. What tests or equipment does a pathologist use?
5. What conclusions is a pathologist able to make?
6. Make a plan to investigate this crime scene just like a pathologist. Remember to start with the right questions, and you are not alone. After you receive some information, you will work with the entire team to solve the crime.

**Odontologist**

Your job is to locate a practicing professional in this field and find out what the professional does. Get to it, sleuth!

*Resources*

- www.discoverychannel.co.uk/crime/forensic_scientists/index.shtml (Click on odontologists.)
- www.virtualmuseum.ca/Exhibitions/Myst/en/rcmp/index.html
- http://forensic.to/links/pages/Forensic_Medicine/Odontology/

*Directions*

1. Name and biographical information of an odontologist:
2. What does an odontologist study in the field?
3. What kinds of questions would an odontologist ask?
4. What tests or equipment does an odontologist use?
5. What conclusions is an odontologist able to make?
6. Make a plan to investigate this crime scene just like an odontologist would. Remember to start with the right questions, and you are not alone. After you receive some information, you will work with the entire team to solve the crime.

### Entomologist

Your job is to locate a practicing professional in this field and find out what the professional does. Get to it, sleuth!

*Resources*

- www.discoverychannel.co.uk/crime/forensic_scientists/index.shtml (Click on entomologists.)
- www.virtualmuseum.ca/Exhibitions/Myst/en/rcmp/index.html
- www.forensicpage.com/new26.htm
- http://forensic.to/links/pages/Forensic_Medicine/Entomology/
- www.research.missouri.edu/entomology/
- http://en.wikipedia.org/wiki/Forensic_entomology

*Directions*

1. Name and biographical information of an entomologist:

2. What does he/she study in the field?

3. What kinds of questions would an entomologist ask?

4. What tests or equipment does an entomologist use?

5. What conclusions is an entomologist able to make?

6. Make a plan to investigate this crime scene just like an entomologist would. Remember to start with the right questions, and you are not alone. After you receive some information, you will work with the entire team to solve the crime.

### Literary Forensic Scientist

Your job is to locate a practicing professional in this field and find out what the professional does. Get to it, sleuth!

*Resources*

- www.virtualmuseum.ca/Exhibitions/Myst/en/rcmp/index.html (Click on document identification and forgery.)
- http://forensic.to/links/pages/Forensic_Sciences/Field_of_expertise/Documents/
- www.tncrimlaw.com/forensic/f_docum.html
- www.fbi.gov/hq/lab/fsc/backissu/jan2000/olson.htm#introduction

*Directions*

1. Name and biographical information of a literary forensic scientist:

2. What does a literary forensic scientist study in the field?

3. What kinds of questions would a literary forensic scientist ask?

4. What tests or equipment does a literary forensic scientist use?

5. What conclusions is a literary forensic scientist able to make?

6. Make a plan to investigate this crime scene just like a literary forensic scientist would. Remember to start with the right questions, and you are not alone. After you receive some information, you will work with the entire team to solve the crime.

### Psychologist

Your job is to locate a practicing professional in this field and find out what this professional does. Get to it, sleuth!

*Resources*

- http://forensic.to/links/pages/Forensic_Psychiatry_Psychology/ (This site links to a plethora of other sites.)

*Directions*

1. Name and biographical information of a psychologist:
2. What does a psychologist study in the field?
3. What kinds of questions would a psychologist ask?
4. What tests or equipment does a psychologist use?
5. What conclusions is a psychologist able to make?
6. Make a plan to investigate this crime scene just like a psychologist would. Remember to start with the right questions, and you are not alone. After you receive some information, you will work with the entire team to solve the crime.

*Group Conclusion*

Victim:

Crime and evidence leading to conclusion:

Motive:

Main events of the crime:

Suspect to be prosecuted:

*Teacher Guiding Answers*

These are the clues to give your students when they ask you the appropriate questions and use the appropriate tools. They do not have to ask these questions word for word.

## Pathologist

What evidence is found on the body? (Tool: autopsy)

Pockets: key with 2763 imprinted, watch, and a dime

Body: a piece of green cloth in victim's mouth and a bullet in the victim's chest.

## Odontologist

Whose teeth records does the victim match? (Any of these tools: digital analysis of teeth; past dental records; ruler, protractor, or grid ruler)

Teeth of the victim: Robert Greene

Were there any other bite marks found? (Same tools as previously mentioned)

There is a bite mark on Jerry Limesta. The bite mark matches Robert Greene's bite.

## Entomologist

What were the type and quantity of bugs found on the body? (Tools: photography, an entomologist book [just ideas and may be hard to find])

The crime scene investigator arrived at the scene at 7:30 p.m. on July 10, 2010. She called you right away. You surveyed the scene and found a small quantity of flies and moths native to the area. You concluded that the body was not moved and that the time of death was only one hour prior to the investigator's arrival.

## Literary Forensic Scientist

Were there any notes or paperwork found at the victim's home? (Tools: handwriting analysis, chromatography, code reference book, fingerprint analysis)

Yes! There were two notes found at the victim's home, but they were in code. You need to go back to your research and figure out how to break the code. Fingerprints found on the stationary belong to the suspect, Jerry Limesta.

*Note 1*

Date: July 6, 2010

We are looking good for tomorrow. Get ready for some action.

*Note 2*

Date: July 9, 2010

This is my last warning. Give me my share of the dough, or else.

Note to teacher: For more information, examples, and solutions for codes and ciphers see http://nrich.maths .org/public/viewer.php?obj_id=5822.

### Psychologists

Were any eyewitnesses identified? What were their statements? (Tools: tape recorder, textbook [many options])

Yes. Two eyewitnesses came forth to offer information. You did a great job remembering that the kind of questions you ask them may taint their stories. You did not ask them leading questions, so you got some great information.

*Witness 1:* It was all such a blur. I turned around because I heard arguing. The two men were in each other's face and wrestling. Just then the man in the green T-shirt pulled a gun and shot the other man. Then the shooter noticed me and took off. That's all I know.

*Witness 2:* I saw several men arguing at around 12:00 p.m. They were all drinking sodas. One man punched the other man. I recognized the one who punched the other man as an old friend, Roger Hill. I really hope you get him.

Does either the victim or the suspect have a history of crime or anything to note from their past?

Great question! Here is a newspaper article on both the suspect and the victim found just three days prior to the incident.

### Final Group Time

Here is the synopsis of the story. If students ask any more questions, you can make up the answers based off this story. The students need to identify the suspect and victim, provide proof and motive, and delineate the main events of the crime.

July 6, 2010: Jerry writes Robert telling him that their plan is still on.

July 7, 2010: Jerry and Robert rob the Brick's Building.

July 9, 2010: Jerry wants his share of the money, but Robert won't give it to him.

July 10, 2010: Jerry argues with Robert, and he tries to get the safety deposit box key from Robert. Robert puts up a good fight and bites Jerry. Jerry's green T-shirt is stuck in Robert's throat (found during the autopsy). Jerry gets frustrated and shoots Robert. Jerry notices witness 1, ditches the gun in the trash can, and runs.

Witness 2's testimony is not true or not relevant to this crime. The witness has the wrong time, the wrong number of people, and mentions someone who does not even live in the area.

If the students ask, the key goes to a safety deposit bank at First Mason Bank. When opened, the investigators find $1,218,211.19 in cash and more than $1.5 million in checks, money orders, and other securities.

## RESOURCE 6.4: RAFT ASSIGNMENT AND ASSESSMENT

| Role | Audience | Format | Topic |
| --- | --- | --- | --- |
| Entomologist | The bug club | Lecture | Bugs in crime |
| Pathologist | Medical student | Persuasive letter | Cause and manner of crime |
| Engineer | Local museum exhibit creators | Exhibit proposal | Structures: are they to blame? |
| Psychologist | CSI fanatics | TV plot | Mental problems in criminals |
| Toxicologist | Police officers | Brochure | Smells and sights at the scene: what to document |

## RESOURCE 6.5: THE FORGED CHECK

| | |
|---|---|
| Butler Area School District | Date: October 10, 2010 |

Pay to the Order of <u>Mrs. Alicia Zoey Davis</u>          $ 850.00

Amount <u>*eight hundred fifty and OO*</u>          Dollars

*Dr. E. Goover*
<br>
Dr. Edmund Goover

Superintendent of Butler Area School District

## RESOURCE 6.6: THE CELL

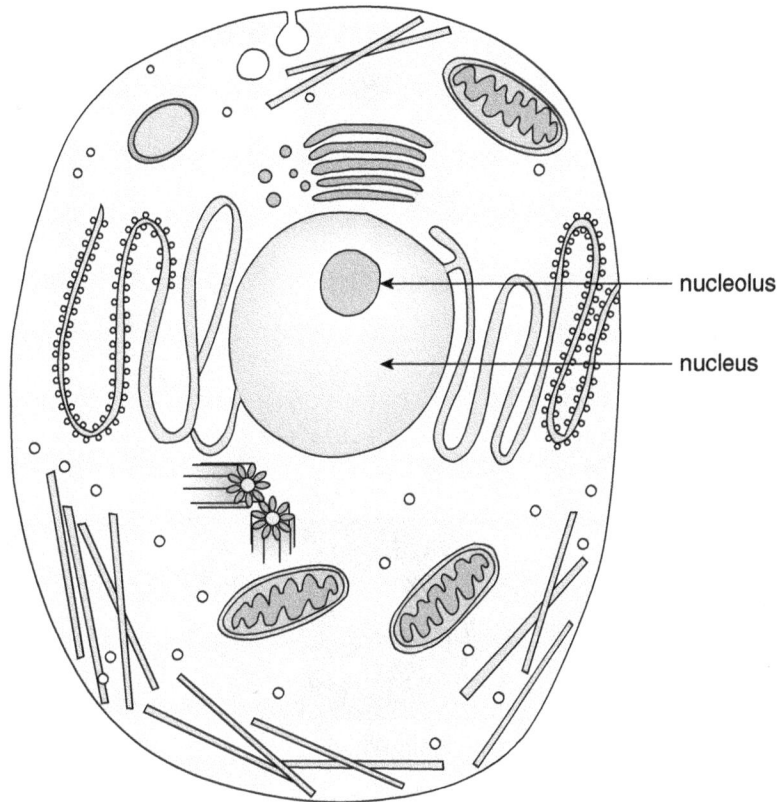

nucleolus

nucleus

*DNA Strips*

Directions: Make many more strips by randomly selecting patterns of G, A, T, and C. Here are just six random examples.

ggactttttggactctctctaggactatacgctagctccaggcggat

ggctggaggctgactgcaggatgcgatgcagtgcagcgcgggt

gtcgctgcagtcgaccagttcaggctggcagttgcaggctaggct

gactcggatgcggatgctgacggaggctgcggaggtcagtcga

aactgcagctgacggctagcagcctagcggcatgcaccaggac

tgaggctggagcggaggagctgcggagctgaggcatggcgga

## RESOURCE 6.7: FINGERPRINT PATTERNS

Plain Arch

Tented Arch

Radial Loop

Ulna Loop

Plain Whorl

Double Loop
Whorl

Central Pocket
Loop

Accidental
Whorl

*Source:* Created from images found at FBI.gov. (n.d.). *Fingerprint identification.* Retrieved November 8, 2010 from http://www.fbi.gov/about-us/cjis/fingerprints_biometrics/fingerprint-overview

# RESOURCE 6.8: STUDENT CHOICE PROJECT

First, choose a type of evidence from this list: documents, fingerprints, DNA analysis, blood, hairs, fibers, firearms and ballistics, microbes, chemicals, and contact traces (paint, glass, soil, etc.). Feel free, also, to pick a type of evidence that is not on this list. Just make sure and check with your teacher first. Then pick one of the following projects to complete.

## Creative Choice

Create a mural that tells the story of the type of evidence you chose. You can include what that type of evidence is used for, pictures of real examples, and tools used to analyze the evidence. Feel free to add your creative touches or additional information.

## Practical Choice

A confused new police officer has just come to you for help. The officer doesn't know what to do with the evidence found at the scene. Your job is to outline a method for analyzing the specific type of evidence you selected. Include specific examples of the evidence, the tools necessary, and what the evidence may be able to tell the officer. Feel free to add your own ideas or additional information that may help.

## Analytical Choice

There is an ongoing debate at the police station. You have been called in to decide which type of evidence is most valuable. Narrow the debate to just two types of evidence, and then compare and contrast these two types of evidence. Which one is more helpful? Which one is easier to analyze? What tools are needed? How have they been used in history? Present your findings in a mini-speech you can present at the station's staff meeting to help ease the tension. Feel free to add your own touches or additional information that may help.

## RESOURCE 6.9: CRIME SCENE SYNOPSIS

Liz can't believe it. How could she have let this happen? For some reason, she cannot get the song "How Much Is That Doggie in the Window?" out of her head. How can a song from her first piano recital when she was seven—half a lifetime ago—be lodged in her head? Liz can even hear her piano teacher saying, "D-G-D-B-G-E-D-C-D-A" as she played it. True, she has a great memory, but why does it have to be of that particular song?

Actually, it is no great mystery. Liz has been hired by her neighbors, the Jeffersons, to take care of their dog, Magic, while they are on vacation. She doesn't know how much Magic cost, but she knows the dog was very expensive. Magic is a purebred Afghan—one of those big dogs with really long blond hair. He is like a child to the Jeffersons. In fact, the only reason the Jeffersons didn't take Magic with them on vacation is because he had been sick. They almost canceled their vacation, but Liz has proven herself to be very responsible. She takes care of many people's pets in the neighborhood. She babysits. She "house-sits." Whenever a family needs help, they hire Liz Lincoln.

"How much is that dog . . ." Thankfully, Liz's singing is interrupted, but only because she is startled. She is at the Jeffersons' back door, and the spare key she has been using is still in the lock. She wonders how in the world she could have left it in the door when she was there earlier that day. She can picture herself putting the key back in its hiding place, but was that earlier that morning? Or yesterday? She has been going to the Jeffersons' house four times a day for almost four days, so it all kind of runs together. At least Liz has arrived a little earlier than she normally does, so she knows that the key has been in the doorknob for just a short time. Usually, she does an afternoon check on Magic around one o'clock, but today she plans to meet her friend Maria at that time, so this afternoon's Magic check is about 45 minutes early.

When Liz opens the back door into the kitchen, her concerns about the key briefly vanish. As soon as she steps inside, she steps in a very small puddle. Oh, no! Magic must have had a little accident! He had been sick because of problems with his kidneys—problems that mean he will most likely need some expensive surgery in the near future. Had he stood at the back door wanting to go out and just couldn't hold it any longer? Liz feels awful. She carefully enters, walking on her heel.

"Magic! Magic! Are you okay, boy?" Before she can say anything else, Liz hears a thud upstairs, like something had been knocked over. She starts to feel a little nervous. "Magic? Is that you? C'mere boy!" Liz stops holding her breath when Magic comes down the stairs. She pets him even more energetically than she normally does.

"You feel all right?" He seems fine. Liz debates calling the Jeffersons but decides to hold off. She is still a little concerned about the noise she heard, though, so she calls her father. Magic barks at anybody he doesn't know, and since he hadn't been barking, she is pretty sure that Magic must have made the noise. Still, she doesn't want to take any chances. While she waits for her dad to come over, Liz takes Magic outside. She wants to let him do his thing, so she can clean her shoe as quickly as possible. Surprisingly, Magic goes to the bathroom immediately. Liz laughs, thinking, "Boy, dogs must go a hundred times a day!" She also keeps a close eye on him to make sure that he stays away from the part of the yard on the other side of the house. The Jeffersons had been having problems with fire ants, and according to Mr. Jefferson, the best way to get rid of ants is with bleach water. (One of Liz's other jobs for the Jeffersons is to pour bleach water—a lot of it—on any anthills she finds. She is a little worried that she is doing more than just killing the ants. But she performs that duty each day when she checks on Magic in the morning.)

Liz's father comes over while she and Magic are still outside. She describes everything that happened. He is glad she called him over to check things out upstairs. Liz leaves him to do that while she cleans up her shoe and the little puddle on the kitchen floor. She is surprised how dirty and cloudy it is. Had she brought that much dirt in with her? Since it is so cloudy and since Magic is having kidney problems, Liz realizes that Magic's vet might want to see a sample of the "accident." Liz collects a little of it using a paper towel and puts that towel in a plastic zip-top bag. She wipes up the rest to put in the trash. As she is about to throw away the dirty paper towels, Liz notices a single piece of paper in the trash. Before they left, the Jeffersons took out the trash, and Liz knows for sure that she hasn't thrown anything away. She pulls the piece of paper out and tosses in the paper towels. The paper is "from the desk of Sally Jefferson." It has the words "I have taken" written on it. Puzzled, Liz assumes that Mr. or Mrs. Jefferson must have started to write a note after they had already emptied the trash. She puts the note in her pocket to take home to be recycled.

As Liz thinks about what a weird day it has been, her father comes downstairs, announcing that the noise was a plant being knocked over. Nothing else seems to be out of place. And since it is almost one o'clock, Liz and her father leave, making sure that the key is back in its hiding place.

Normally, Liz brushes Magic when she checks on him at one, but that gets postponed until she comes back around five. Liz did not want to leave the mall so early, but with all of the strange stuff that happened earlier, she isn't about to risk the possibility of more accidents. "Magic! Magic! C'mere, boy! Let's go outside! Magic! Time to eat!" For Magic, the word *eat* is even more exciting than *outside*. "Magic?"

Suddenly, Liz is scared. She continues to call out his name while she walks around the house. She goes upstairs. Nothing. He isn't on his bed. He isn't anywhere. But Liz doesn't totally panic. There has to be an explanation. And there is. A note she hadn't noticed at first is on the kitchen table. Written in large font, the note says

We have taken your dog. We will keep him unless you pay us ransom money. If you except our conditions and pay the money, he will be fine.

Magic has been dognapped? Liz can't believe it. How could she have let this happen? Dognapped and by bad spellers to boot. (Liz is an excellent student and sees immediately that the dognappers wrote "except" when it should have been "accept.")

The first thing Liz does is call her parents. While she waits for them to arrive, she replays in her mind the events that happened earlier. As she remembers the key in the door and the noise in the house, it starts to come together for her. Maybe even the little puddle is connected. Had she startled the dognappers earlier that day?

Liz's parents immediately offer to call the Jeffersons and then the police. "No. I need to be the one to do it. The Jeffersons put me in charge of Magic," she says calmly.

"My Magic?" Sally Jefferson is stunned. Liz has to explain it twice before she finally reacts. The reality of the situation begins to set in. "We'll pay whatever they want!" Then, Mrs. Jefferson remembers how "frugal" her husband is. "Well, I mean, I'll need to talk to Hal first." She continues as if she is thinking out loud. "First the news of the expensive operation, now a ransom payment. He's not going to be happy about having to spend more money on 'that mutt,' as he sometimes calls my precious Magic. I overheard him talking to Gerald, his best friend, about how ridiculous this dog is. Costing us a fortune. He is going to be so mad." Then, Sally snaps back to the matter at hand. "But you don't need to worry about that. Hal's playing golf right now, and, uh, I can't reach him. He turns off his cell phone, so no one can disturb him."

Liz gets the sense that Mrs. Jefferson is a little embarrassed by the fact that she is unable to immediately get in touch with her husband. Is she worried he won't pay the ransom?

"Um, Mrs. Jefferson, do you want us to go ahead and call the police?"

"Please." And with that, Sally Jefferson begins to bawl. "As soon as Hal gets back, we'll come home," she says between sobs. Liz doesn't know how long Mr. Jefferson will be on the golf course, but she knows that it will take them almost three hours to drive home.

Liz and her parents are surprised at how quickly the police arrive. Bernie Woodward is in charge of the investigation. It is obvious from the way he acts that he is taking this very seriously. While another officer looks around inside the house, Detective Woodward stays outside with Liz and her parents.

"Liz, I need you to tell me everything that happened." She appreciates that Detective Woodward speaks to her as if she is an adult.

"Four days ago, I started looking after Magic . . ." Liz impresses Detective Woodward with her very detailed description. As she is describing the noise and the knocked over plant, however, she gets a little distracted.

She sees Otis Nixon coming across the yard from his house nextdoor. The way he is, Liz thinks, he'll probably step right on an anthill and not even realize it. Liz doesn't really like Otis. For the first time, she realizes that the Jeffersons have people on both sides of their house she doesn't care for that much. Melinda Johnson is their other neighbor. She is Liz's age, and Liz suspects that Melinda is jealous of her status in the neighborhood (and the money that comes with it). People always hire Liz, never Melinda. Liz could never prove it, but she suspects Melinda is the one who spread a rumor around last year that Liz was caught at school cheating on a big science test. Of course Liz and her parents knew it wasn't true, but the rumor has always bothered her. Liz has to stop thinking about Melinda, though, because Otis has made his way over to them.

"What's going on?" Otis asks everybody. "Where's Magic? I mean, Liz, you're usually out here with him and all." Liz can tell that Detective Woodward is as annoyed as she is at the interruption.

Detective Woodward says, "Interesting that you should ask. It appears that he's been stolen. Do you know anything about that?"

"Me? Uh, no, of course not." Otis answers. "But I'm a private eye, so I might be able to help out with the investigation. Otis Nixon's my name." Liz almost laughs out loud. Is he serious? Private eye? Otis is something like twenty-five years old and lives with his parents, and she doesn't think he has ever had a job for more than a few months. And now he is calling himself a private eye? "Magic's a very valuable dog. Did she tell you that?" Otis points to Liz. "Any clues inside? What's the ransom note say? I assume the perp took the dog to get the Jeffersons to pay a ransom." Otis talks very quickly. Liz can only shake her head as she imagines Otis on the case using words like *perp* to try to impress people. Detective Woodward tries to get Otis to slow down a little. "Mr. Nixon, have you noticed anything suspicious or out of the ordinary over the last few days?"

"Why, I'm glad you asked." This should be interesting, Liz thinks. "As a matter of fact, there was a white van—you know, one of those without any windows in the back. One of those rental vans." Then Otis pauses, scratching his nose. "It just seemed a little out of place. I've got ESP for those things. That's why I'm such a good PI. That's short for private eye, you know." Liz smiles politely but sarcastically thinks, "Oh, really?" "And when they don't leave any clues from breaking in, that's when you've gotta have a . . ."

"Sixth sense?" Detective Woodward doesn't seem to question Otis's special abilities. Otis nods. The detective, though, is ready to move on, wondering, "I don't suppose you got a plate number or anything?"

"Oh, I was ready to rememorize it, but it didn't have a plate on it."

Rememorize? What a weirdo, thinks Liz as she again fights back the urge to laugh out loud. How will Detective Woodward ever get to the bottom of Magic's disappearance without Otis here to "help"? If Liz didn't feel so confident in the detective's ability to get Magic back, she might not find Otis so funny and ridiculous—just ridiculous.

By the time the Jeffersons return home, Detective Woodward has canvassed the neighborhood for any possible eyewitnesses. Other than Otis, no one reported seeing anything suspicious. There is no sign of forced entry, and Liz touched the key most recently, so her prints are on it. But without Liz, the police would have very little physical evidence. There are the wet paper towels that she was saving for Magic's vet. She had assumed the mess came from Magic, but now she isn't so sure. She also had the beginnings of that note in her pocket. Maybe that is something?

To solve the case, investigators have to think about who had access to the hidden key or another key, and at the same time, who had a motive for taking Magic. Investigators can't wait on the dognappers to make their next ransom demand, so they start testing the physical evidence immediately.

### Fingerprints for Final Case

DNA fingerprints (from five suspects): These can be cut apart and one copied twice so that one will have been found at the scene of the crime. Only three are needed for this crime because there are only three suspects.

| Otis Nixon | Melinda Johnson | Gerald Hanso |
|---|---|---|
| _____ | | _____ |
| | _____ | _____ |
| | _____ | |
| | | |
| | _____ | _____ |
| _____ | | |
| _____ | | |
| _____ | _____ | |
| _____ | _____ | |
| | | |
| | _____ | _____ |
| _____ | | _____ |
| _____ | | _____ |
| _____ | | _____ |
| | _____ | |

## RESOURCE 6.10: GENERAL RUBRIC

This rubric can be used on a lesson-by-lesson basis.

|  | 1 Novice | 2 Practitioner | 3 Expert |
|---|---|---|---|
| *Content* | The student does not grasp the main content ideas presented in the lesson. | The student grasps the main content ideas well enough to explain it in his or her journal or through a discussion. | The student grasps the main content ideas well enough to explain it *and apply it to other situations* in his or her journal or through a discussion. |
| *Process* | The student does not understand the methodological process that a forensic scientist utilizes. The student is not able to delineate the process verbally by his or her actions or by written or spoken words. | The student understands the methodological process that a forensic scientist uses in various situations. The student is able to delineate the process by his or her actions or by written or spoken words. | The student not only understands the methodological process that a forensic scientist uses in various situations but also is able to apply the process in other situations. The student is able to delineate the process by his or her actions or by written or spoken words. |
| *Products* | The student's product is not reflective of the content knowledge the student has gained or should have gained. The product does not exhibit any thought processes the student should have gained. The student has not exhibited any effort or growth. | The student's product demonstrates both the content knowledge and the methodological skills a forensic scientist uses. The student clearly demonstrates his or her understanding of the field through the product. | The student's product demonstrates both the content knowledge and the methodological skills a forensic scientist uses. The student clearly understands the field's connection to him- or herself or to other fields. The student explains or conveys in detail the evidence that supports the conclusion. |

# Index

Action-Planning Guide, 179, 192–193
Addition table, 127–128 (figure)
Additive scenarios, 123, 144
Adhesion, 219
Adventures of a Seed (Plants Alive unit), 33–34
    lab report, 50
Agarose gel, 223
Algorithms, 128–132, 137, 138, 144
American Civil War unit, 4–8
Analytical intelligence:
    Conundrums in Criminalistics unit, 251
    Plants Alive unit, 52
Arithmetic unit. *See* Getting to the Heart of
        Mathematical Numbers and Operations unit
Artifacts, 157, 173
Artwork, 172
Ascending levels of intellectual demand (AID).
        *See* Differentiation based on learner need
Assessment:
    about, 3 (figure)
    Civil War unit, 4, 5, 6
    Conundrums in Criminalistics unit, 200–201
    Experience Poetry unit, 81–82
    Getting to the Heart of Mathematical Numbers
        and Operations unit, 119, 121, 140–141
    Plants Alive unit, 19
    Point of View Under Transition unit, 59
    Preserving Our Identity unit, 155, 160–161
Associative property, 126–127

"Between Walls" (Williams), 92, 103
Biology unit. *See* Plants Alive unit
Bishop, Elizabeth, 91
Blood analysis, 226
"Blues Fantasy" (Hughes), 89
Bouchard, David, 175
Brown, Jeremy, 207
Bruner, Jerome, 21–22
Building Conceptual Understanding of
        Algorithms (Getting to the Heart of
        Mathematical Numbers and Operations
        unit), 128–132
    sample activities, 144

Calculators, 139
Calculators to Reinforce Place Value activity, 152

Cell (Conundrums in Criminalistics unit), 249
Changing Point of View (Point of View Under
        Transition unit), 64–66
Chromatograms, 219
Chromatography, 219
Civil War unit, 4–8
Classroom community, 15
Closure, 3 (figure)
Cohesion, 219
Combination scenarios, 123–124, 142, 144
Community, 157
Commutative property, 126, 127–128 (figure)
Comparative scenarios, 123, 144
Concepts, organizing:
    Conundrums in Criminalistics unit, 199
    Experience Poetry unit, 77–78
    Getting to the Heart of Mathematical Numbers
        and Operations unit, 117
    Plants Alive unit, 15–16
    Point of View Under Transition unit, 56–57
    Preserving Our Identity unit, 158
Conflict unit, 5–6
Connecting Problem Solving to the Real World
        (Getting to the Heart of Mathematical
        Numbers and Operations unit), 134–135
    sample activities, 146–147
Connecting Writing to Science lab report, 52
Connections, Curriculum of. *See* Curriculum of
        Connections
Content:
    about, 3 (figure)
    Civil War unit, 4, 5, 6, 7
    Conundrums in Criminalistics unit, 199–200
    Experience Poetry unit, 77–81
    Getting to the Heart of Mathematical Numbers
        and Operations unit, 117–120
    Plants Alive unit, 15–18
    Point of View Under Transition unit, 56–59
    Preserving Our Identity unit, 155, 158–160
Conundrum journals, 204
Conundrums in Criminalistics unit, 195–256
    assessment, 200–201
    concepts, organizing, 199
    content framework, 199–200
    guiding questions, 196
    introduction to the unit, 195–198

Lesson 6.1: The Universe of Knowledge, 197, 201–205
Lesson 6.2: Thoughts and Tools of the Trade, 197, 205–208
Lesson 6.3: Who's Who in Forensic Science?, 197, 208–211
Lesson 6.4: Scene Analysis and Evidence Documentation, 197–198, 211–214
Lesson 6.5: Document Analysis, 198, 214–220
Lesson 6.6: DNA and Imprints, 198, 220–224
Lesson 6.7: Fingerprinting, Blood, Questions, and Evidence, 198, 225–228
Lesson 6.8: Meet a Forensic Scientist, 198, 228–230
Lesson 6.9: Solve a Simulated Crime, 198, 230–234
materials needed, 197–198
overview, 11
principles, 199
Resource 6.1: Preassessment Graphic Organizer, 235
Resource 6.2: Thinking like a Forensic Scientist, 236–237
Resource 6.3: Interactive Crime Simulation, 238–246
Resource 6.4: RAFT Assignment and Assessment, 247
Resource 6.5: The Forged Check, 248
Resource 6.6: The Cell, 249
Resource 6.7: Fingerprint Patterns, 250
Resource 6.8: Student Choice Project, 251
Resource 6.9: Crime Scene Synopsis, 252–255
Resource 6.10: General Rubric, 256
standards, 199–200
unit sequence and teacher reflection, 201–234
Core Curriculum:
about, 4–5, 8 (figure)
Conundrums in Criminalistics unit, 195, 196
Experience Poetry unit, 76–77
Getting to the Heart of Mathematical Numbers and Operations unit, 116, 119–120
Plants Alive unit, 13–14
Preserving Our Identity unit, 154, 155, 156
Counting to 1 Million activity, 151–152
Creating a Plastic Bubble Greenhouse, 54
Creative intelligence:
Conundrums in Criminalistics unit, 251
Plants Alive unit, 52
Creech, Sharon, 94
*Crime Files, Four-Minute Forensic Mysteries* (Brown), 207
Crime Scene Synopsis (Conundrums in Criminalistics unit), 252–255
Criminalistics unit. *See* Conundrums in Criminalistics unit
Culture, 157
Curators, 178, 191

Curriculum components, 3 (figure)
Curriculum of Connections:
about, 5–6, 8 (figure)
Conundrums in Criminalistics unit, 195, 196
Getting to the Heart of Mathematical Numbers and Operations unit, 117, 119
Plants Alive unit, 14, 15
Preserving Our Identity unit, 154, 155, 156
Curriculum of Identity:
about, 7–8, 8 (figure)
Conundrums in Criminalistics unit, 195, 196
Experience Poetry unit, 77
Getting to the Heart of Mathematical Numbers and Operations unit, 117, 119
Plants Alive unit, 14, 15
Preserving Our Identity unit, 154, 155, 156
Curriculum of Practice:
about, 6–7, 8 (figure)
Conundrums in Criminalistics unit, 195–196
Experience Poetry unit, 76
Getting to the Heart of Mathematical Numbers and Operations unit, 116–117
Plants Alive unit, 14–15
Preserving Our Identity unit, 154, 155, 156
Curriculum Project, 165

Dactylographers, 226
Dactylography, 227
Dickinson, Emily, 88, 107
Differentiation based on learner need:
about, 3 (figure)
Civil War unit, 4–5, 6, 7
Getting to the Heart of Mathematical Numbers and Operations unit, 120
Preserving Our Identity unit, 157
Discovery learning, 21–22
Distributive property, 127, 131–132
Distributive scenarios, 124, 144
DNA analysis, 222–224
DNA and Imprints (Conundrums in Criminalistics unit), 198, 220–224
Document Analysis (Conundrums in Criminalistics unit), 198, 214–220

Egg Carton Observations lab report, 46
Electrophoresis, 223–224
Elements of Poetry (Experience Poetry unit), 86–90
Engineers, 247
Entomologists, 242, 245, 247
Ethics of the Use of the Tools of Mathematics (Getting to the Heart of Mathematical Numbers and Operations unit), 138–139
Exhibit designers, 178–179, 191
Exit cards:
Point of View Under Transition unit, 63
Preserving Our Identity unit, 162
Experience Poetry unit, 75–113

assessment, 81–82

concepts, organizing, 77–78

content framework, 77–81

introduction to the unit, 75–77

Lesson 3.1: Preassessment: "What I Know" Interest Inventory and "What I Love" and the Five Senses, 82–86

Lesson 3.2: Elements of Poetry, 86–90

Lesson 3.3: The Junk Festival and William Carlos Williams Poem Imitation, 90–93

Lesson 3.4: *Love That Dog* and Why Write Poetry?, 93–94

Lesson 3.5: Roller 'Roo Story and Poem Differentiation and Found Poems, 95–97

Lesson 3.6: Interactive Poetry Museum, 97–100

overview, 11

principles, 78

Resource 3.1: What I Know, 101

Resource 3.2: Five Senses Activity, 102

Resource 3.3: "Between Walls," 103

Resource 3.4: "The Red Wheelbarrow," 104

Resource 3.5: "The Locust Tree in Flower," 105

Resource 3.6: "This Is Just to Say," 106

Resource 3.7: "Why Write Poetry?," 107

Resource 3.8: "Rollin' with My Peeps" Poem, 108

Resource 3.9: Roller 'Roo at Skatetown, USA, 109

Resource 3.10: "Rollin' with My Peeps" Dissected, 110

Resource 3.11: A Fictionalized First-Person Speech about Mary Oliver, 111

Resource 3.12: Interactive Poetry Museum Note-Taking Guide, 112

Resource 3.13: Interactive Poetry Museum: The Roles, 113

skills, 80–81

standards, 78–80

unit sequence and teacher reflection, 82–100

Experimenting With the Basic Needs of Plants lab report, 49

Extension activities:

about, 3 (figure)

Civil War unit, 4, 5, 6, 7

Getting to the Heart of Mathematical Numbers and Operations unit, 120

Preserving Our Identity unit, 157

*See also* Homework/individual challenges

Facilitating Easy Recall of Mathematical "Facts" (Getting to the Heart of Mathematical Numbers and Operations unit), 124–127, 127–128 (figure)

sample activities, 143

Fictionalized First-Person Speech about Mary Oliver, 111

Figurative language, 87–88

Fingerprinting, Blood, Questions, and Evidence (Conundrums in Criminalistics unit), 198, 225–228

Fingerprint Patterns (Conundrums in Criminalistics unit), 250

"Fish, The" (Bishop), 91

Five Senses activity (Experience Poetry unit), 82–86, 102

"Fog" (Sandburg), 88

Folklore, 157

Forensic unit. *See* Conundrums in Criminalistics unit

Forged Check (Conundrums in Criminalistics unit), 248

Formative assessments:

Conundrums in Criminalistics unit, 200, 201

Getting to the Heart of Mathematical Numbers and Operations unit, 121

Plants Alive unit, 19

Point of View Under Transition unit, 59, 71

*See also* Assessment

Found poems, 96, 97

Found sculptures, 91–92

Fractured fairy tales, 56

Frasier, Debra, 164, 165

Frayer Diagram for Conceptual Knowledge, 160, 176, 180

General Rubric (Conundrums in Criminalistics unit), 256

Getting to the Heart of Mathematical Numbers and Operations unit, 115–152

assessment, 119, 121, 140–141

concepts, organizing, 117

content framework, 117–120

guiding questions, 116–117

introduction to the unit, 115–117

Lesson 4.1: Know When to Add, Subtract, Multiply, or Divide, 122–124

Lesson 4.2: Facilitating Easy Recall of Mathematical "Facts," 124–127, 127–128 (figure)

Lesson 4.3: Building Conceptual Understanding of Algorithms, 128–132

Lesson 4.4: Relationships between Operations, 132–133

Lesson 4.5: Connecting Problem Solving to the Real World, 134–135

Lesson 4.6: What Is a Mathematician?, 135–136

Lesson 4.7: The Tools of a Mathematician, 137–138

Lesson 4.8: The Ethics of the Use of the Tools of Mathematics, 138–139

overview and background of the unit, 11, 115–116

parallels for the unit, 116

principles, 117

prior to Lesson 4.1: Preassessment, 121
Resource 4.1: Preassessment, 140–141
Resource 4.2: Lesson 4.1 Sample
    Activities, 142
Resource 4.3: Lesson 4.2 Sample
    Activities, 143
Resource 4.4: Lesson 4.3 Sample
    Activities, 144
Resource 4.5: Lesson 4.4 Sample
    Activities, 145
Resource 4.6: Lesson 4.5 Sample
    Activities, 146–147
Resource 4.7: Lesson 4.6 Sample
    Activities, 148–150
Resource 4.8: Lesson 4.7 Sample
    Activities, 151–152
skills, 119
standards, 118–119
unit sequence and teacher reflection,
    121–139
Grade 2 units. *See* Experience Poetry unit;
    Getting to the Heart of Mathematical
    Numbers and Operations unit
Grade 3 units. *See* Experience Poetry unit;
    Getting to the Heart of Mathematical
    Numbers and Operations unit; Point of
    View Under Transition unit
Grade 4 units. *See* Conundrums in Criminalistics
    unit; Experience Poetry unit; Getting to the
    Heart of Mathematical Numbers and
    Operations unit; Point of View Under
    Transition unit
Grade 5 units. *See* Conundrums in
    Criminalistics unit; Experience Poetry unit;
    Getting to the Heart of Mathematical
    Numbers and Operations unit; Point of
    View Under Transition unit
Graphic organizers:
    Conundrums in Criminalistics unit, 235
    Getting to the Heart of Mathematical
        Numbers and Operations unit, 145
    Point of View Under Transition unit, 67, 73
    Preserving Our Identity unit, 165, 171, 172,
        173, 183
Graphing My Plants' Growth lab report, 47
Grouping strategies:
    about, 3 (figure)
    Civil War unit, 5, 6, 7
    Getting to the Heart of Mathematical
        Numbers and Operations unit, 120
    Preserving Our Identity unit, 157
Guiding questions:
    Conundrums in Criminalistics unit, 196
    Getting to the Heart of Mathematical
        Numbers and Operations
        unit, 116–117
    Plants Alive unit, 14–15
    Preserving Our Identity unit, 154–155

Harjo, Joy, 88
History unit. *See* Preserving Our Identity unit
Homework/individual challenges:
    DNA and Imprints (Conundrums in
        Criminalistics unit), 224
    Document Analysis (Conundrums in
        Criminalistics unit), 220
    Fingerprinting, Blood, Questions, and
        Evidence (Conundrums in Criminalistics
        unit), 228
    Meet a Forensic Scientist (Conundrums in
        Criminalistics unit), 230
    Scene Analysis and Evidence Documentation
        (Conundrums in Criminalistics unit), 214
    Solve a Simulated Crime (Conundrums in
        Criminalistics unit), 234
    Thoughts and Tools of the Trade
        (Conundrums in Criminalistics unit), 208
    The Tools of a Mathematician (Getting to the
        Heart of Mathematical Numbers and
        Operations unit), 138
    Understanding the Tools of a Public Historian
        (Preserving Our Identity unit), 164
    The Universe of Knowledge (Conundrums in
        Criminalistics unit), 205
    Who's Who in Forensic Science?
        (Conundrums in Criminalistics unit), 211
    *See also* Extension activities
"Hope Is a Thing with Feathers" (Dickinson), 88
How Is This Like Me? chart, 73
Hughes, Langston, 88–89

Identity, 157
Identity, Curriculum of. *See* Curriculum of
    Identity
Identity element, 125–126
"If I Can Stop One Heart from Breaking"
    (Dickinson), 107
If You're Not From . . . , You Don't Know . . .
    (Preserving Our Identity unit), 174–176
    brainstorming sheet, 175, 186
    template, 175, 187
*If You're Not From the Prairie . . .* (Bouchard), 175
Incremental scenarios, 123, 142, 144
Interactive Crime Simulation (Conundrums in
    Criminalistics unit), 210, 238–246
Interactive Poetry Museum (Experience Poetry
    unit), 97–100
    museum roles, 113
    notetaking guide, 112
Intermediate grades. *See* Preserving Our Identity
    unit; *specific grades*
Introducing the Historical Method (Preserving
    Our Identity unit), 161–162
Introduction:
    about, 3 (figure)
    Civil War unit, 4
    Conundrums in Criminalistics unit, 195–198

Experience Poetry unit, 75–77
Getting to the Heart of Mathematical
　　Numbers and Operations unit, 115–117,
　　119–120
Plants Alive unit, 13–15
Point of View Under Transition unit, 55–56
Preserving Our Identity unit, 153–158, 156
Is It Alive? (Plants Alive unit), 20–22
lab report, 40
"It's Raining in Honolulu" (Harjo), 88

Jigsaw activity:
　Plants Alive unit, 31
　Preserving Our Identity unit, 171
Journals:
　Conundrums in Criminalistics unit, 227
　Experience Poetry unit, 86, 97
　Point of View Under Transition unit, 61, 63,
　　66, 68, 70
Junk Festival and William Carlos Williams Poem
　　Imitation (Experience Poetry unit), 90–93

Kentucky science standards, 16–18
Know When to Add, Subtract, Multiply, or
　　Divide (Getting to the Heart of
　　Mathematical Numbers and Operations
　　unit), 122–124
　sample activities, 142
KWL (know, want to know, learned),
　　15, 19–20, 37

Lab coats, 20
Lab reports (Plants Alive unit):
　The Adventures of a Seed, 50
　Is It Alive?, 40
　The Needs of Every Living Thing, 49
　Observing Germinating Plants, 44–47
　Plant Parts!, 48
　What Do Seeds Need to Grow?, 42–43
　What's in a Seed?, 41
　What's Inside Our Fruit?, 51–52
Language arts units. *See* Experience Poetry unit;
　　Point of View Under Transition unit
Learning activities:
　about, 3 (figure)
　Civil War unit, 4, 5, 6, 7
　Getting to the Heart of Mathematical
　　Numbers and Operations unit, 120
　Preserving Our Identity unit, 156
　*See also* Teaching methods
Lesson and unit closure, 3 (figure)
Library of Congress (LOC), 173
Literary forensic scientists, 242, 245–246
Literature unit. *See* Experience Poetry unit; Point
　　of View Under Transition unit
Living or Nonliving lab report, 40
"Locust Tree in Flower, The"
　　(Williams), 93, 105

Look . . . I Am an Author! (Point of View Under
　　Transition unit), 66–68
*Love That Dog* (Creech), 94
*Love That Dog* and Why Write Poetry?
　　(Experience Poetry unit), 93–94

Making Our State Public: Culminating Project
　　(Preserving Our Identity unit), 176–179
Manipulative materials (Getting to the Heart of
　　Mathematical Numbers and Operations
　　unit), 122, 135
Materials needed:
　The Adventures of a Seed (Plants
　　Alive unit), 33–34
　Conundrums in Criminalistics
　　unit, 197–198
　Is It Alive? (Plants Alive unit), 21
　The Needs of Every Living Thing
　　(Plants Alive unit), 32
　Observing Germinating Plants
　　(Plants Alive unit), 28
　Plant Parts! (Plants Alive unit), 30
　What Do Seeds Need to Grow?
　　(Plants Alive unit), 25
　What Do We Know about Plants? (Plants
　　Alive unit), 20
　What Do We Know about Plants? Revisited
　　(Plants Alive unit), 37
　What's in a Seed? (Plants Alive unit), 23
　What's Inside Our Fruit? (Plants
　　Alive unit), 35
Mathematics unit. *See* Getting to the
　　Heart of Mathematical Numbers and
　　Operations unit
Meet a Forensic Scientist (Conundrums in
　　Criminalistics unit), 198, 228–230
Mexico unit, 5
Missouri grade-level expectations for reading
　　and writing, 57
Multiplication table, 128 (figure)
Museum docents, 179, 191
Museum Exhibit Group Rubric (Preserving
　　Our Identity unit), 179, 194
Museum Exhibit Roles, 127–179, 191
Music, 88–89
　*See also* Experience Poetry unit
Mute evidence, 171, 172, 173
My Baggie Garden lab report, 43
My Plant Grows Up! lab reports, 42, 44
My Science Notebook, 39–54

National Council for Teachers of English
　　(NCTE) standards, 79–80
National Council for the Social Studies
　　standards, 159
National Council of Teachers of English and the
　　International Reading Association (NCTE/
　　IRA) Standards, 57–58

National Council of Teachers of Mathematics standards, 118–119
National science standards:
Conundrums in Criminalistics unit, 200
Plants Alive unit, 16
Natural resources, 157
Needs of Every Living Thing (Plants Alive unit), 31–33
lab report, 46
Nye, Naomi Shihab, 83, 107

Observation/classification, 22
Observing Germinating Plants (Plants Alive unit), 27–29
lab report, 44
Odontologists, 241, 245
Oliver, Mary, 98–99, 111
*On the Day You Were Born* (Frasier), 164, 165
Oral history, 172

Parallel Curriculum Model (PCM):
books about, 1–2
Core Curriculum overview, 4–5, 8 (figure)
curriculum components, 3 (figure)
Curriculum of Connections overview, 5–6, 8 (figure)
Curriculum of Identity overview, 7–8, 8 (figure)
Curriculum of Practice overview, 6–7, 8 (figure)
history, 1–2
overview, 2–3
Parent letters, 184
Partitioning scenarios, 123, 144
Pathologists, 241, 245, 247
Pathway to Discovery Chart, 164, 177, 181
PCM. *See* Parallel Curriculum Model
Pennsylvania state standards, 199–200
Photography/camera use, 60–61
Photos, 171–172
Plant fair, 37–38
Plant Parts! (Plants Alive unit), 29–31
lab report, 48
Plants Alive unit, 13–54
assessment, 19
concepts, organizing, 15–16
conclusion: plant fair, 37–38
content framework, 15–18
guiding questions, 14–15
introduction to the unit, 13–15
Lesson 1.1: What Do We Know about Plants?, 19–20
Lesson 1.2: Is It Alive?, 20–22
Lesson 1.3: What's in a Seed?, 23–24
Lesson 1.4: What Do Seeds Need to Grow?, 25–27
Lesson 1.5: Observing Germinating Plants, 27–29

Lesson 1.6: Plant Parts!, 29–31
Lesson 1.7: The Needs of Every Living Thing, 31–33
Lesson 1.8: The Adventures of a Seed, 33–34
Lesson 1.9: What's Inside Our Fruit?, 35–36
Lesson 1.10: What Do We Know about Plants? Revisited, 36–37
My Science Notebook, 39–54
overview, 10
principles, 16
Resource 1.1: Living or Nonliving, 40
Resource 1.2: Seed Dissection, 41
Resource 1.3: My Plant Grows Up!, 42
Resource 1.4: My Baggie Garden, 43
Resource 1.5: My Plant Grows Up!, 44
Resource 1.6: Writing About My Potted Plant, 45
Resource 1.7: Egg Carton Observations, 46
Resource 1.8: Graphing My Plants' Growth, 47
Resource 1.9: Plant Parts: Labeling the Parts of a Plant, 48
Resource 1.10: Experimenting With the Basic Needs of Plants, 49
Resource 1.11: The Adventures of a Seed, 50
Resource 1.12: What's Inside Fruit?, 51
Resource 1.13: Connecting Writing to Science, 52
Resource 1.14: Rubric for Science Notebook, 53
Resource 1.15: Creating a Plastic Bubble Greenhouse, 54
standards, 16–18
unit sequence and teacher reflection, 19–37
Poetry unit. *See* Experience Poetry unit
Point of View Under Transition unit, 55–73
assessment, 59
concepts, organizing, 56–57
content framework, 56–59
introduction to the unit, 55–56
Lesson 2.1: What Is My Point of View?, 59–61
Lesson 2.2: What Is Point of View?, 62–63
Lesson 2.3: Changing Point of View, 64–66
Lesson 2.4: Look . . . I Am an Author!, 66–68
Lesson 2.5: Wrapping up That Changing Point of View, 68–70
overview, 10–11
principles, 57
Resource 2.1: Story Map, 71
Resource 2.2: Writing Rubric, 72
Resource 2.3: How Is This Like Me?, 73
skills, 58–59
standards, 57–58
unit sequence and teacher reflection, 59–70
Postassessment:
Point of View Under Transition unit, 59, 72
Preserving Our Identity unit, 160–161
*See also* Assessment

Practical intelligence:
  Conundrums in Criminalistics unit, 251
  Plants Alive unit, 52
Practice, Curriculum of. *See* Curriculum of
    Practice
Preassessment:
  Conundrums in Criminalistics unit,
    200, 201, 235
  Experience Poetry unit, 82–86
  Getting to the Heart of Mathematical
    Numbers and Operations unit, 140–141
  Plants Alive unit, 19
  Point of View Under Transition unit, 59
  Preserving Our Identity unit, 160
  *See also* Assessment
Preassessment Graphic Organizer worksheet
    (Conundrums in Criminalistics unit), 235
Predictions, making, 26
Present Your Findings, 182
Preserving Our Identity unit, 153–194
  assessment, 160–161
  concepts, organizing, 158
  content framework, 158–160
  guiding questions, 154–155
  introduction to the unit, 153–158
  Lesson 5.1: Introducing the Historical Method,
    161–162
  Lesson 5.2: Understanding the Tools of a
    Public Historian: Learning about Our
    Own Lives, 163–165
  Lesson 5.3: Understanding the Tools of a
    Historian: Learning about Our State
    History, 166–168
  Lesson 5.4: Using Primary Sources, 169–173
  Lesson 5.5: If You're Not From . . . , You Don't
    Know . . . , 174–176
  Lesson 5.6: Making Our State Public:
    Culminating Project, 176–179
  overview, 11
  principles, 158
  Resource 5.1: Frayer Diagram for Conceptual
    Knowledge, 180
  Resource 5.2: Pathway to Discovery Chart, 181
  Resource 5.3: Present Your Findings, 182
  Resource 5.4: Graphic Organizer for Step 3 in
    the Pathway to Discovery, 183
  Resource 5.5: Parent Letter, 184
  Resource 5.6: Rubrics, 185
  Resource 5.7: If You're Not From . . .
    Example Brainstorming Sheet, 186
  Resource 5.8: If You're Not From . . .
    Template, 187
  Resource 5.9: Spot the Stereotype, 188
  Resource 5.10: Right There, or History and
    Me, 189
  Resource 5.11: Primary Source Lesson-Task
    Directions, 190
  Resource 5.12: Museum Exhibit Roles, 191

  Resource 5.13: Action-Planning
    Guide, 192–193
  Resource 5.14: Museum Exhibit
    Group Rubric, 194
  skills, 159–160
  standards, 159
  unit sequence and teacher reflection, 161–179
Primary grades. *See* Plants Alive unit; *specific
    grades*
Primary sources:
  defined, 158, 170
  Primary Source Lesson-Task Directions, 190
  Using Primary Sources, 169
Principles:
  Conundrums in Criminalistics unit, 199
  Experience Poetry unit, 78
  Getting to the Heart of Mathematical
    Numbers and Operations unit, 117
  Plants Alive unit, 16
  Point of View Under Transition unit, 57
  Preserving Our Identity unit, 158
Probes, 224
Products:
  about, 3 (figure)
  Civil War unit, 5, 6, 7
  Getting to the Heart of Mathematical
    Numbers and Operations unit, 120
  Preserving Our Identity unit, 157
Psychologists, 243, 246, 247
Public historians, 178, 191

RAFT Assignment and Assessment
    (Conundrums in Criminalistics
    unit), 247
Reading units. *See* Experience Poetry unit; Point
    of View Under Transition unit
"Red Wheelbarrow, The" (Williams), 92, 104
Regions, 158
Relationships between Operations (Getting to
    the Heart of Mathematical Numbers and
    Operations unit), 132–133
  sample activities, 145
Repeated addition scenarios, 123, 144
Resources:
  about, 3 (figure)
  Civil War unit, 4, 5, 6, 7
  Experience Poetry unit, 77
  Getting to the Heart of Mathematical
    Numbers and Operations unit, 120
  Plants Alive unit, 24, 26, 30, 34, 36
  Point of View Under Transition
    unit, 56, 63, 65
  Preserving Our Identity unit, 157, 177
Restriction enzymes, 223
Rhyme, 89–90
Rhythm, 89
Right There, or History and Me, 168, 189
Roller 'Roo at Skatetown, USA, 109

Roller 'Roo Story and Poem Differentiation and Found Poems (Experience Poetry unit), 95–97

"Rollin' with My Peeps," 108

"Rollin' with My Peeps" Dissected, 110

Row-by-column scenarios, 144

Rubrics:
 Conundrums in Criminalistics unit, 256
 Getting to the Heart of Mathematical Numbers and Operations unit, 147
 Plants Alive unit, 53
 Point of View Under Transition unit, 72
 Preserving Our Identity unit, 179, 185, 194
 *See also* Assessment

Sandburg, Carl, 88

Scene Analysis and Evidence Documentation (Conundrums in Criminalistics unit), 197–198, 211–214

Science standards, national:
 Conundrums in Criminalistics unit, 200
 Plants Alive unit, 16

Science units. *See* Conundrums in Criminalistics unit; Plants Alive unit

Secondary sources, 158, 170

Seed Dissection lab report, 41

Self-assessment:
 Experience Poetry unit, 81
 Plants Alive unit, 19
 *See also* Assessment

Sensory images, 88

Serologists, 226

Shoe print impressions, 221–222

Skills:
 Experience Poetry unit, 80–81
 Getting to the Heart of Mathematical Numbers and Operations unit, 119
 Point of View Under Transition unit, 58–59
 Preserving Our Identity unit, 159–160

Social studies unit. *See* Preserving Our Identity unit

Socratic questioning (Point of View Under Transition unit), 61, 68

Solve a Simulated Crime (Conundrums in Criminalistics unit), 198, 230–234

Sound, 89

Spot the Stereotype, 167–168, 188

Standards:
 Conundrums in Criminalistics unit, 199–200
 Experience Poetry unit, 78–80
 Getting to the Heart of Mathematical Numbers and Operations unit, 118–119
 Plants Alive unit, 16–18
 Point of View Under Transition unit, 57–58
 Preserving Our Identity unit, 159

State history unit. *See* Preserving Our Identity unit

States, 158

Static scenarios, 123, 142, 144

Sternberg's analytical intelligence:
 Conundrums in Criminalistics unit, 251
 Plants Alive unit, 52

Sternberg's creative intelligence:
 Conundrums in Criminalistics unit, 251
 Plants Alive unit, 52

Sternberg's practical intelligence:
 Conundrums in Criminalistics unit, 251
 Plants Alive unit, 52

Story maps (Point of View Under Transition unit):
 Changing Point of View, 65
 Wrapping up That Changing Point of View, 70, 71

Student Choice Project (Conundrums in Criminalistics unit), 251

Subtractive scenarios, 124, 144

Summative assessment:
 Conundrums in Criminalistics unit, 200, 201
 Experience Poetry unit, 81
 Getting to the Heart of Mathematical Numbers and Operations unit, 121
 Plants Alive unit, 19
 *See also* Assessment

"Summer Day, The" (Oliver), 98–99

Surveys, 148–149

Take-away scenarios, 123, 144

Teaching methods:
 about, 3 (figure)
 Civil War unit, 4, 5, 6, 7
 Getting to the Heart of Mathematical Numbers and Operations unit, 120
 Preserving Our Identity unit, 156
 *See also* Learning activities

Thinking like a Forensic Scientist worksheet (Conundrums in Criminalistics unit), 236–237

"This Is Just to Say" (Williams), 93, 106

Thoughts and Tools of the Trade (Conundrums in Criminalistics unit), 197, 205–208

Tools of a Mathematician (Getting to the Heart of Mathematical Numbers and Operations unit), 137–138
 sample activities, 151–152

Toxicologists, 247

Transitivity of equality, 133

Understanding the Tools of a Historian: Learning about Our State History (Preserving Our Identity unit), 166–168

Understanding the Tools of a Public Historian: Learning about Our Own Lives (Preserving Our Identity unit), 163–165

Universe of Knowledge (Conundrums in Criminalistics unit), 197, 201–205

Using Primary Sources (Preserving Our Identity unit), 169–173

Van Allsburg, Chris. *See* Point of View Under Transition unit

Virginia's sixth-grade standards of learning for English, 78–79

Walk, schoolyard, 22

What Do Seeds Need to Grow? (Plants Alive unit), 25–27
lab report, 42–43

What Do We Know about Plants? (Plants Alive unit), 19–20

What Do We Know about Plants? Revisited (Plants Alive unit), 36–37

"What I Know" Interest Inventory and "What I Love" and the Five Senses (Experience Poetry unit), 82–86

What I Know worksheet, 101

What I Love activity (Experience Poetry unit), 83

What Is a Mathematician? (Getting to the Heart of Mathematical Numbers and Operations unit), 135–136
sample activities, 148–150

What Is My Point of View? (Point of View Under Transition unit), 59–61

What Is Point of View? (Point of View Under Transition unit), 62–63

What's in a Seed? (Plants Alive unit), 23–24
lab report, 41

What's Inside Our Fruit? (Plants Alive unit), 35–36
lab report, 51–52

Who's Who in Forensic Science? (Conundrums in Criminalistics unit), 197, 208–211

"Why Write Poetry?," 107

Williams, William Carlos, 92–93, 103–106
*See also* Experience Poetry unit

Wrapping up That Changing Point of View (Point of View Under Transition unit), 68–70

Writing About My Potted Plant lab report, 45

Writing Rubric (Point of View Under Transition unit), 72

Writing units. *See* Experience Poetry unit; Point of View Under Transition unit

Written history, 172

**CORWIN**

A SAGE Company

The Corwin logo—a raven striding across an open book—represents the union of courage and learning. Corwin is committed to improving education for all learners by publishing books and other professional development resources for those serving the field of PreK–12 education. By providing practical, hands-on materials, Corwin continues to carry out the promise of its motto: **"Helping Educators Do Their Work Better."**

www.ingramcontent.com/pod-product-compliance
Lightning Source LLC
Chambersburg PA
CBHW080246030426
42334CB00023BA/2714